BHUTAN

Françoise Pommaret—Tibetologist, lecturer and writer—has travelled extensively in Asia and particularly in Bhutan, where she has lived and worked since 1981. She was a Research Assistant for the Bhutan Tourism Corporation (1981–6) and is now working in the Department of Education of the Royal Government of Bhutan as a History Research Officer.

Françoise Pommaret-Imaeda was born in Poitiers, France. Her strong historical and linguistic interests are reflected in her academic achievements. She has taken a master's degree in the classics, in the history of art and archaeology, as well as a diploma in Tibetan studies. This she followed up with an arts doctorate. In 1989 she was awarded the *Prix Jean-Mermoz de l'Union culturelle et technique de langue française* by the President of the French Senate in Paris.

She speaks French, English, Tibetan and Dzongkha. Among her publications are: *Bhutan, A Kingdom of the Eastern Himalayas* (Shambhala, USA—Olizane, Geneva); *The History of Bhutan—A Handbook for Teachers* (Department of Education, Thimphu, Bhutan) and *Les Revenants de l'Au-delà dans le Monde tibétain* (CNRS, Paris). She has also written several articles on the religious culture of Bhutan.

BHUTAN

Françoise Pommaret

Photography by
Françoise Pommaret & Yoshiro Imaeda

Translated by
Elisabeth B Booz

 **PASSPORT BOOKS**

Trade Imprint of National Textbook Company
Lincolnwood, Illinois U.S.A.

Published by Passport Books in conjunction with
The Guidebook Company Ltd

This edition was first published in 1991 by Passport Books,
Trade Imprint of National Textbook Company,
4255 WestTouhy Avenue, Lincolnwood (Chicago),
Illinois 60646-1975 U.S.A.

Printed in Hong Kong

Consultant Editors: Bikram Grewal and Toby Sinclair
Series Editors: Ralph Kiggell and Rose Borton
Photography: Françoise Pommaret & Yoshiro Imaeda
Photo Editor: Caroline Robertson
Maps: Bai Yiliang
Design: Unity Studio

Contents

(following pages) The spectacular landscape near Lingshi dzong with the Jichudrake and Tsheringang mountains both more than 7,000 metres high

Note on Pronunciation

u is pronounced *oo* as in boot

ü is pronounced like a French *u*

e is a short vowel as in b*e*t

ph is pronounced as an aspirated *p* not f

tsh is pronounced as *ts* not ch

c is pronounced *ch* as in cheek

Preface

This is the first guide in English to the little-known country of Bhutan and it is therefore necessary to explain the spirit in which it was conceived.

Bhutan is a tightly closed country which receives very few tourists in a year. Its policy is to control tourism and place emphasis on its traditional values. This guide is written both for tourists who have the curiosity to discover an extraordinary land, and for foreigners who come to work in Bhutan and contribute to its development. That will help to explain why more in-depth information is offered than is usually found in guidebooks of this kind. It attempts to introduce Bhutan's culture and way of life. In addition, it pays more attention to cultural characteristics that are strictly Bhutanese than to aspects of its culture that are held in common with other Himalayan countries. It also hopes to be a ready reference for all foreigners in Bhutan, whether tourists or residents.

Quite simply, this guide will have served its purpose if it succeeds in fostering a better understanding between foreign visitors and the Bhutanese people.

I owe a debt of gratitude to the volunteer teachers, English, Irish and Canadian, who have given me shelter and assistance during my peregrinations through different regions of Bhutan.

I would like to thank all my Bhutanese friends who have helped to give me a deeper understanding of this country, in particular my friends Namgyel, Norzom, Dago, Kunga and Karma; Lopen Chencho who worked with me in the Department of Tourism and who, with the greatest humility, taught me so well the traditions of his country; and the great historians Lopen Pemala and the late Lopen Nado.

Without them, this guide could never have come into being and it is to them and to the Bhutanese people that I dedicate it. My very best wishes! *Tashidele!*

Françoise Pommaret 1990

Introduction

'Bhutan? Where's that?' This is the response you can expect if you say you are going to Bhutan. Most people have never heard of it. Bhutan does not make headlines—it hardly makes a small paragraph in a Western newspaper once every ten years. From time to time a full-scale article on Bhutan does appear, but it reaches only a limited audience.

Yet, a handful of people around the world, who form a sort of 'initiates' club', eagerly follow events there by carefully reading the weekly journal *Kuensel*, published by the Bhutanese government. Some of them have visited Bhutan on professional trips, some as official guests, and others as tourists. All of them have come back enthralled by this secret land.

Hidden in the eastern Himalayas between India and China (Tibet), as big as Switzerland but sparsely inhabited (population barely one million), Bhutan certainly exudes charm—magic, its devotees would say. The mountains are magnificent, the forests are dense, the people are delightful, the air is pure and crystalline, the architecture imposing, the religion exciting, the art superb. There are no beggars, very few thefts, virtually no violent crime, and a traveller's personal safety is guaranteed. Public relations hype, you may be thinking; guidebooks always inflate their subject. But the surprising fact is that it's all true. For the occasional visitor, Bhutan is truly Shangri-la, a mythical country hidden deep in the mountains.

But while the Bhutanese themselves are aware that they live in a privileged land, surrounded by nations beset with terrifying economic and social problems, they also know that they are not living in Shangri-la. Their day-to-day reality allows no time for dreaming. The hard life of the peasants, made up of household chores, work in the fields and care of livestock, is scarcely mechanized as yet. Religious festivals, pilgrimages and secular holidays are the only moments of rest, anticipated pauses punctuating the agricultural calendar.

With 90 percent of the population engaged in agriculture or raising livestock, Bhutan remains a rural country devoid of industry, except in the south. The beauty of the pastoral landscape sometimes seems unreal to travellers from the industrialized world: houses with brightly decorated window frames and shingled roofs, patchworks of green paddy fields, plots of tawny buckwheat, oak forests, a covered

bridge, fences of intricately woven bamboo, a man leaning on a
wooden rail trampling his harvest, a woman weaving in the open air,
a baby laced into a horse's saddle bag, yaks browsing in a grove of
giant rhododendron.
    Such scenes remain in the memory forever. But it is the symbols of
Bhutan's religion which leave the deepest impression: the *chortens*
(commemorative monuments) dotting the landscape, fluttering prayer
flags, prayer wheels turned by the swift water of mountain streams,
the monasteries. Buddhism is everywhere, determining attitudes,
moulding thoughts. Red-robed monks, high *lamas*, the religious men
in a village; everybody is aware of their moral and spiritual influence
on the population. They preside over all events: weddings, departures
on trips, official ceremonies, promotions, not to mention the
fundamental role they play in religious initiations, mass blessings and
festivals. Their importance is underlined further by the fact that
Bhutan is the only country in the world where the Tantric form of
Mahayana Buddhism is the official state religion.
    Religion, tradition and ancestral custom constitute Bhutanese
etiquette, the most visible elements of which are respect for all
religious institutions and the wearing of national dress. This emphasis
on traditional values is as much a deliberate policy of the government
as is its concern with social and economic development.
    These aims, which at first may seem contradictory, are reconciled
through the desire to develop local resources and promote self-
reliance. The two objectives merge in a totally harmonious way: a
monk photocopies the pages of a text he needs for a ritual; a high
official, wearing a heavy raw silk garment with a sword at his side,
discusses a report on improved rice production or yak-breeding. The
report has been produced on a computer in the dark offices of a
fortress where, across the courtyard, monks perform a ceremony for
the guardian deities of Bhutan.
    The Bhutanese do not reject their cultural and spiritual heritage in
favour of modern imported values. Never having been colonized,
always fiercely independent and proud of their traditions, they see no
need to adopt ideas simply because they come from more developed
and powerful countries. Using common sense, they accept only those
ideas that help them to improve their way of life and develop their
country within the framework of their own traditions without
destroying the environment. Uninhibited, they continue to follow

customs that many other countries would condemn as archaic. The Bhutanese have no desire for cultural assimilation. They are different and intend to remain so.

Above and beyond the beauty of the land, the architecture, the human kindness, it is this quiet self-confidence, this pride of the people in their values and faith in their religion that holds the secret of Bhutan's charm, the ineffable quality that evades definition and provides endless fascination.

Facts for the Traveller

Bhutan's policy of restricting tourism has three purposes. First, it aims to preserve the natural environment and the lifestyle of the people without upsetting their existing socio-economic balance. Second, it recognizes the lack of infrastructure and tourist facilities, the rugged character of the terrain and problems of communication. Third, by charging all travellers a daily fee for tourist services (hotels, transport, meals, guide, etc.), Bhutan is able to earn the foreign currency it needs for expenditure in other areas of development. Bhutan receives an average of 2,500 tourists a year.

Getting to Bhutan

It is impossible to visit Bhutan as an individual traveller except by official invitation from the government. You must come in a group of at least six persons, or else sign up with a tour group organized in Europe or America. The Bhutan Tourism Corporation (BTC), an office of the government, provides tourist services within the country and manages all tourist affairs (except for Indian nationals, who enjoy a special status). Rates vary according to the season and type of accommodation, but you should count on at least US$170 per day. Diplomats can take advantage of slightly different conditions. For further information about arrangements, rates or methods of payment, write in English to the Bhutan Tourism Corporation (see Useful Addresses, page 256).

Individuals travelling in India and Thailand can join special groups to Bhutan organized by the BTC, leaving either from Calcutta on Fridays and returning on Tuesdays, or from Bangkok, where a 'Three Kingdom Tour' is offered through Thai International, starting from Thailand and taking in both Nepal and Bhutan. A five-day tour departs from Bangkok on Wednesdays and a four-day tour departs on Sundays.

By Air The only practical way for tourists to enter Bhutan is by air. Druk Air, Bhutan's national airline, has been in operation since 1983 and has its headquarters at the airport at Paro. Outside the country it is sometimes known by the name of Royal Bhutan Airlines. The fleet currently consists of one twin-engine Donier 228 propeller aircraft carrying 17 passengers, and one BAe 146 four-engine jet

carrying 70 passengers.

From October to April, when the skies are generally clear, the flight into Bhutan provides fantastic views over the Himalayas (Ganesh Himal, Cho Oyu, Everest, Lhotse, Makalu, Kanchenjunga, Chomolhari, Gangkar Phunsum, Kula Kangri). Upon landing at Paro Airport you will be met by a tour-guide and a bus. Druk Air also operates a bus between the airport and Thimphu. The bus ride from Paro to Thimphu takes 1 hour 15 minutes and costs 25 *ngultrums*, or US$2.

Druk Air timetables are often subject to change without prior notice, so you should confirm times by telex from Druk Air Thimphu, or ask the Druk Air agent in Bangkok (Thailand), Dhaka (Bangladesh), Delhi, Calcutta (India) or Kathmandu (Nepal). To give a general idea, in July 1989 the flight Paro–Dhaka–Bangkok–Dhaka–Paro took place on Wednesdays; the flight Paro–Delhi–Paro on Monday and Thursday mornings; the flight Paro–Calcutta–Paro on Tuesday and Friday mornings; and Paro–Kathmandu–Paro on Sunday mornings.

Paro Airport is in the mountains, where weather conditions sometimes prevent flights from landing or taking off. You should therefore try to avoid tight connections, if possible allowing a full day between the flight out of Bhutan and any ongoing flights. If Druk Air is unable to fly, it normally takes no responsibility for passengers' expenses while they wait (hotel, food, etc.), except on the Bangkok flights.

All air costs into or out of Bhutan must be paid in US dollars, either in cash or travellers' cheques. Credit cards are not accepted. The only exception is when Druk Air tickets are bought in Thimphu. Chundu Travel and Yu Druk Travel both accept American Express.

Tourist groups travelling by arrangement with BTC receive a 30 percent discount on Druk Air. The reduced prices were as follows in 1989: Paro–Bangkok = US$209; Paro–Kathmandu = US$105; Paro–Delhi = US$182; Paro–Calcutta = US$105; Paro–Dhaka = US$105. For further information, write in English to the Managing Director of Druk Air (see Useful Addresses, page 256).

Visas

Bhutan requires visas but it does not issue them abroad. Details about your passport must be given to the travel organization arranging your trip at least 15 days before you leave for Bhutan, and the BTC handles all formalities from then on. You will not be permitted to board the plane into Bhutan unless the clearance has come from Thimphu. The visa itself will be stamped into your passport on arrival at Paro Airport. It costs US$20, which must be paid in cash.

Leaving Bhutan

Airport Tax There is an airport tax of 50 *ngultrums* per person upon departure from Paro. The airports from where you catch your flight into Bhutan may also charge a tax. The amount varies from one country to another, so it is a good idea to inquire in each country.

Customs It is strictly forbidden to export antiques. It is also forbidden to take out religious objects such as statues, prayer wheels, reliquaries, bells or *vajras*, whether old or new. It is better to avoid trouble and buy what you want in India, Nepal or Sikkim. If you have already bought a religious object before entering Bhutan, declare it on your customs form and mention it to your Bhutanese guide. However, an exception is made for new *thangkas* (painted religious scrolls) purchased at the state store, the Handicrafts Emporium, in Thimphu, but they must be accompanied by a certificate from the Department of Antiquities. Your guide will take care of that formality for you. Tourists are strongly discouraged from buying anything directly from villagers in order to safeguard Bhutan's cultural heritage. It is advisable to ask for sales receipts from all shops to show to customs inspectors when you leave Bhutan. Purchases without sales slips run the risk of being confiscated. It is also forbidden to take out any butterflies, plants or flowers.

Money

Bhutan's unit of currency is the *ngultrum* (Nu.), which equals 100 *chetrum*. A *ngultrum* has the same value as an Indian rupee, which is also legal tender. As of July 1989, one US dollar equalled roughly 16 Nu. Tourists can exchange travellers' cheques or cash at the Bank of Bhutan in Thimphu or in their hotels. American dollars, pounds sterling, French or Swiss francs, German marks or Japanese yen are the accepted currencies.

Credit cards are still unknown in Bhutan except in Thimphu where a few shops and travel agencies will take American Express cards.

(The BTC does not accept credit cards for payment of any of its services such as hotels and meals.) Personal cheques are not accepted anywhere in Bhutan.

Communications

The Bhutanese postal system is slow but relatively reliable. The honesty and goodwill of Thimphu's postmen are worth a mention. As of 1989, postcards for all destinations except India, Nepal and Bhutan require a 3 Nu. stamp. Letters for Europe require 4.50 Nu., for Asia 4 Nu., for America 5 Nu., for India, Nepal or Bhutan 50 *chetrum*. A letter takes about ten days to reach Europe, one week to Japan and three weeks to America. Packages (up to 5 kg or 11 lb) should be sent by registered mail.

Bhutanese stamps are beautiful and a joy to stamp collectors. If this is your interest, ask at the philatelic office of the Thimphu Post Office to see the stamp albums and also buy first-day covers there.

There is a public telex in Thimphu, in addition to telex lines used by government offices. The rates are for a minimum of three minutes but the lines are frequently out of order. Likewise, if the telephone lines are working, it is possible to make international calls but there is likely to be a long delay as calls have to go through two exchanges, one in Bhutan and another in India. If you should get through and are not cut off, a clear connection is rare. Telephoning can be a trying experience for the nerves and a waste of time. Moral: only try telephoning in a real emergency and don't count on a good connection!

Bhutan's country code is 975. The government is in the process of installing a satellite telephone system, which will greatly facilitate communications.

From Thimphu you can place a call through an operator to Paro, Punakha, Wangdi Phodrang, Ha and Phuntsholing. Telephone calls can also be made between Tashigang, Samdrup Jongkhar and Kanglung. However, communications within the country are usually made by radio.

Local Time

Bhutan's time is six hours later than Greenwich Mean Time. When it is 12 noon GMT, it is 6 pm in Bhutan. Bhutan's time is half an hour later than India's. When it is 12 noon in New Delhi, it is 12.30 pm in Bhutan.

Health

Inoculations

Although no inoculations are compulsory, it is advisable to have tetanus and typhoid shots (TAB). In addition, gamma globulin is recommended against viral hepatitis A. The inoculations should be spread out over a period of six weeks. If you expect to stay in Bhutan for an extended period, you should also be vaccinated against polio, diphtheria, meningitis and measles.

Precautions

Amoebas and giardias (parasites that cause dysentery) are rife. Avoid drinking unboiled water or ice cubes, and never eat unpeeled fruit or raw vegetables. Bear in mind that tablets for disinfecting water are not effective against all types of amoeba. Bottled mineral water can be purchased in Thimphu and some of the hotels.

People susceptible to car sickness should not travel in Bhutan unless they bring adequate medicine. The roads have thousands of curves and turns and the straight stretches can be counted on the fingers of two hands.

Malaria

Malaria is endemic in the southern region and chloroquine is not totally effective. In case of an attack, take one dose (three tablets) of Fansidar. In any event, keep plenty of mosquito repellent, cream or lotion on any exposed areas of skin when you are outdoors and burn mosquito coils, when possible, indoors (available in Thimphu and in the south).

Altitude

The average altitude during a trip is 2,300 metres (7,500 feet) but on a trek it may reach as high as 5,400 metres (17,500 feet). It is advisable to drink considerably more liquids at high altitudes than at sea level as dehydration is common. If you have heart problems or high blood pressure, you should consult your own doctor before undertaking a trip to Bhutan. A mild sleeping pill can be helpful against insomnia

BHUTAN

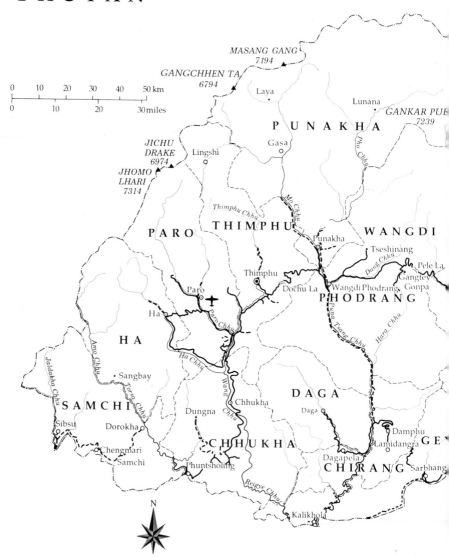

MASANG GANG
7194

GANGCHHEN TA
6794

Laya

Lunana

GANKAR PUE
7239

PUNAKHA

JICHU
DRAKE
6974   Lingshi

Gasa

JHOMO
LHARI
7314

Thimphu Chhu

THIMPHU

PARO

WANGDI

Punakha

Tseshinang

Pele La

Thimphu   Dochu La   Gangtey
Gonpa

Paro   Wangdi Phodrang

PHODRANG

Ha

HA

Sangbay

DAGA

Daga

Damphu
Lamidangra   **GE**

SAMCHI   Dungna   Chhukha

Sibsu   Dorokha

CHHUKHA   Dagapela

Chengmari   Phuntsholing   **CHIRANG**   Sarbhang
Samchi

Kalikhola

N

0 10 20 30 40 50 km

0 10 20 30 miles

International Boundary

Dzongkhag (District) Boundary

Paved Road

Unpaved Road/ Under Construction

River

▲ Mountain

◉ Capital

Dzongkhag (District) Headquarter

Dungkhag (Sub-district) Headquarter

· Town, Village

✈ Airport

)(Pass

KULA KANGRI
7554

Lhedang·

LHUNTSHI

Lhuntshi

BUMTHANG

Kurjey
Jakar
Yutong La

Ura

Thumsing La

GSA

Shemgang

MONGAR

Mongar

Tashi Yangtse

Dametsi

Gamri Chhu

Radi

Tashigang

Sakteng

Merak

TASHIGANG

Bumthang Chhu

Kuru Chhu

Kulong Chhu

Bumthang Chhu

Wamrong Thrimshing

HUG

SHEMGANG

PEMA-GATSEL

Pemagatsel

SAMDRUP

JONGKHAR

Daifam

Panbang

Nganglam

Samdrup Jongkhar

Bangtar

phug

Manas Chhu

Badi Chhu

Dhansiri Chhu

Drangme Chhu

Mongde Chhu

caused by the altitude. Headaches are common during the first days of a trip; it is best to keep away from any alcoholic drinks until you are acclimatized.

Medication

Bring all your customary medicines with you plus a laxative, an anti-diarrhoea medicine (an oral rehydration solution is also very helpful in case of diarrhoea), antihistamine tablets, anti-nausea tablets (in case of mountain sickness), eye lotion, lip salve and one or two syringes with disposable needles. Thimphu has three pharmacies that are well stocked with antibiotics and analgesics.

Hospitals

The hospital at Thimphu is a far cry from hospitals with Western facilities but it is the best equipped in the country, with general physicians, specialists and dentists, a laboratory for tests and an operating room, but no intensive care unit. Simpler hospital units exist in all major centres throughout the country. Medical care is free.

Climate

It is hard to generalize about Bhutan's weather since the mountain climate varies enormously from one region to another. It varies with the altitude and can also reach extremes of heat and cold within the same 24 hours at any given altitude.

Southern Bhutan is tropical, with a monsoon season. The east is warmer than the west. The central valleys of Punakha, Wangdi Phodrang, Mongar, Tashigang and Lhuntshi enjoy a semi-tropical climate with very cool winters, whereas Ha, Paro, Thimphu, Tongsa and Bumthang have a much harsher climate, including occasional snowfalls in winter. The north of the country is inhabited up to 5,000 metres (16,400 feet) in summer. The climate there is rough, with monsoon rains in summer and heavy snowfalls in winter that block the passes leading into the central valleys.

In these valleys, where most tourist activities are concentrated, the winters (mid-November to mid-March) are dry, with daytime temperatures of 16–18°C (60–65°F) if the sun is shining. By contrast, the evenings and early mornings are cold, with night-time temperatures falling below freezing. Snow covers the mountain tops but reaches the valleys only two or three times each winter.

Spring lasts from mid-March to the beginning of June, with temperatures warming gradually to 27–29°C (80–84°F) by day and 18°C (64°F) at night. However, cold spells are possible up until the end of April, with a chance of new snow on the mountains above the valleys. Strong, gusty winds start blowing almost every day from noon to about 6 pm, raising clouds of dust. (Many roofs get blown off in this season!) The first storms break, and they become more and more frequent with the approach of the monsoon which arrives in mid-June.

This brings the rainy season. Bhutan then receives abundant rain, especially in the south, as it gets the full force of the monsoon coming up from the Bay of Bengal, to which its mountains form a barrier. However, apart from the first days of the monsoon when it rains without stopping, the rain falls mainly in the late evening and at night. Temperatures get a little cooler—23–24°C (73–75°F) by day and 15–16°C (59–61°F) at night, but the sun often comes out from behind the clouds and the days are very pleasant. It is worth noting that, unless you are extremely lucky, it is almost impossible to get a clear view of the high Himalayas from the end of March until the end of September.

At the end of September, after the last of the big rains, autumn suddenly arrives. All at once the sky clears, a brisk breeze picks up and temperatures start falling towards freezing at night although bright sunshine continues to keep the days warm. Autumn is a magnificent season that lasts until mid-November.

Clothing

The wide range of temperatures does not make dressing easy. The best solution is to wear several layers, such as a cotton shirt, pullover, wool cardigan and jacket, which can be taken off or added as needed. Do not bring delicate clothes: conservative sportswear is the appropriate style for a traveller in Bhutan.

Even in summer you will need a sweater or a light jacket in the evening. An umbrella is a 'must' in all seasons. It is more useful than a raincoat and acts as protection not only against the rain but also against the sun, which can be fierce at these altitudes. Comfortable sports shoes are strongly recommended; mountain boots are not necessary unless you plan to go trekking.

From May to September, cotton clothes are sufficient, plus a woollen sweater or light jacket. From November to the end of April, on the other hand, you will need very warm clothes including long underwear or woollen tights to wear under trousers, and a down jacket or coat. Houses and hotels are very poorly heated; the electricity is often cut off and rooms can become icy cold, especially at night when the temperature indoors can drop to 3–4°C (37–39°F). It is dangerous to leave the small electric heater running all night because of the risk of a short-circuit and fire.

Clothes dry fast and you are able to get your laundry returned, washed and ironed, on the following day in all the hotels at Thimphu, Paro, Phuntsholing, Bumthang and Tashigang. Dry cleaning takes two weeks!

The Bhutanese are conservative and wear their own national costume. Clothes that are too tight-fitting, short or revealing, such as shorts, miniskirts or low-cut T-shirts, cause offence, especially in the countryside, and should be avoided by visitors. If you are going to meet a member of the government, city clothes are recommended (jacket and tie for men, skirt for women).

Equipment and Supplies

As well as the medical supplies mentioned on page 27, you may want to bring with you: sunscreen lotion, sunglasses, a water flask, a torch (flashlight) with extra batteries, a folding pocket knife, a hat or headscarf in summer, cap and gloves in winter, disinfectant tablets for water, insect repellent (summer) and paper tissues. Toilet paper and talcum powder can be purchased in the main towns. Sanitary towels for women can be found but are expensive and mediocre in quality— better to bring your own.

Coffee-lovers may want to bring their own preferred brand. Packets of dried soup and herbal teabags are very comforting when you are not feeling well. Dried fruit is available but expensive and of poor quality. Salami, cheese, etc. brought from abroad help to liven up ordinary picnics.

Cigarettes imported from India are available but expensive. In Thimphu only, you can find Western cigarettes (555, Rothmans, Dunhill, Marlboro) but at prohibitive prices. If you smoke, you would do better to bring your own.

Photography

You should plan to bring all your own photographic equipment, including film and batteries. You can find film for prints in Thimphu but rarely for slides. There is no way to get a camera repaired in Bhutan. Video cameras are permitted but 16 mm movie cameras are not, the latter being considered professional equipment and subject to very high duty.

Photography is not allowed inside religious monuments or *dzongs*!

Electricity

Bhutan's electricity is 220 V but it is erratic. Power cuts are frequent, even in Thimphu. In the rest of the country, the power supply depends on so many factors that it tends to be very irregular. Always keep a torch (flashlight) handy. Do not rely on an electric razor.

Food and Drink

Lack of variety prevents Bhutanese cooking from ranking among the world's great cuisines, but it is nonetheless quite interesting.

There are three conditions for fully appreciating Bhutanese cooking: you should like hot, spicy food, you should like meat fat, and you should like dried meat. However, to set your mind at rest, there are many vegetable dishes that do not contain the last two ingredients though hot chilli peppers are to be found in some form in all of them. The national dish, *hemadatsi*, is made entirely of chillies (*hema*), treated as a vegetable rather than as seasoning, and served in a cheese sauce.

Nowadays, a typical Bhutanese meal consists of a mountain of rice (the Bhutanese eat up to a kilo of rice a day) and two or three dishes with various stews, the number of which increases with the status of the family.

The rice may be white or red; the latter is a special variety, not whole-grain rice. Rice is becoming increasingly the staple food throughout the country whereas, until quite recently, buckwheat pancakes (*kule*) and noodles (*buta*) were the main component of the diet of Bumthang in Central Bhutan, and maize in the eastern regions.

Melted, soft fresh cheese (*datsi*) is used to make the sauce in which many vegetables are cooked, especially potatoes, mushrooms, asparagus and fiddlehead ferns. The Bhutanese are skilled at using wild food products from the forests: fiddleheads, bamboo, mushrooms, taro, yams, sweet potatoes, wild beans, banana-flower buds, and even orchids and dried river weed. Soya is only eaten in certain areas of Eastern Bhutan.

Most stews contain a little meat or small bones. The favourite meats of the northern Bhutanese are yak and pork. Beef and chicken are the second choice, while mutton and lamb are not eaten at all. Meat can be eaten fresh or dried and, except in summer, it is common to see strips of meat drying on lines or hanging from windows. Pork-fat is considered a delicacy, and the best of all and the second most popular national dish after *hemadatsi* is undoubtedly *phagshapa*, strips of pork-fat, often dried, stewed with radishes or turnips and dried chillies.

Scrambled eggs cooked in butter are the main ingredient of *gondomaru*, while Bhutanese salad, *eze*, composed of hot peppers, soft cheese, tomatoes and finely chopped onions, complements other dishes. Fresh fish is rare because religious considerations rule out fishing, but dried fish brought up from the plains makes a tasty stew mixed with hot peppers.

Small pieces of liver dredged in chilli powder, lung stuffed with a special variety of pepper, pig's feet and blood sausages filled with hot peppers are specialities that the casual visitor will probably not have an opportunity to taste.

Rice is eaten with the right hand, pressed into a small ball and dipped in the stew, or alternated with bits of meat or vegetable. The powerful hot peppers often cause noses and eyes to run, but this just provides proof of a properly seasoned meal. Sweets and desserts barely exist except for *kabze*, dried fritters in various shapes that are prepared for festivals.

Roasted flour, called *pchie* (similar to *tsampa*), toasted rice (*zao*), flattened rice (*sip*) and flattened maize (*gesasip*) are served with tea as an appetizer or for breakfast. They can be eaten dry or dipped in the tea.

Tea is generally considered to be the most widely consumed beverage, but it is surprising to note that in parts of Central and Eastern Bhutan, *ara*, a drink with 20 percent alcohol content, is the commonest drink. There are two kinds of tea: *seudja*, which is tea churned with salt and butter, and *nadja*, tea brewed with milk and sugar in the Indian style. Coffee, or rather Nescafé, is a recent innovation and a luxury which is not to be found in village homes.

Drinking pure milk is also a new habit that has not become widespread. Traditionally, milk has always been turned into butter and cheese. *Datsi*, the small, round, soft cheeses on sale in the market, are never eaten raw but are used to thicken sauces. Another kind of cheese is *churpi*, which you will see as a loop of big white cubes strung together. This cheese, made in yak-breeding areas, is nibbled between meals and is unbelievably hard. The last kind of cheese, and the most sought-after because it is the most difficult to find, comes from Eastern Bhutan and is called *seudeu*. It resembles a greyish green blob and is sold in leather containers. Its pervasive smell and unappetizing appearance may repel foreign cheese-lovers. It is never eaten raw but is mixed in small quantities into broth to make soup.

Among specialities of Tibetan origin, by far the most popular are *momos*, little raviolis stuffed with meat, vegetables or cheese. *Thukpa* is a noodle soup that many people enjoy in winter. *Shabale* are fried dumplings stuffed with minced meat. The more rarely found *trimomo* is steamed bread served with a soup.

A meal must always end with the passing around of *doma*. *Doma* is a quid of betel, but in Bhutan this is much more than a simple aid to digestion. To offer *doma* to somebody is to express friendship and it is a symbol of sociability. Ready-made quids of betel wrapped in little paper cones can be bought perfectly easily but the true betel-lover prepares his own, which involves a whole ritual.

Apart from its social significance, *doma* is an intoxicating substance on about the same level as tobacco, and also has harmful effects. The government is now trying to limit the use of *doma* and young people are eating less and less of it.

In the south of Bhutan, *supari* or *pan* takes the place of *doma*. There the regional cooking is much less distinctive, being very close to the cuisines of India and Nepal. There are more vegetables, lentils and onions, and the favourite meats are mutton and chicken.

Indian beer is available in all urban centres, as well as whisky, gin and rum, produced in Bhutan at reasonable prices. According to connoisseurs, Special Courier and Bhutan Mist pure malt whiskies are good. There is no wine but there are local alcoholic drinks made from grains, *ara* and *chang*, which are not always produced under the most hygienic conditions.

A distillery in the Bumthang Valley produces very reasonably
priced cider, apple wine and apple and peach brandy. These products
can be bought in Thimphu at Lhatshog, shop No. 7. It is impossible
for tourists to buy Western alcoholic drinks.

Shopping

Bhutan has very fine handicrafts. Objects are fashioned from bamboo,
wood and silver, and there are many kinds of fabric and even
thangkas. Bhutanese handicrafts differ from those of other Asian
countries in two respects: they are not oriented to the tourist market,
thereby remaining authentic, and they are relatively expensive.
Bargaining is not a custom in Bhutan so you cannot hope to get more
than a 10 percent reduction.

There are no handicraft shops except in Thimphu, so shopping
elsewhere is difficult and there is very little choice. You might meet
somebody while you are travelling across the country who will sell
you something typical of that region, but it is by no means certain.
Thimphu is without question the best place to find a variety of goods
from all over Bhutan; here you can make comparisons and choices.
One word of advice: if you see something you like, buy it at once
because shops do not keep any stocks. (For more information on
handicrafts, see page 88.)

Thangkas

Religious banners that are new but painted according to the strict
rules of traditional iconography are sold primarily at the government-
run Handicrafts Emporium. They can be mounted on brocade or not,
as you like. Without brocade, the lowest price is around US$25; a
large thangka with brocade can run up to US$335.

Fabrics and Clothing

Handwoven fabrics are the pride of Bhutan and will remind textile-
lovers of weavings from Laos, from the tribes of northeastern India or
the Amerindians of Central America and Peru. Prized around the
world, some pieces are collector's items. Handwoven fabrics cannot
be bought by the metre or yard.

The cheapest fabrics are plain cotton, while the most expensive are
masterpieces, representing many months of intensive work, which are

covered with silk designs on a base of either cotton or silk. There are different types of textile for different purposes: belts; the women's national dress (*kira*); the men's garment (*go*); the women's ceremonial scarves (*rachung*); and the men's (*kabne*); ceremonial cloths (*chasipangkhep*); bags (*pechung* or *bundi*); and rolls of woollen cloth from Bumthang called *yatra* which, when sewn, serve as coverlets, sofa covers or jackets.

A woman's dress, or *kira*, is a simple rectangular piece of cloth 2.5 by 1.5 metres (roughly 2.5 by 1.5 yards). It is wound around the body, secured at the shoulders by two silver clasps and gathered in at the waist by a wide belt. A *kira* is usually made up of three pieces of cloth sewn together to form the rectangle, but it can also be made from a dozen narrow strips which in this case are always of wool. A man's *go* is cut somewhat like a kimono and reaches the ankles. It is pulled up to the knees and fastened at the waist by a narrower belt than the woman's, forming a large pouch over the abdomen.

In 1989, a simple cotton *kira* was worth about US$20, a *kira* with silk designs on cotton cost US$300 and US$800, and a *kira* of silk on silk cost US$1,150–2,500. A *go* made of raw silk cost US$130–170; a *go* or *kira* of wool was between US$60 and US$75. A *yatra* was US$50 and US$80. A man's belt cost US$5, and a woman's varied between US$2.50 for the cheapest and US$50 for a fine silk one. Shops in Thimphu which sell excellent traditional textiles are the Handicrafts Emporium, Tshering Drolkar, Ethometo, the shop at the Hotel Motithang, and Peljorkhang (located at the main crossroads of the town).

You can also buy a *kira* or *go* made of Bhutanese machine-woven material at Gyeltsen Tsongkhang (shop No. 30 with large glass windows on a lower level than the bank opposite it). There are also Bhutanese children's clothes of machine-woven material which are cheap and make delightful gifts.

It is sometimes possible to find large pieces of raw silk at the Handicrafts Emporium, either natural in colour or dyed maroon, orange or dark blue (they are actually men's ceremonial scarves).

Jewellery and Silverwork

The most popular products are wooden alcohol-receptacles mounted and decorated with beaten silver, and containers for ingredients used in the preparation of betel nut: these are rectangular boxes to contain the betel leaves and areca nut (about US$135), and little round boxes to hold the lime.

Bhutanese jewellery is limited but spectacular: large clasps of chased silver connected by a chain, earrings of gold and turquoise, heavy silver bracelets with simple engraving or set with coral and turquoise, silver belt ornaments and elaborate pearl necklaces.

Bhutanese and Tibetan jewellery can be bought at the Handicrafts Emporium, Ethometo (ground floor of the tourism building), Tshering Drolkar (at the end of the hall, ground floor of the tourism building), the shop in the Hotel Motithang, and Zangmo (shop No. 16 located just beyond the Emporium on the opposite side of the road). The first three shops mentioned also sell 'ethnic' jewellery at easily affordable prices, especially rings set with coral, lapis lazuli or turquoise. This kind of jewellery is in fact imported from Nepal and India.

Woodwork

The most beautiful woodcarving is found on wall panels and small folding tables that are nearly always painted. Masks represent human characters, animals or gods who appear in sacred dances. They can be made of wood or papier-mâché and are always painted. They come in two sizes: normal and miniature.

Lacquered bowls and receptacles vary considerably in price depending on the quality of the wood (ordinary wood or gnarled) and whether or not they are mounted with silver. Woodwork and masks can be found at the Handicrafts Emporium and Ethometo.

Carved Slate

You can sometimes find etched slate objects of excellent quality at the Handicrafts Emporium but their weight can create a problem if you are travelling by air.

Bamboo and Rattan Wares

Common objects for everyday use are the cheapest, most authentic souvenirs you can purchase. In certain shops in Thimphu and in the Sunday market you will find tea or alcohol strainers, conical hats, quivers, tall baskets for serving rice, rectangular mats for sorting rice and other grains, or slender bamboo cylinders covered with braided

strips and pierced with a hole—they are for carrying alcohol.
Rectangular baskets with lids, called *zem*, are meant to be slung over
the flanks of pack animals. They are now very rare except in
miniature. Finally, there are the famous *banchung*, light round baskets
decorated with coloured geometric designs whose two parts stack one
inside the other and close tightly: they are very practical for carrying
food and can also be used as plates.

Paper and Books
Bhutanese paper (see also page 113) is handmade in large, square
sheets with flecks of bark still visible. It is excellent for painting on,
for doing calligraphy or for making original gift-wrapping. It can be
bought by the sheet at the Handicrafts Emporium.

The National Library Shop, a little way beyond the Emporium on
the opposite side of the street, sells traditional Bhutanese books at
affordable prices, as well as religious postcards. The shop is open at
unpredictable times but, in general, it follows office hours.

Rugs
Most of the good rugs that you find in Thimphu are made locally.
Bhutan has always produced outstanding fabrics but never rugs. They
are imported from Tibet. The best choice of rugs is at Tshering
Drolkar, at the Motithang Hotel and sometimes at Zangmo. Although
rugs are starting to be woven in Bhutan, the quality is poor.

Other Things to Buy
Some other interesting things you may find at the Handicrafts
Emporium are waterproof black hats, made of yak hair, which come
from the eastern region of Merak Sakteng. The appendages that stick
out around them allow the rain to run off without getting your face
wet. Wallets and other articles made out of traditional fabrics are
very popular.

The only non-religious musical instrument, which can sometimes
be purchased at the Handicrafts Emporium, is the *dranyen*, a kind of
lute made of painted wood. In the Sunday market it is often possible
to buy the long, copper, telescopic trumpets that are used for religious
ceremonies.

Bundles of incense are available everywhere. The quality is better than that of Indian incense as it is composed of pure incense without added sticks of wood for strength, but that means it is also much more fragile.

Bhutan's stamps (see also page 22) are greatly prized by collectors and are very cheap since they are sold at their postal value.

Excellent maps of Bhutan and the town of Thimphu are available, as well as cassettes of secular and religious Bhutanese music, although they are not professional recordings. The Ethometo shop sells maps and cassettes, also postcards, T-shirts and sweat shirts with emblems of Bhutan, and magnificent Bhutan calendars. A good selection of Tibetan and Bhutanese calendars and modern religious paraphernalia can also be found at shop No. 132, Sangay Department Store (on the main street, opposite the road to the Post Office).

Darjeeling tea is a good buy. The best brands are Lopchu (pink and blue package) or Makaibari Apoorva (green and yellow package). These can be found at Lhatshog, shop No. 7, where you can also find the alcoholic drinks produced in Bumthang: cider, apple wine and apple brandy. Out of curiosity, take a look at the blackish cones and bricks of tea leaves that are used for making butter-tea. Shop No. 8 of Dawa Tshering (to the left of No. 7) has a whole assortment of such typical goods and is worth a visit if you do not have a chance to see the Sunday market.

Boots made of leather or felt look attractive but are fairly uncomfortable because they are cut very wide.

Bhutanese machine-woven check material made of mixed wool and polyester can be bought by the metre at Gyeltsen Tsongkhang, mentioned above. Warm and strong, it is intended for school uniforms and costs about US$5 per metre. It makes excellent winter shirts, skirts or dresses. You can also find printed flannelette (ask for *pooche*) at about US$1.25 a metre. You can have a shirt made for US$2.50 in 24 hours by the Indian tailors located on the left side of the tourism building or at the Emporium. Unfortunately, they do not know how to make skirts or dresses.

The two pieces of a Bhutanese woman's costume, which can be easily worn in the West, are the blouse (*onju*) and the little jacket (*toego*). Neither one fastens, both are cut on the same pattern and one size fits all, more or less. They can be found most easily at Gyeltsen Tsongkhang, Ugyen Dorje Tsongkhang and Karmapa Tsongkhang. They are usually made of polyester and cost about US$7 for the blouse, US$14 for the jacket. When they are made of silk or imported brocade, the price goes up to US$40 or more.

Ceremonial white scarves (*kata*) for presentation (see page 105) are found, among other places, at Gyeltsen Tsongkhang, Karmapa Tsongkhang and Ugyen Dorje Tsongkhang. The least expensive cost a few cents but they are made of coarse tulle and are not really presentable. The ones called *ashi kata* cost about US$1 and are of a much better quality. The most expensive, which are offered on exceptional occasions, can cost up to US$16.

Areas Open to Visitors

Since January 1988, foreign visitors have been forbidden to visit most of Bhutan's temples, fortresses and monasteries. This decision was taken in order to protect the works of art, to prevent any commercialization of the religion, and to preserve the sanctity of its ceremonies. In exceptional cases and for a particular site, written permission may be granted by the Secretary of the Special Commission for Cultural Affairs. The list of religious monuments where tourists were still permitted to enter was as follows in 1989:

Western Bhutan

Paro district: Ta Dzong (National Museum), Drukyel Dzong, viewpoint looking at Taktsang from the tourist inn, Bitekha Dzong.

At Thimphu: Tashichoedzong (in winter when the monks are at Punakha), Memorial Chorten of the Third King, Temples of Changlimithang and Jigmeling.

Chukha district: Temples of Zangdopelri and Kharbandi at Phuntsholing, Temples of Kamji, Chasilakha and Chime, and Chapcha Dzong.

Chirang district: Temples of Damphu and Lamidara.

Punakha district: Punakha Dzong (in summer when the monks are in Thimphu).

Central Bhutan

Jakar (Bumthang) district: Wangdichoeling Dzong, Sacred Lake of Mabartsho, Temple of Ura.

Geylegphug district: Monasteries of Tharpaling and Nyimalung, Temples of Sershong and Sergang.

Eastern Bhutan

Mongar district: Mongar Dzong.

Tashigang district: Temple of Zangdopelri at Kanglung, Temples of Radi, Merak and Sakteng, Tashi Yangtse Dzong.

Samdrup Jongkhar district: Temple of Zangdopelri.

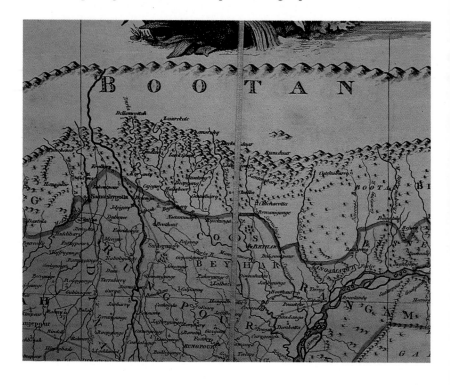

The Land of Bhutan

Geography and Population

Bhutan's isolation from the Western world can be explained in large part by its geography. Located between India and the autonomous region of Tibet, China, between 88°45' and 92°10' longitude east and between 26°40' and 28°15' latitude north, the country covers 47,000 square kilometres (18,147 square miles). It has a population density (1987) of 28.9 people per square kilometre (74.8 per square mile). Population growth is 2 percent per annum.

Bhutan forms a gigantic staircase from a narrow strip of land in the south at an altitude of 300 metres (985 feet) up to high Himalayan peaks in the north with an altitude of over 7,000 metres (23,000 feet).

Access

The most densely populated and fertile regions are the southern borderlands, the foothills of the Himalayas, with an altitude between 300 and 1,600 metres (985–5,250 feet) and the central valleys, with an altitude between 1,100 and 2,600 metres (3,600–8,530 feet). Until the 1960s, the central valleys were very hard to reach from the south because a formidable mountain wall rises 2,000 metres (6,500 feet) from the plain, cut through with jungle-filled gorges that made travel dangerous and slow. It took five days to cover the hundred-odd kilometres (150 miles) of paths that separated the capital of Thimphu from Buxa Duar on the Indian border.

Paradoxically, until the closing of the border with Tibet in 1959, the High Himalayas provided easy access in several places, with certain passes open even in winter. There were numerous cultural and economic exchanges between the two countries, going all the way back to the seventh century.

In the first half of the 20th century, some of the more accessible regions of Bhutan were settled by people of Nepalese origin who could tolerate low altitudes. In 1962, a paved road was constructed for north–south traffic linking Thimphu with Phuntsholing in the southwest, and in 1963 another was completed between Thimphu and Samdrup Jongkhar in the southeast.

Southern Bhutan

With the coming of the paved road, the narrow southern plain, formerly called the Duars, 'the Gates', and the Himalayan foothills — up to 1,700 metres (5,575 feet) — could now be made productive. The proximity of markets in northern India and Bangladesh contributed to the development of these areas and small trading towns came into existence: Phuntsholing, Geylegphug and Samdrup Jongkhar. Small industries producing such goods as alcohol, bricks, clothes, matches, fruit juice and jam started up in this border region. Two big cement plants, Panden in the west and Nanglam in the east, and a calcium carbide factory at Pasakha, export the major part of their production. Apart from rice grown for local consumption, other crops, including oranges and cardamom, are directed towards foreign markets.

The southern regions are inhabited mainly by peasants of Nepalese origin, high-caste people and tribal populations who continued to immigrate from the end of the 19th century until about 1950. They are full Bhutanese citizens, officially designated as Southern Bhutanese.

The Central Himalayas

In the central Himalayas where Bhutan is located, summer rice and winter wheat are grown in the valleys of Paro, Thimphu, Punakha, Wangdi Phodrang, Lhuntshi and part of Tashigang, while barley, buckwheat and wheat are the crops of Ha and Bumthang which lie above 2,600 metres (8,500 feet). Since the beginning of the 1980s, potatoes have made a remarkable breakthrough in areas that are too high or too poor for rice. Thus, Chapcha, south of Thimphu, Bumthang, the glacial valley of Gantey (Phobjika) near the Pele La (*la* means pass), and the Kanglung region near Tashigang are experiencing an economic boom thanks to this tuber that has made itself at home in Bhutan. In the east, where the soil is poorer, maize is the main crop, with the best soil saved for rice cultivation. Millet is grown everywhere and turned into alcohol. The Thimphu and Paro areas also produce peaches and plums but specialize in apples and asparagus. A large part of the two latter crops goes for export. Oranges and bananas, consumed locally, grow in Punakha, Wangdi Phodrang, Mongar, Lhuntshi and Tashigang.

The raising of livestock — pigs, cattle and poultry — is widespread both in the central valleys and the south, but the purpose is home *(following pages)* Remains of the Drukyel dzong *(burnt down in the early 1950s) guarding an entrance to Paro valley, with Jhomolhari Mountain's snowy peak in the background*

45

consumption rather than mass production. Sheep are raised in Bumthang to produce wool rather than meat, as the Bhutanese do not like mutton. Moreover, religious beliefs prevent the killing of animals for meat.

The central Himalayan region is the home of the Drukpa people, mainly peasants and livestock breeders, who are of Mongoloid stock and speak languages of the Tibeto-Burman family. Their dwellings are normally scattered but towns are now developing around the *dzongs* (monastery-fortresses) which formerly defended each valley. Their appearance is directly related to the improved network of communications, the growth of an administrative infrastructure and the birth of a middle class made up of civil servants and small shopkeepers.

In addition to the High Himalaya's which run east–west, mountain chains also run north–south at a height of 4,000–5,000 metres (13,000–16,400 feet), traversing the country and forming veritable barriers between different regions. Each of the central valleys is thus a microcosm separated from the next valley by a high pass (average altitude 3,000 metres, or almost 10,000 feet), a great hindrance to communications within the country. A main road now links up all the central valleys but it still takes three days under the best weather conditions to go from Ha to Tashigang.

The Black Mountains form the main watershed separating two river basins on either side, where the rivers are oriented north–south, watering the valleys. The rivers are turbulent, rushing through gorges before they empty on to the Indian plains to become large tributaries—the Torsa, Raidak, Sankosh and Manas—of the Brahmaputra. Their hydroelectric potential is enormous and a 336 megawatt power station, Chukha Hydel, has been built with Indian assistance on the Wang Chhu (*chhu* means 'river').

The Central Himalayas, inhabited by the Drukpas, can thus be divided into three parts with very distinct characteristics, enhanced by the fact that each has its own language which is mutually incomprehensible to the others.

Western Bhutan

Western Bhutan is made up of the valleys of Ha, at 2,700 metres (8,850 feet), Paro, at 2,200 metres (7,200 feet), and Thimphu, at 2,300 metres (7,500 feet), while Punakha and Wangdi Phodrang, at 1,300 metres (4,260 feet), form a single long valley. Except for the

Ha valley, which has a climate suited more for livestock raising and which used to be very active in trade with Tibet, Western Bhutan is a land of rice paddies and orchards.

The relative wealth of the people can be seen in the very large houses that accommodate several generations. The walls are of rammed earth and straw, the upper storeys boasting remarkable woodwork with paintings frequently seen on the frames of the three-lobed windows and on the ends of beams. Wooden shingles, the traditional roofing material, have often been replaced by corrugated iron. However, traditional roofs have come back into favour and the recent opening of a slate mine provides a totally satisfactory alternative to shingles.

The mountain slopes are covered by fine coniferous and deciduous forests where logging is strictly controlled by the government. All the valleys are rich in reminders of the past: monasteries, temples and fortresses abound, and the country's permanent capital has been located in the Thimphu valley since the early 1950s.

The five valleys which make up Western Bhutan are the domain of the *Ngalong*, 'the first to rise', meaning the first to convert to Buddhism, who speak Dzongkha, the 'language of the Dzong (fortress)', now the national language of Bhutan. Although closely related to Tibetan, it has many differences, particularly in the pronunciation of final syllables and the conjugation of verbs.

The Black Mountains, at 5,000 metres (16,400 feet), have traditionally marked the boundary between Western and Central Bhutan. The main road, which goes from Paro to Tashigang, crosses them via the Pele La, 3,300 metres (10,800 feet) high.

Central Bhutan

Central Bhutan is made up of several regions, all of which speak a language (*kha*) with local variations (Bumthangkha, Khyengkha, Kurtoekha). Its archaic usages place it linguistically in the eastern Proto-Bodish subgroup.

The most southerly district of central Bhutan is called Khyeng, a region blessed with a semi-tropical climate and famous for its dense jungle. The inhabitants of Khyeng understand the forest well and include in their diet all sorts of wild plants: yams, orchids, ferns, rattan shoots, tiny wild mangoes, banana flowers and even poisonous roots and seeds, which they are able to treat in ways that make them edible. The people produce splendid bamboo and rattan basketwork.

Tongsa, north of Khyeng, lies along the main road. It is in a gorge cut by the Mangde River with a few cultivated areas terraced on its steep slopes. Bhutan's most impressive *dzong* holds a strategic and privileged position here.

A 3,300-metre- (10,800-foot) high pass, the Yutong La, leads to Bumthang which is a group of four valleys at altitudes of 2,700–4,000 metres (8,850–13,000 feet): Chumey and Choekhor are mainly agricultural, Tang and Ura practise yak- and sheep-herding. The mountainsides are covered with dark coniferous forests, rice gives way to buckwheat, and the houses are built of stone rather than rammed earth and are more sparsely decorated than in Western Bhutan. Bumthang is very proud of its rich art and history. Its religious traditions are very much alive and each monastery, each holy place, is the subject of long stories that blend myth with reality.

The region of Kurtoe (Lhuntshi) to the northeast is separated from Bumthang by a pass at 4,000 metres (13,100 feet), the Rodong La. Kurtoe is closely connected to Bumthang by language and family-kinship, but geographically it belongs to Eastern Bhutan. At lower altitudes (1,600–2,500 metres or 5,250–8,200 feet) rice and maize are grown, but the area in general is best known for its production of fine fabrics with varied and extremely intricate designs.

Eastern Bhutan

From Bumthang, the motor road crosses into the eastern region by a more southern pass than the Rodong La, the 4,100-metre- (13,500-foot-) high Thumsing La. Bhutan's east consists of the regions of Mongar, Tashigang and a southern part that extends as far as Samdrup Jongkhar on the Indian border. This eastern region is the land of the Sharchopas, the 'people of the east', who speak their own language. The climate is generally warmer and drier, the forests thinner and the altitudes lower than in the west. It is a region of deep V-shaped valleys, with fields and dwellings clinging to the bare slopes. The main crop is maize, though rice and wheat can also be grown. Numerous cattle, especially the famous *mithun*, a native bull with spectacular horns, graze alongside the roads, roaming freely and rarely put in barns. Most of the houses are built in traditional Bhutanese style, but one can see many made of bamboo matting and raised on stilts, a reminder of the region's close proximity to Southeast Asia.

The Sharchopas are well known for their piety, and the land is dotted with small temples where *gomchens*, laymen trained in religious practices, live with their families away from monastic communities. As in Kurtoe, the women possess matchless weaving skills and produce magnificent fabrics of raw silk and cotton.

At the eastern tip of the country, three days' walk from Tashigang, lie the high valleys of Merak and Sakteng inhabited by herdsmen, semi-nomadic people belonging to a special ethnic group, the Dakpas.

Northern Bhutan

Lying above 3,500 metres (11,500 feet), Northern Bhutan is the beginning of the High Himalayas. Lingshi, Laya and Lunana are inhabited only by yak-herders and, as such, could be considered as similar to the high valleys of Merak and Sakteng in the east and of Gantey (Phobjika) in the Black Mountains. The high altitude limits cultivation to barley and root crops. Potatoes have recently made their appearance and are an important addition to a diet made up essentially of milk, butter, cheese and yak meat. The inhabitants are semi-nomadic yak-herders. They spend most of the year in black tents woven from yak hair, but they also build drystone-walled houses, which serve as shelter during the coldest months of the year and as storehouses for the goods and grains that they barter with the central valleys.

Flora and Fauna

The three relief zones (the foothills, the central Himalayan valleys and the High Himalayas) also define three climatic regions: tropical, temperate with monsoon, and alpine with monsoon. These climatic variations, coupled with the huge changes in altitude, make Bhutan a country with an extremely rich flora: within a distance of 70 kilometres (44 miles) one passes from rice paddies, banana and orange groves at 1,300 metres (4,200 feet) in the Punakha region, through deciduous forests and then an alpine forest (at Gasa), finally arriving in the Laya area where yaks graze and only barley and winter wheat can be grown.

The wealth of floral variety includes rhododendrons, junipers and magnolias several metres (yards) high, carnivorous plants, rare orchids, blue poppy, edelweiss, gentian, medicinal plants, daphne,

giant rhubarb, high-altitude plants, tropical trees, pine and oak. Bhutan is such a botanical paradise that one of its ancient names meant 'Southern Valleys of Medicinal Herbs'.

The fauna also varies with the different types of vegetation and is abundant since, in accordance with their religion, the great majority of Bhutanese neither hunt nor fish. The dense forests of the south offer a haven to elephants, tigers, buffaloes, snakes and monkeys, one species of which, the Golden Langur, is unique in the world. In the rivers, the *masheer* is sometimes compared to tropical salmon. The central Himalayas are the domain of pheasants, hornbills, red pandas, monkeys, wild boar and, above all, fearsome black bears with white fur 'collars'. Black-necked cranes migrate to Tibet to winter in the isolated valleys of Gantey and Bumdeling. The desolate high valleys belong to yaks, mountain goats or tahr (*Hemitragus jemlahicus*), timid blue sheep, the extremely rare snow leopard and the strange takin (*Budorcas taxicolor*).

History

Ancient Times

No archaeological research has yet been carried out in Bhutan, but stone implements found on the surface of the ground seem to indicate that the country was inhabited fairly early, probably around 2000 BC.

Secular and religious history in Bhutan are so intertwined that the religious school—the *Drukpa*—which prevailed from the 17th century on even gave its name to the country it unified and its inhabitants. It is thus that in the Dzongkha language, Bhutan is called *Druk yul* and the Bhutanese people *Drukpas*. The poetic translation of *Druk yul* is 'Land of the Dragon', which can be explained by the following anecdote. When Tsangpa Gyare Yeshe Dorje (1161–1211) was consecrating a new monastery in Central Tibet at the end of the 12th century, he heard thunder, which popular belief holds to be the voice of a dragon (*druk*). He therefore decided to name this monastery 'Druk', and the religious school which he founded was likewise called 'Drukpa'. In the 17th century, when the Drukpas unified Bhutan, they gave it their name.

Before becoming Druk yul, Bhutan was called by various other names: *Lho Jong*, 'The Valleys of the South'; *Lho Mon Kha Shi*, 'The Southern Mon Country of Four Approaches'; *Lho Jong Men Jong*, 'The

Southern Valleys of Medicinal Herbs'; and *Lho Mon Tsenden Jong*, 'The Southern Mon Valleys where Sandalwood Grows'. '*Mon*' was a generic term applied by Tibetans to the Mongoloid, non-Buddhist populations who lived on the southern slopes of the Himalayas. The origin of the name 'Bhutan' is unclear, but the most plausible guess is that it comes from the Indian term *Bhotanta*, which refers to all the regions bordering on Tibet.

Bhutan's ancient history is known through written Tibetan sources but unfortunately they are not explicit about the population or type of government that existed in those times.

Buddhism Reaches Bhutan

According to Bhutanese tradition, the history of Bhutan began in the seventh century AD when the Tibetan king, Songtsen Gampo, constructed the first two Buddhist temples: Kyichu in the Paro valley and Jampa in the Choekhor valley at Bumthang. In the eighth century, a Tantrist from Swat (in present-day Pakistan) arrived in Bhutan. His name was Padmasambhava but he is generally known in Tibet and Bhutan as Guru Rinpoche, the 'Precious Master'. Here, as in Tibet, he introduced Tantric Buddhism. He is considered by the Nyingmapa religious school (*pa* means school or sect) to be their founder and the Second Buddha. All the places he visited and in which he meditated are places of pilgrimage for the Bhutanese, who also worship his Eight Manifestations in almost all the temples in the country. The story of the conversion to Buddhism of a king reigning in Bumthang indicates that, at the time of Padmasambhava, the valleys of Bhutan were already inhabited by a population of unknown origin (but probably Mongoloid if one is to believe the ancient names for Bhutan) who practised an animistic type of religion.

After this first introduction of Buddhism, the ninth and tenth centuries constitute an obscure historical period. Tibet itself plunged into great political turmoil following the assassination in 842 of the Tibetan king, Langdarma, whom tradition depicts as anti-Buddhist. Countless texts disappeared and Buddhism survived only in remote regions. No contemporary information exists now about these troubled centuries. However, later sources give reason to believe that many people, particularly aristocrats, fled from Tibet and settled in the valleys of Central and Eastern Bhutan, where they assumed power.

The Monastic Community and Other Religious Orders

Ordained monks are called *gelong*. They live in dzongs or monasteries and wear a characteristic dark red robe. They are usually placed in a monastery at the age of five or six, an act that brings great prestige and religious merit to their family. They follow monastic academic courses which in earlier times used to be the only form of education available. After a few years of study, and depending on their aptitude, the monks are then directed into purely scholastic roles or into more artistic–religious pursuits (dancers, musicians, painters, tailors).

At present there are about 3,400 subsidized monks in Bhutan under the authority of the *Je Khenpo*, the head of all religious affairs, who presides over the monastic organization, the *Dratshang Lhentshog*. His principal assistant at the national level is the *Dorje Lopen*, who is in charge of religious teachings. The Dorje Lopen is one of four high Lopens or masters, the others being the *Drape Lopen* , 'master of grammar', who is in charge of literary studies, the *Yangpe Lopen* , 'master of songs and liturgy', and the *Tsenyi Lopen* , 'master of philosophy'. To these four masters, who have the rank of minister, are added a *Khilkhor* who is the 'master of arts' and a *Tsipe Lopen* who is the 'master of astrology'. Moreover, in each monastery there is the *Umdze* or 'choirmaster' and the *Kudun* or 'master of discipline' who carries a rosary of large ivory beads and a symbolic whip.

The state takes care of basic needs, but any money the monks earn by performing rituals remains their own property. The monks carry out daily rituals and perform special ones at fixed times in the dzongs and monasteries. They also respond to the needs of people outside and perform the types of ceremonies that are called for either in the monastery or in the homes of the faithful.

Monks progressively take different categories of vows, from novice to fully ordained monk. They are celibate and must abstain from smoking and drinking, but they are not vegetarian and even eat in the evening, unlike their brothers in Southeast Asia. A few monks join monastic orders after adolescence, but they are rare. Monks can renounce their vows at any time in order to start a family, but they have to pay a fine. They are then called *getre*, 'retired monk', and there is no social stigma attached to this condition.

The great majority of ordained monks belong to the Drukpa clergy, but ordained monks of the Nyingmapa school also exist.

About 3,000 other monks, not supported by the state, live from private patronage.

A *tulku* or *rinpoche* is the reincarnation of a great master whose different incarnations form a line of descendants. All the successive incarnations bear the same name as the founder of the line. Such a person is called a tulku, which means 'Body of Emanation', but the term by which he is addressed is Rinpoche, 'Great Precious One'. Certain tulkus are fully ordained monks and therefore celibate, while others marry and are in no way held in less respect because of their family life. Moreover, once a person has been declared a tulku, he remains so all his life even if his activities appear to be incompatible with a religious existence. Being a tulku is an inherent quality, almost a genetic trait, like being tall or having brown eyes.

At the present time, there are about 500 tulkus in all the countries that practise Tibetan Buddhism. Bhutan has some highly prestigious tulkus. The Bhutanese throng to receive teachings or blessings from important tulkus who have been granted an intense religious education and have, since childhood, occupied a high position in the religious hierarchy.

Gomchens are a very special category. They are half-laymen, half-clergy, most of whom (15,000) belong to the Nyingmapa school. They differ from ordained monks in that they live at home and have a family. They earn their living in secular occupations, as farmers or civil servants, but they have received religious teachings that permit them to perform ceremonies for the faithful. They dress in a *go* that is slightly longer than that of the other laymen. In addition, they sometimes have long hair knotted in a ponytail and have a very wide, dark red ceremonial scarf that closely resembles a monk's cloak. *Gomchens* play an extremely important role in isolated villages where they stand in for monks in all the rituals that villagers need to have performed.

A lama is not another name for a monk, as is often believed in the West. ***Lama*** means 'religious master', a translation of the Sanskrit word *guru*. A lama may be an ordained monk or he may be a married lay religious person. He may be a gelong or a gomchen or a tulku, either married or not (except in the first case). The term 'lama' implies a religious status and is an honorary title given to a man by virtue of his knowledge and wisdom about religious rather than social questions. Frequently the title is transmitted along with religious teachings from father to son. A Westerner should not be too surprised to find a lama serving as the principal of a village primary school high in eastern Bhutan, wearing ordinary clothes and surrounded by his own offspring. But there are also lamas to be found who conform more closely to the Western image of a venerable religious master.

Nuns, or ***anims***, are less numerous than monks in a culture where monastic life is essentially male. There are about 250 nuns, both state-supported and not, but their communities are always under the supervision of a monastery of monks. There are a few isolated women's monasteries where young nuns learn rituals and the basic texts. They move away when a high lama comes into the region to give teachings or blessings. The state supports about 50 of them.

The beginning of the 11th century saw a revival of Buddhism in Tibet which was reflected in Bhutan by the activity of *tertons*, the 'discoverers of hidden religious treasures', in Paro and Bumthang. These treasures were texts or objects hidden by Padmasambhava and other saints, to be discovered by predestined persons at a favourable moment. The Nyingmapa school produced most of the *tertons*.

The end of the 11th century and the beginning of the 12th was a period of religious expansion in Tibet, and several different religious schools came into being including the Kadampa, Kagyupa and Sakyapa schools. The missionary activities of these new schools were also directed towards the 'Southern Valleys'.

Schools of Religion Spread in Bhutan

At the end of the 12th century, Gyelwa Lhanangpa (1164–1224) arrived in Western Bhutan where he had special links with the Paro valley, having inherited land there from his great-great-grandfather. He was the founder of the Lhapa school, a branch of the Kagyupa school.

In the first half of the 13th century, a religious man named Phajo Drugom Shigpo (1208–76) also arrived in Western Bhutan. He belonged to another branch of the Kagyupa, the Drukpas, founded in Central Tibet by Tsangpa Gyare Yeshe Dorje (1161–1211) who, shortly before his death, had prophesied that Phajo would convert the Southern Valleys. As soon as he arrived, Phajo Drugom Shigpo came into conflict with the Lhapas, who by then were firmly established in Western Bhutan. Phajo finally won the struggle and, having married a woman from the Thimphu valley, he founded the first Drukpa monasteries at Phajoding and Tango. The Lhapa school continued nonetheless until the 17th century when it was totally crushed by Shabdrung Ngawang Namgyel, who unified Bhutan under Drukpa authority.

In spite of the growing political and religious influence of the Drukpa, many religious men, whether they belonged to the Drukpa school or not, continued to come to Western Bhutan between the 12th and 17th centuries. Barawa (1320–91), for example, founded a sub-sect of the Drukpas, the Barawas. Others who came were the Nenyingpas and the Chagzampas, the latter named after their founder, Thangton Gyelpo (1385–1464), also known as Chagzampa, 'builder of iron bridges'.

*(following pages) Three traditional paintings:(top left) 'Man leading a yak';
(bottom left) 'Mongol leading the tiger'; (right) Padmasambhava
(Guru Rinpoche) from the Thangka of Wangdi Phodrang*   57

Saints and Scholars

Finally, in the 15th century, came Drukpa Kunley, 'the divine madman'
(1455–1529). Drukpa Kunley is without doubt the most popular figure
of Bhutanese history and everybody in the country is familiar with his
adventures. He belonged to the Drukpa school, and was even a member
of the great Gya family from which came the Drukpa hierarchs, who
served also as successive abbots of Ralung, the most important Drukpa
monastery. Though he refused to take monastic vows, his wandering
life, his eccentric, shocking behaviour and the songs with which he
taught the essence of the religion, guaranteed him a special place in the
history of Tantric Buddhism. His descendants played an important role
in Bhutanese history, especially Tenzing Rabgye (1638–96) who became
the famous Fourth Temporal Ruler, *Desi*, of Bhutan.

Drukpa influence finally made itself felt in the centre and east of the
country after the 16th century when Ngagi Wangchuck, a brother of the
Drukpa hierarchs, and later Tenpe Nyima, his grandson who fathered the
future *Shabdrung* (see below), came from Tibet and founded temples in
the east and centre of the country. Up until then, Nyingmapa monks had
been the most active in that part of the country.

Longchen Rabjampa (1308–63), the greatest philosopher of the
Nyingmapa school, chose exile in the Bhutanese region of Bumthang
following a quarrel with the Tibetan master of his time. In the Bumthang
valleys, he founded the monasteries of Tharpaling, Samtenling, Shinkar
and Ugyenchoeling and also carried on missionary activities in Shar
(now the district of Wangdi Phodrang). One of the foremost Tibetan
tertons, Dorje Lingpa (1356–1405), followed in his footsteps, and he
likewise settled in the Bumthang valleys, at Chakar and Ugyenchoeling.

The most famous Nyingmapa saint, Pema Lingpa, was born in
Bumthang in 1450 and died there in 1521. He was the reincarnation
not only of Guru Rinpoche but also of Longchen Rabjampa, the
philosopher. Famous among Tibetans far beyond the borders of
Bhutan for his activities as a *terton*, Pema Lingpa also founded the
monasteries of Petsheling, Kungzandra and Tamshing in Bumthang.
He was the originator of numerous sacred dances, which came to him
in visions, and he left behind him several important writings.

Many descendants of Pema Lingpa scattered throughout Eastern
Bhutan, where they strengthened the hold of the Nyingmapas. One of
them founded the great monastery of Dametsi not far from Tashigang,
and one of Pema Lingpa's grandsons, Pema Trinley, established the

Gantey monastery in the Black Mountains, on the border between Central and Western Bhutan. Through the descendants of his son Kunga Wangpo, who settled in Kurtoe, Pema Lingpa is the ancestor of Bhutan's royal family.

This brief outline shows how from the 12th century until the end of the 16th century, Bhutan was an important field of missionary activity for the Buddhist religious schools, but it also shows clearly the lack of political unity which characterized the country.

The Unification of Bhutan

Under the politically and religiously charismatic Ngawang Namgyel (1594–1651), Bhutan became a unified state in the 17th century. Ngawang Namgyel was a religious leader of the Drukpa school, who took the honorary title of *Shabdrung*, 'at whose feet one submits'. Persecuted in Tibet, he fled to Bhutan in 1616 and, over the next 30 years, succeeded in crushing all opposition and unifying the 'Southern Valleys' into Druk Yul, 'the Land of the Drukpas'.

Ngawang Namgyel was born into the princely Gya family, and he became the 18th abbot of Ralung, the great Drukpa monastery in Tibet near the northern border of Bhutan. He had been recognized as the incarnation of a famous Drukpa scholar, Pema Karpo (1527–92), but this recognition was challenged by the Tsang *Desi*, the ruler of Tibet's province of Tsang, who had his own candidate. Fearing for his life, Ngawang Namgyel fled from Ralung and sought refuge in Western Bhutan. Here he accepted an invitation by followers of the Drukpa school which had been firmly established in the region since the 13th century.

Ngawang Namgyel, using the title of Shabdrung, constructed his first dzong at Simtokha in the valley of the Wang River. Subsequent dzongs not only symbolized the power of the Drukpa school, since each dzong contained a monastery, but also constituted a matchless instrument of government, as each also served as centres of administration for the provinces.

However, before the Shabdrung could bring about the unification of Bhutan, he had to fight against enemies from abroad as well as inside the country. Shortly after his arrival, the Shabdrung had to contend with a Tibetan invasion. Forced back, the Tibetans attacked again in 1634 and 1639 but with no greater success. In 1645 and 1648, the Tibetans made equally vain attempts at conquest.

The enemies within were the 'Five Groups of Lamas'—the long-established religious schools in Western Bhutan, headed by the Lhapas, old foes of the Drukpas. The Shabdrung battled successfully against this coalition and firmly established the political and religious power of the Drukpas in Western Bhutan. He was not able, in his lifetime, to fulfil his ambition of unifying Central and Eastern Bhutan, but his wish was carried out shortly after his death in 1651. In 1656, after a difficult military campaign, Central and Eastern Bhutan were drawn into the Drukpa sphere of political influence and Bhutan took on its definitive shape.

The Shabdrung's Legacy

Shabdrung Ngawang Namgyel gave Bhutan a remarkable system of administration and law. He established a state clergy under a religious leader, the *Je Khenpo* ('Chief Abbot') and a theocracy administered by monks at whose head he placed a temporal chief, the *Desi*. This dual system of government was to be unified and transcended in the person of the Shabdrung and it lasted until the monarchy took over in 1907. The country was divided into three large provinces—Dagana, Paro and Tongsa—headed by governors, or *Penlops*. Each dzong was directed by a *Dzongpon*. Thus, a whole hierarchy of officials was established. Shabdrung Ngawang Namgyel also gave the country a legal system based on Buddhist moral principles and customary rules in general use at that time.

In 1651, the Shabdrung went into retreat at Punakha Dzong and died soon afterwards. His death was kept secret for over half a century in case turmoil should erupt in the newly created country while a worthy successor to the Shabdrung was being sought.

In the first half of the 18th century, the theory of the triple reincarnation—the Body, Speech and Mind of the Shabdrung—was finally established. However, only 'Mind' incarnations were recognized as providing official successors to the Shabdrung as heads of state.

From the middle of the 18th century to the end of the 19th century, the Penlops increased their power to the detriment of the central government. Furthermore, the dual system of government, devised to be run by a strong man, favoured political inertia in the absence of a reincarnation of the Shabdrung's forceful personality. Terrible power struggles took place among the Desi, the Penlops and the Dzongpons

as a consequence. The combination of these factors led to instability
and increasingly frequent internal disputes that ended in incessant
civil wars.

The Coming of the British

Up until the middle of the 18th century, the Bhutanese government
had conducted foreign relations only with the kingdom of Cooch
Behar on its southern border and with regions within Tibet's cultural
sphere (Tibet, Ladakh, Sikkim). Now it was faced with a new factor
in the form of British hegemony in Assam and their expansion into
the Himalayas.

In the second half of the 18th century, British missions seeking
preferential trade agreements with Tibet and Bhutan succeeeded in
establishing good relations with the Bhutanese without, however,
gaining the concrete results that they hoped for. But the conflicting
interests between the two countries over the question of the Duars
(the narrow southern plain) rapidly soured these good relations and
the expeditions in the 19th century were marked by hostility.
Continual skirmishes on the southern border from the 1830s onward
escalated until they broke out, in 1864, into a conflict known as the
Duar War. In November 1865, the Treaty of Sinchula restored
friendly relations: Bhutan lost the fertile strip of land that made up the
Duars, but in exchange it received an annuity from the British.

New Leadership

During this time, the progressive weakening of the central
government became more marked and, in the second half of the 19th
century, it contributed to the emergence of the power of the two main
Penlops, in Paro and Tongsa, who in fact controlled Western Bhutan
and Central and Eastern Bhutan respectively. The Penlop of Tongsa,
named Jigme Namgyel, helped by a network of alliances and his own
political genius, became the strong man of Bhutan after 1865. Upon
his death in 1881, he bequeathed the position of Penlop of Tongsa to
his son, Ugyen Wangchuck. The new governor strengthened the
alliances forged by his father and claimed a decisive victory over his
fiercest opponents at Thimphu in 1885. From then on, Bhutan
enjoyed its first period of political stability in many generations.

Ugyen Wangchuck favoured increased co-operation with the

British. On the suggestion of his eminent advisor, Kazi Ugyen Dorje, he served as intermediary in the delicate negotiations between the Tibetans and the British. In 1904, at the time of the British expedition into Tibet under Colonel Francis Younghusband, he won the confidence and respect of the latter who awarded him the title of Knight Commander of the Indian Empire (KCIE) in 1905. The British were consequently very pleased and relieved when an assembly of representatives of the monastic community, civil servants and the people elected Ugyen Wangchuck to be the First King of Bhutan on 17 December 1907. Thus ended the dual system of government established by Shabdrung Ngawang Namgyel, and a hereditary monarchy was inaugurated.

Monarchy and Modernization

King Ugyen Wangchuck died in 1926 and was succeeded by his son, Jigme Wangchuck, who reigned until his death in 1952. The reigns of the first two kings were marked by political stability and a degree of economic prosperity after the years of internal conflict that had drained the country's economy. A desire to open the country to the outside world, the influence of enlightened men such as Kazi Ugyen Dorje and his son Gongzim Sonam Tobgye, and aid from Great Britain permitted the establishment of the first Western-style schools and the sending of the first Bhutanese students to India for advanced training.

The Third King, Jigme Dorji Wangchuck (r. 1952–72), is considered the father of modern Bhutan. Inheriting a country at peace, he understood that the world was changing and that Bhutan, if it wished to survive, could no longer continue its political isolation but must start developing.

In 1961, with the help of India, the king launched the first five-year plan of development, with particular emphasis on road-building. In 1962, Bhutan joined its first international organization, the Colombo Plan, and in 1971 it joined the United Nations. After the sovereign's death in 1972, his son, Jigme Singye Wangchuck, ascended the throne at the age of 17. Brought up by the late king with an eye to his future role as monarch, King Jigme Singye Wangchuck had no trouble in taking over the reins of state, and has dedicated himself to a policy of socio-economic development for the country while maintaining its ancestral traditions and cultural heritage. With emphasis on the well-being of the

National Symbols of Bhutan

The rectangular **national flag** of Bhutan is divided diagonally and depicts a white dragon across the middle. The upper part of the flag is golden yellow, representing the secular power of the King, while the lower part is orange, symbolizing the Buddhist religion. The dragon, whose white colour is associated with purity, represents Bhutan. The jewels held in its claws stand for the wealth and perfection of the country.

The **national emblem**, contained in a circle, is composed of a double diamond-thunderbolt placed above a lotus, surmounted by a jewel and framed by two dragons. The double diamond-thunderbolt represents the harmony between secular and religious power which results from the Buddhist religion in its Vajrayana form. The lotus symbolizes purity; the jewel expresses sovereign power; and the two dragons, male and female, stand for the name of the country which they proclaim with their great voice, the thunder.

National Day is celebrated on 17 December and commemorates the ascension to the throne of Ugyen Wangchuck, the first king of Bhutan, at Punakha Dzong on 17 December 1907.

The **national anthem** became official in 1966. The first stanza can be translated:

> In the Kingdom of the Dragon,
> The southern land of sandalwood,
> Long Live the King
> Who directs the affairs of both state and religion.

The **national flower** is the blue poppy (*Meconopsis grandis*), which grows at high altitudes.

The **national tree** is the cypress (*Cupressus torolusa*), which is often associated with religious places. The Bhutanese identify with it because it is straight and strong and can grow in inhospitable soil.

The **national bird** is the raven (*Corvus corax*) because it adorns the royal hat. It represents the deity Gonpo Jarodonchen (Mahakala with a raven's head), one of the most important guardian deities of Bhutan.

The **national animal** is the takin (*Burdorcas taxicolor*), an extremely rare bovid mammal of the ovine-caprine family. It lives in flocks in places 4,000 metres (over 13,000 feet) high, and eats bamboo. It can weigh as much as 250 kilograms (550 lb).

people, and their ability to profit from the advances of the modern world without losing their sense of identity, the King is challenging the classic process of modernization and he fully intends to succeed.

At the same time, the King began a diplomatic offensive which, while remaining unobtrusive, has nonetheless been effective. By 1989, Bhutan was a member of nearly all the organizations affiliated with the UN. Bhutan has belonged to the Movement of Non-aligned Countries since 1973 and to the South-Asian Association for Regional Cooperation since 1985. It has diplomatic relations with 21 countries including India, Bangladesh, Japan, Switzerland and the countries of the European Community.

The Monarchy and National Institutions

Central Government

The system of government is a monarchy. His Majesty the King is the Head of State and the Head of Government. He is assisted by a Cabinet which is the main executive body. It consists of the Ministers of Home Affairs, Foreign Affairs, Communications and Social Services; of Representatives of His Majesty in the Ministries of Finance and Agriculture; the Vice-Minister of Industry and Commerce; State Secretaries of the Commissions of Cultural Affairs, Planning and Civil Service; the Chief of the Army and Police, and other high officials. Each ministry is divided into departments headed by a Director.

The National Assembly

The National Assembly was created in 1953 and consists of 150 members — 100 representatives of the people, elected for three years, ten representatives of the clergy and 40 representatives appointed by the King from among his ministers, royal counsellors, district heads and other high officials.

The National Assembly meets twice a year in the Assembly Hall of Thimphu's Tashichoedzong. Sessions are of variable length, depending on the importance of the subjects being dealt with.

Royal Advisory Council

Set up in 1965, the Royal Advisory Council is an advisory body that is always in session. Its purpose is to advise the King and also to make sure that resolutions passed by the National Assembly are properly carried out. It has a three-year mandate and consists of nine members who must be approved by the Assembly: two members appointed by the King, one representative of the state clergy chosen by the Assembly, and six members appointed by the National Assembly.

The Judicial System

Judicial power is held in the last resort by the King, to whom all Bhutanese may appeal. A High Court of six judges was established in 1968 with its seat in Thimphu. Four of the judges are appointed by the King and two represent the people, elected by the Assembly. All districts have a local court presided over by a magistrate who is appointed by the King, but village headmen still try the less important cases.

The Code of Law is based on the one established by Shabdrung Ngawang Namgyel. While still keeping its Buddhist foundations, it has been adapted to meet modern problems. Bhutan is certainly a country with one of the lowest crime rates in the world. Court cases deal essentially with family disputes or quarrels over property rights. There are no lawyers and each litigant pleads his own case.

Local Administration

Inherited from Shabdrung Ngawang Namgyel's administrative system of the 17th century, local administration has undergone modifications during the 20th century. The most far-reaching changes have been the abolition of the post of Penlop following the inception of the monarchy and the creation instead of 18 *Dzongkhag* (districts), each headed by a *Dzongdag* (district chief) who is appointed by the King and is responsible to the Ministry of Home Affairs. In 1988, four *Dzongde* (zones) were set up as administrative units between the district level and the central government. A group of four districts make up one zone, which is headed by the *Dzongde Chichab* (a top Zonal Administrator), with authority over the district chiefs in his area.

The Dzongdag is aided in his duties by an assistant who deals with internal administration. The most heavily populated districts are divided into *Dungkhag* (sub-districts). All districts are divided into blocks, administrative units that include several villages. A District Development Committee made up of representatives of the people and high district officials meets to discuss development projects. At the block level, government orders are transmitted through the *Gup* (village headman). He is elected by the villages in the block and doubles as a magistrate for settling minor disputes.

The State Monastic Community

The state clergy includes the monks of the official Drukpa Kagyupa school who make up the central and regional monastic communities. The state clergy formerly owned vast land holdings from which it drew its revenue, but since 1968 it has been subsidized by the government. In 1982, the government began buying up monastic land and redistributing it to the most needy peasants.

The Je Khenpo heads the clergy and controls all religious affairs. He is chosen from among the highest monks in the hierarchy and retains his position for life, if he so wishes. He is assisted in his administrative duties by four high-ranking monks chosen by the central monastic community (Thimphu/Punakha). The Je Khenpo also administers religious teachings throughout the country. The state clergy is represented in the National Assembly and on the Royal Advisory Council.

The *Rabde* (regional monastic communities) have their seat in the local dzong and are under the direction of a high-ranking monk assigned by the central monastic community.

The *Dratshang Lhentshog* is an independent organ of the state clergy, headed by the Je Khenpo. It looks after the interests of the 3,400 monks in Bhutan, both Drukpa and Nyingmapa, and maps out broad areas of religious policy. The Je Khenpo is aided in these duties by a high lay official.

The Economy

Agriculture and livestock raising are still the main pillars of the economy, with 90 percent of the population dependent on these two sectors for their livelihood. However, in the gross national product they only account for a little less than half the total (45 percent). Forestry represents 15 percent, while industry and mining, still in the early stages of development, account for 10 percent but are expanding rapidly. Trade is also expanding at a spectacular rate. Tourism and the Druk Air company, although very important for earning foreign currency, only constitute a small part of the gross national product.

While the gross national product is one of the lowest in the world, placing Bhutan in the group of Least Developed Countries, this does not reflect the reality of life there. The economic condition of the Bhutanese cannot be compared with that of people in Africa or Asia who fall in the same category. Some 98 percent of Bhutanese peasants own their land, there is a favourable ratio of population to cultivable area, housing is of good quality, and even though malnutrition exists due to poor eating habits and the unavailability of certain products, there is no famine. A small middle class has been developing since the beginning of the 1980s.

A Cautious Road to Development

Thanks to its small population and relatively fertile land, Bhutan has never had to face the insurmountable problems that beset some of its neighbours. Its problems are human in scale and can be worked out, a factor which contributes to the optimism and enthusiasm of those involved in the development process. King Jigme Singye Wangchuck sets an example by devoting much of his time to travelling about the country, visiting the districts and making sure that programmes are being carried out to everyone's satisfaction.

In 1961, the present King's father initiated the first five-year plan of development. Top priority was given in the first two five-year plans to the building of roads and the formation of a technical and administrative framework. Once the basic infrastructure was created, natural resources could then be turned to economic account. The third and fourth plans, covering the years 1971–81, included development programmes in such varied sectors as agriculture, forestry, electricity, mines and public health.

The fifth plan (1981–6) was a turning point in government policy. It was no longer a question of simply executing projects but also of achieving economic growth in order to gain greater economic self-reliance, of making the administration more effective through decentralization, of ensuring that the population received its fair share of the progress being made, and that it was involved in carrying out the projects.

The sixth plan, which began in 1987, continues the objectives of the fifth, with supreme importance being laid on national values, which takes the form, for instance, of the 'Bhutanization' of the

school curriculum. Traditional etiquette, the development of the national language and the cultural heritage are receiving particular attention. Concern about ecology is widespread among Bhutanese leaders. They feel that the late development of Bhutan has allowed them time to learn from the mistakes of other countries.

In the leaders' view, socio-economic development should not lead to a deterioration of the people's way of life nor of their traditional values. Each project is scrutinized carefully and may be slowed down or even abandoned if it affronts religious faith or the environment. In this way, Bhutan follows a cautious road to development.

The foremost donor of aid, in the form of both technical and financial assistance, is India. From the inception of the five-year plans, India has played a major role in Bhutan's development, especially in the construction and upkeep of roads, communications, hydroelectricity and the furthering of technical and administrative skills.

Bhutan also receives aid in various forms from the UN, particularly through UNDP (United Nations Development Programme) which opened an office in Thimphu in 1979) and other UN organizations such as UNICEF, FAO, WFP, WHO, UNESCO, IFAD and Volunteers. The European Community started a programme of agricultural assistance in 1985. Switzerland, in particular, has developed special ties with Bhutan.

Several non-governmental organizations from various countries work through volunteers in the high-priority sectors of agriculture, livestock, health and education.

Bhutanese Arts

Like other Himalayan regions, Bhutan was influenced for centuries by Tibetan art but has developed its own art forms and themes.

Bhutanese art has three main characteristics: it is anonymous, it is religious and, as a result, it has no aesthetic function by itself. A Bhutanese does not view a painting or a sculpture as a work of art but as a religious work. Paintings and sculptures are consecrated through a special ceremony whereby they come to personify the deities. In general, the term 'image' is preferred to the word 'statue', which has no spiritual connotation. When a Bhutanese commissions a painting or statue, he looks on this as a pious act which will earn him merit, and thus his name is sometimes inscribed on the work to commemorate his act. This

The Dzongkha Language

Dzongkha, Bhutan's national language, means 'the language spoken in dzongs'. Historically it is the language of Western Bhutan, and was not spoken beyond the Pele La Pass in the Black Mountains. Today, however, it is Bhutan's language of administration and it is taught in all schools. Teachers are trained at the school in Simtokha Dzong in the Thimphu valley.

Dzongkha was formerly only an oral language, the written language being Choekey, the 'religious language' known to the outside world as Classical Tibetan. The remarkable feature is that Choekey has remained practically unchanged since the eighth century and was the common written language of a vast geographical area including Bhutan, northern Nepal, Sikkim, Ladakh, Tibet and Mongolia. An enormous literature has been written in this language over the centuries by monks who were the only people with access to education.

Dzongkha has been a written language for the last 30 years or so, and the government has made great efforts since the 1960s to standardize it, and encourage its use. Linguistically related to Choekey (both languages belong to the Tibeto-Burman subgroup of the Sino-Tibetan language family), Dzongkha uses the same writing system. This system, invented around the seventh century, is adapted from an Indian alphabet of that period, with 30 consonants and four vowels, reading from left to right.

One of the big problems of learning Dzongkha, which also holds true for Choekey, arises from the complexity of its orthography, which requires a great deal of memorization. Dzongkha is, in fact, a monosyllabic, two-tone language with an alphabet superimposed on to it.

To tell the difference in writing between words that have the same pronunciation but differing tones, certain 'subterfuges' have been invented. These are additional prefixes and suffixes that are written but not spoken, or letters added above or below a word which can sometimes totally change the sound of the consonant to which they are attached! To deal with this, it clearly becomes necessary to learn each word by heart. Thus, a word pronounced 'la' may in fact be written *lha, bla, la,* or *lags* depending on whether it means 'a god', 'life energy', 'a mountain pass' or 'yes'. The number 'eight', pronounced 'gye', is written *brgyad* and 'Choekey' is simply *chos skad*.

The name of a person, written phonetically in the Latin alphabet as Rinzing Wangchuck and pronounced as it reads, is written *Rigs 'dzin dbang phyug* in Choekey. The inventiveness of the orthography of proper names, written solely as a way to indicate pronunciation, is enough to throw the unprepared mind into total confusion. It turns out that the dzong pronounced Jakar can also be written as Byakar, but in practice is spelled *Bya dkar. Rdo rje* becomes Dorji or Dorje; *Rig 'dzin* becomes Rigzin, Rinzing or Rizzy; *Dpal 'byor* becomes Penjor or Peljor or Paljor; *Chos sgron* becomes Choden, Choeden or Chogron; *Stobs rgyas* becomes Tobgyey, Tobgye or Tobgyel; *Rnam rgyal* becomes Namgye, Namgyel or Namgyal, and so on.

An effort to standardize the orthography is currently being undertaken by a government office called the Consultative Committee for the Development of Dzongkha.

Chortens and Mandalas

A *chorten* (*stupa* in Sanskrit) is a 'receptacle for offerings' and in the Himalayan world it symbolizes Buddha's Mind and is sacred. As a sign of respect, a chorten should always be walked around in a clockwise direction, which also gains merit for believers.

According to Buddhist tradition, the first chortens were built in India and contained Buddha's relics, which had been divided up after his death. They then became places of worship.

In all regions of the Himalayas, thousands of chortens are still built by the faithful, who consider this a virtuous action. Chortens are built in memory of great religious figures, to obtain merit for a deceased person, or to subjugate demons.

A chorten is composed of five parts which symbolize the five elements: the base stands for the earth; the dome for water; the 13 parasols for fire; the moon and sun for air; and the flame on the pinnacle for ether (a rarefied element believed to fill the upper regions of space). The 13 parasols also symbolize the 13 degrees that must be ascended in order to attain Enlightenment.

Chortens are generally compact, closed structures, but some are made in the

attitude, fundamentally different from that of the modern West, explains why new paintings are often donated to temples, covering up old ones. The criterion is faith, not art.

An artist was traditionally a monk who gained merit by doing this work, but his name was never mentioned since he was expected to scorn all vanity. The disciples of a master often prepared the work while only the final, delicate touches were executed by the master himself.

The rules of iconography are firmly established and must be scrupulously respected. Each deity has a colour and special attributes that cannot be changed without altering the meaning and the religious function. The artist, therefore, cannot express himself except in small details or in the painting of minor scenes. (See the Glossary for a list of deities, page 260.)

Painting

Traditional mineral and vegetable pigments are still widely used but they are becoming more expensive than chemical paints. Paintings can be grouped into three categories: paintings on statues, mural paintings and *thangkas*—paintings on banners.

Clay statues are totally painted. Metal statues—incorrectly called 'bronzes'—only have the face painted, enhanced by delicate strokes to point up the moustache or eyes.

form of gateways and others contain chapels (such as Dungtse Lhakhang in the Paro valley and the Memorial Chorten in Thimphu). There are three styles of chorten in Bhutan: the Nepalese style, the Tibetan style and the Bhutanese style (see also page 81).

Building a chorten involves a number of rituals and ceremonies. The most important is installing the 'tree of life'—a piece of a tree inscribed with prayers—and placing statues, books or other precious objects in the interior of the structure, and, finally, the consecration. To break open a chorten is a dreadful crime.

A **mandala** (*khyil khor* in Dzongkha) is a mystic, cosmic diagram. In the centre of the mandala is a divinity with whom the meditating practitioner seeks to merge after traversing various stages incorporated in the mandala. Each divinity has a different mandala and certain monks specialize in making them.

The most usual two-dimensional mandalas are on cotton *thangkas* and are composed of circles and squares; or they are made with coloured powders for certain rituals. Three-dimensional mandalas also exist, many made of gilded copper and placed on altars; there are even entire temples which reflect the structure of a mandala.

The fresco technique is not known. The surface of a wall to be painted is dressed with a layer of earth which is allowed to dry and is then sanded before being painted. Another technique, which is perhaps peculiar to Bhutan, was also widely used in ancient monasteries and temples. A very finely woven cloth was applied to the surface of the layer of earth with such care that it is virtually impossible to detect it unless it becomes damaged and starts to peel off the wall. A special paste made of flour and ground pepper was also applied to prevent insects from eating the cloth. The paintings were then made on the cloth.

Thangkas are very numerous in Bhutan. As they are not hung permanently in the temples but are kept rolled up in boxes and only displayed during important ceremonies, their colours stay remarkably fresh.

The technique of the thangka involves fixing a piece of damp cotton cloth on to a wooden or bamboo frame. A mixture of lime and glue is applied to the cloth which is then sandpapered. A grid of geometric lines is then drawn on it to serve as the framework and measuring gauge for the composition. Sometimes the artist simply prints the cloth with a wooden block that has the design already carved on it, or else he uses a stencil. In the latter case, the cloth is covered with a paper cartoon that has the lines of the desired drawing pierced with small holes. The artist traces over the lines with charcoal, leaving the design laid out in dots on the cloth, ready to be painted.

Most thangkas are painted in different colours, but some have the background completely gilded with the drawing executed in fine red and black lines. Other thangkas reserved for certain terrible deities use a black background with a drawing of red and gold lines. When the thangka is finished, it is mounted with a brocade border of different colours which have symbolic meanings. Finally, two pieces of wood are sewn to the upper and lower edges for hanging.

Two other techniques, unrelated to painting, are used in making thangkas: embroidery and appliqué. Appliqué is primarily used to make the enormous thangkas that are hung on the outside walls of fortresses during religious festivals.

Although painting styles have changed over the centuries, it is difficult to trace a history of Bhutanese painting. The main reason is that most datable mural paintings in temples have been repainted many times by pious donors.

Tamshing, in Bumthang, is one of the rare temples that has kept its original paintings from the beginning of the 16th century (see page 205). They show a central deity who occupies almost the whole field, while the sides are divided into little compartments containing minor deities belonging to the same cycle as the central figure. The commanding proportions of the latter, the general composition, the clothing of the minor figures and the patterns of the jewellery all show the Indian influence of the Pala-Sena dynasties of Bengal (8th–12th centuries). This style also strongly influenced early Tibetan and Central Asian art through the intermediary of Nepal.

Although Chinese influence was reflected in Tibetan art in the 15th century, there is no Bhutanese example surviving from that time. Therefore, it is difficult to draw any firm conclusions since many pieces of artistic evidence from this period have been covered over with new paintings from a later date. Chinese influence by way of Tibetan art does show up in certain paintings, but much later — for instance, at Taktsang and Tango (both end of the 17th century) and Phajoding (mid-18th century). Whether murals or thangkas, the style of painting displaying a central deity surrounded by minor figures survives today.

From the beginning of the 18th century, Chinese influences are well indexed. Artists started to use the whole wall or the whole

surface of cloth to produce asymmetrical compositions, several figures or scenes occupying the space without having a principal figure in the centre. The style became more flowery, the use of gold paint more frequent, and landscapes were treated in the Chinese manner. The names of personages are often written under their images, which helps in dating the paintings.

Sculpture

There is no stone or rock sculpture in Bhutan except for letters carved in bas-relief on stone walls or occasionally on rocks. On the other hand, since slate is an abundant resource, slate flagstones are finely engraved with pictures of deities and religious characters. The most beautiful are found in Simtokha Dzong, and since each one carries an inscription identifying the figure represented, they are extremely valuable for studying Bhutanese iconography.

Clay images can be seen everywhere and are completely painted. Their size varies from the tiny images that are placed inside portable chapels or personal reliquaries to gigantic statues two or three metres (six to ten feet) tall.

A block of fine clay is worked around a core of wood wrapped in pieces of cloth that are inscribed with prayers. This core is the *sogshing,* which is the image's 'tree of life' and which is also found in metal images and chortens. Small votive tablets of clay mixed with the ashes of the dead are placed in sacred spots. They are moulded first and later painted or whitewashed.

Metal images are made of a copper alloy. Images in silver or gold are rare. The *cire perdue,* or 'lost wax', technique, which was introduced to Tibet and Bhutan by Newari craftsmen from the Kathmandu valley, is widely used in making medium-sized images.

Large images and chortens of metal are first hammered out of metal sheets, then worked into shape by repoussé and engraved. The different parts are then assembled with rivets. Most metal images and chortens are gilded, and some are ornamented with coral and turquoise offered by generous donors. The face and jewellery of a deity are sometimes inlaid with silver, and the face and hair are often painted.

From the 18th century onwards, altars and chortens were frequently covered with sheets of delicately worked, gilded copper. Statues then become much more ornate, often encrusted with semiprecious stones and having bases in the form of double rows of lotus petals.

The bindings of religious books are made from two wooden boards, and the upper cover may be carved with divinities in high relief or covered with embossed sheets of copper.

It is hard to talk about different styles of sculpture as no systematic study has been made. Newari influence (itself derived from Indian art) appears in the huge statues that are surrounded by a nimbus of mythical animals such as *garudas* (griffins), *nagas* (dragon-snakes) and *makaras* (giant fish) on a ground of foliage. The nimbus reflects the typical structure of Newari doors. The best examples are found in Simtokha Dzong and in Hedi Monastery in the upper Paro valley.

Architecture

Bhutan's architectural forms are quite diverse. Chortens, stone walls, temples, monasteries, fortresses, mansions and houses make up a unique architectural landscape.

Chortens A *chorten*, which represents Buddha's Mind, is erected in memory of an eminent lama or to ward off evil spirits from places normally considered dangerous, such as crossroads, bridges and mountain passes. There are three types of Bhutanese chorten: great chortens of whitewashed stone modelled after the chorten of Bodnath in Nepal; smaller stone chortens very much in the Tibetan style, found especially in Central and Eastern Bhutan and often protected by a wooden superstructure; and square-shaped chortens with the roof composed of four slopes and the upper part just below the roof decorated by a wide red stripe—these are mostly found in Western Bhutan.

Like statues, chortens are consecrated. They contain a 'tree of life' inscribed with prayers. Statues, religious books, fragrant herbs and even weapons are placed inside them.

Two chortens may be linked together by a stone wall, a 'mani wall' named after the *mantra* of the bodhisattva Avalokiteshvara which is most often inscribed on the stones. One also sees the *mantras* of two other great bodhisattvas, Vajrapani and Manjushri. The stone walls are relatively few in number and fairly short in Bhutan, a circumstance easily explained by the topography, which does not lend itself to lengthy constructions.

Three Frequently Seen Religious Series

In Bhutan you will see three sequences of objects that might be called, for want of a better term, 'religious series'.

The Eight Auspicious Signs

The Treasure Vase symbolizes the contents of the Buddhist doctrine, treasures that will overcome all desire on the part of its believers.

The Endless Knot is a symbol of love.

The Victorious Banner proclaims the victory of Buddhism and the victory of virtue over sin.

The Wheel of Law, as it moves, symbolizes that the Buddhist doctrine is alive and dynamic.

The Golden Parasol offers protection against the sun; in like manner, the Buddhist doctrine protects a person's spirit.

The Golden Fish keep their eyes wide open in spite of the water, and they have knowledge of obstacles and objectives; similarly, the Buddhist doctrine permits the faithful to take correct actions in the world.

The White Conch symbolizes the propagation of the Buddhist doctrine.

The Lotus symbolizes non-attachment; as the lotus does not remain caught in the mud, so the non-attached spirit does not remain caught in the life of this world.

The Seven Treasures of the Universal Buddhist Monarch *Gyelsi Nadun*

The Flaming Wheel allows the Monarch to travel wherever he wishes at great speed and thus to vanquish his enemies.

The Precious Jewel is made of lapis lazuli and dispels the gloom of night. It fulfils the wishes of the Monarch and his subjects.

The Precious Queen is adorned with all the virtues and is a perfect companion for the Monarch.

The Precious Minister is strong, brave, and takes good care of the kingdom while remaining perfectly loyal to the Monarch.

The Precious Elephant is as strong as a thousand elephants and an irreplaceable helper in battle.

The Precious Horse can fly in the sky and enables the Monarch to circle the world three times in a day.

The Precious General possesses great physical and mental strength, and does not wantonly harm others but only fights to save his Monarch.

The Eight Kinds of Chortens *Chorten Degye*

The Eight Chortens commemorate eight different events in Buddha's life and each is different from the others:

Desheg Chorten To celebrate the birth of his son at Lumbini, Buddha's father ordered a chorten to be built.

Changchub Chorten To commemorate Buddha's Enlightenment at Bodhgaya, the king of the region ordered a chorten to be built.

Choekhor Chorten To commemorate Buddha's first sermon in the Deer Park at Sarnath near Benares, his five disciples had a chorten built named after the Wheel of Religion.

Chotrul Chorten To celebrate Buddha's victory over the non-Buddhist masters at Sravasti, the king of the region ordered a chorten to be built named after miracles.

Lhabab Chorten To celebrate Buddha's return to earth after he had ascended to the Heaven of the Thirty-Three Gods to preach the doctrine to his mother, the king of the region ordered a chorten to be built named after the descent from the godly heaven.

Yendum Chorten To celebrate Buddha's victory at Rajagriya over his wicked cousin who had sown discord among the monks, the king of the region ordered a chorten to be built named after reconciliation.

Namgyel Chorten To commemorate Buddha's voluntary prolongation of his life at Vaisali, the gods built a chorten named after victory.

Nyende Chorten To commemorate Buddha's *Nirvana* at Kusinagara, the people of this country built a chorten named after extinction.

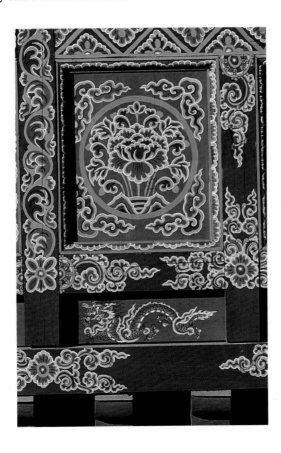

Bhutanese architecture is a remarkable adaptation of Tibetan architecture to different ecological conditions. As in Tibet, the walls of fortresses slope inwards and are whitewashed, with the windows becoming larger in the upper storeys. However, in Bhutan, the need to cope with heavy precipitation and the availability of wood have given its architecture a flavour all its own.

Wood is widely used. The assembling of windows and doors is so complicated that the work is done at ground level, the finished elements being fitted into the upper walls later. Windows are characterized by trilobed crossbars at the top and by complicated lintels that carry symbolic meaning in all of their parts. Lintels and windows are painted with floral or geometric designs.

The roofs of houses are pitched above a flat floor. They are mortised and covered with shingle held in place with heavy stones. These pitched roofs are completely original in style and help give an impression of lightness to the whole building. This is clearly an innovative adaptation — made necessary by rain and snow — of the flat Tibetan roof. Traditionally, all wooden elements were joined by tenon and mortise but nails have also come into use in the past 30 years. Buildings are often destroyed by fire and reconstructed just as they were before.

Lhakhang *Lhakang* (temples) are fairly small buildings of simple design which are likely to comprise one storey around a small enclosed courtyard. They differ from ordinary houses by the red band painted on the upper part of their walls and an ornament of gilded copper on the roof. Inside, the walls are completely covered with paintings, and the interior space is sometimes divided by pillars into an antechamber and the sanctuary proper. These buildings seem to have been the first forms of religious architecture and some of them are centuries old. Lhakhang are maintained by a caretaker who may be a member of the owner's family if it is private, or be assigned by the state clergy if it is state property.

Gompas *Gompas* (Bhutanese monasteries) can be divided into two types: one that we will call the 'cluster' type and the other the 'dzong' type.

The 'cluster' type is probably the older. It consists of a core formed by one or two temples with various dwelling structures grouped around it. Examples of this type are Dzongdrakha in the Paro valley, Phajoding in the Thimphu valley, and Tharpaling in the Bumthang valley.

The 'dzong' type is built like a fortress with a central tower enclosing the temples and surrounded by exterior walls against which are built monks' cells and service rooms. The most impressive examples of this type are the monasteries of Gantey, near Pele La, Tango in the upper Thimphu valley, Talo near Punakha and Dametsi in Eastern Bhutan. Cheri Monastery, built in the upper Thimphu valley in 1619–20, has characteristics of both styles. The central building is a dzong and around it are clustered houses for meditation and retreat.

Dzongs Bhutanese fortresses are known as dzongs and were constructed at strategic points for political reasons. They contain both regional Drukpa monastic communities and the administrative offices of the district government. The solidity and elegance of the sloping walls, combined with richly detailed woodwork and the ethereal character of the pitched roof, make the dzong one of the most beautiful architectural forms of Asia. The basic pattern of a dzong consists of a central tower, *utse*, built in the middle of a courtyard, while monks' cells and administrative offices back up against the walls that surround it. Gasa, Tashigang and Dagana dzongs are good examples. However, certain dzongs, such as Punakha, Wangdi Phodrang and Thimphu, have two separate courtyards delimited by the central tower, one encompassed by administrative buildings and the other by buildings belonging to the clergy.

Courtyards and buildings are sometimes constructed on different levels following the slope of the terrain. Paro, Jakar and Tongsa dzongs are built in this way. Tongsa is the most complex of all, with its maze of courtyards, buildings and passages on different levels.

Secular Architecture Secular architecture reflects many features of religious or fortress architecture. Lordly residences seem to have appeared during the period at the end of the 19th century when the country began to enjoy relative peace and the lords of Bumthang acquired great political power. The construction of these residences continued during the reigns of the first and second kings. Their basic layout was, in fact, very similar to that of a fortress: the lord and his family lived in a central building surrounded by an enclosed courtyard with service buildings backed up against its walls. However, the architecture of these residences was less severe than that of dzongs, which were built for defence. There was considerably more decoration on the woodwork, and windows opened even from the exterior walls. The upper floor of the central building was always turned into a private chapel. This room was decorated with painted murals and contained numerous statues as well as the religious books needed for rituals. The most noted examples of this type of architecture are Lamey Gompa, Wangduchoeling, Domkhar, Prakhar and Ugyenchoeling in the Bumthang valley, Kunga Rabten and Samdrupchoeling to the south of Tongsa, and Gantey in the Paro valley.

All dzongs, lordly residences and important temples are built of stone, while village houses are constructed of different materials depending on their locations. In Western Bhutan, cob (rammed earth) is the commonest building material, whereas in the centre and east, stone is the choice. In Eastern Bhutan, woven bamboo matting is also used for building, and it often serves as roofing for small houses on stilts.

Throughout Bhutan, houses have the same characteristics: they are rectangular, with one or two storeys. The upper floors are constructed almost universally as an open wooden framework with bamboo lathing filling the spaces, covered by white plaster. Although in former times the wooden framework and the plaster were left as they were, the tendency nowadays is to paint them and decorate them with various designs.

Windows traditionally had no permanent protective screening; sometimes bamboo screens were put up to shut out bad weather without excluding light, but today glass is used in the more populated areas. At night, windows are closed from the inside by sliding shutters.

The roof is the same as for other buildings, and the space between the flat roof and the two-sided sloping roof is used for drying vegetables or meat and for storing hay. In towns, this space is closed off with bamboo mats.

In farmhouses, formerly never whitewashed, the ground floor is dimly lit by narrow windows and used for the farm animals and as a storeroom. The upper floors are reached by a ladder with steps hollowed out from a tree trunk. If there is a middle floor, it can be

used for storage or to provide rooms for servants and visiting relatives. The top floor, which receives light from many windows, is where the family lives. It is divided into small rooms which do not have specialized uses except for the latrines (if they exist), the kitchen and the little private chapel, which sometimes doubles as a bedroom for distinguished guests.

Furniture is rudimentary: a few small low tables, mattresses which are rolled up by day along with the bedcovers, some rugs, shelves for the dishes, metal or wooden trunks for keeping clothes in, a wooden altar in the chapel, and one or two looms for weaving.

The house gives on to a courtyard (sometimes covered), forming a terrace where all sorts of daily activities take place. This type of farm is found throughout the country, with regional variations. These days they are likely to be whitewashed.

In towns, the houses are similarly arranged but the ground floor has windows and contains the kitchen, the storeroom and the servants' rooms. It can also be transformed into a small shop. The kitchen and the bathroom are sometimes located in a small annexe attached to the rear of the house.

The beauty of its proportions and decorations make a Bhutanese house one of the loveliest examples of popular architecture.

Crafts

The fact that Bhutanese crafts are relatively expensive and not made for the tourist trade can be explained by social and economic factors. Most Bhutanese still live in semi-isolation and produce for themselves any objects and clothing that they need. Except for goldsmiths, silversmiths and painters, craftsmen are peasants who make things in their spare time. It is the surplus production of the peasants which is sold, the daily articles and fabrics of their traditional life.

Most products, particularly fabrics, are relatively expensive compared to those of other Asian countries. This is because demand exceeds supply, there is a shortage of available labour, and a new upper social class came into existence at the beginning of the 1980s. In addition, there is little mechanization. Every step of production is performed by hand, from dyeing hanks of thread or hacking down bamboo in the forest to weaving or braiding the final product. The time spent in producing handicrafts is considerable and can involve as much as a year for certain textiles.

A final factor contributing to high prices is that there is no competition, which explains why there is so little bargaining. People know how much an item costs because the price is fixed by local demand and things cost the same for everybody, tourists and local people alike, so visitors never feel cheated. On the other hand, they don't have the satisfaction of driving a good bargain. Some fabrics can cost US$1,000, while others can be found for as little as US$15! Not all prices are so high, bamboo products in particular are very reasonable, but in general they are higher than elsewhere in Asia.

Each region has its specialities: raw silk comes from Eastern Bhutan, brocade from Lhuntshi (Kurtoe), woollen goods from Bumthang, bamboo wares from Khyeng, woodwork from Tashi Yangtse, gold- and silverwork from Thimphu, and yak-hair products from the north or the Black Mountains.

Fabrics Fabrics are woven at home by women, mostly from Central and Eastern Bhutan who are famous for their skills; each region produces its own specialities.

There are four kinds of loom: a horizontal frame with pedals, a fixed vertical frame with backstrap, a card loom (used only for making belts), and a fixed horizontal frame with backstrap, the latter being used only by the women of Laya, in Northern Bhutan.

The fibres used are cotton, wool, silk (raw and refined), yak hair and nettle fibre (which is still used to make very strong bags but was formerly used for making clothes as well). Yak hair is used by the semi-nomads of Northern Bhutan for weaving tents, waterproof coats and clothing. Dyes are usually vegetable or mineral and are made by the weaver herself. Chemical dyes also exist and are easily recognizable by their vivid colours.

Every fabric has a name which describes its particular combination of fibre, colour and pattern. Thus, check woollen material is called *mathra*, *serthra* or *tsangthra* depending on its colour. Fancy women's dresses with a white background covered with brocade designs of silk are called *kushutara,* and those with a blue background are called *onsham*. Material with a yellow background and green and red stripes with additional warp patterns is *mensimathra.*

Material is either striped (horizontal for women, vertical for men in wool, cotton or silk) or check (unisex, always woollen). Extra designs are obtained by the brocade technique (supplementary weft threads) or by adding warp threads. All patterns have a symbolic meaning: the tree, the swastika, the wheel, the *vajra*, the diamond, etc.

Raw silk is often imported from Assam. The silkworm is the *Philosoma cynthia* and not the *Bombyx mori* that produces Chinese silk. For religious reasons, the Bhutanese hate to kill the silkworms in their cocoons, so they let them escape and in doing so let the thread break before it is unrolled. This, and the different species of worm, explain why the silk looks and feels much rougher than Chinese or Indian silk.

Jewellery Jewellery, gold-and silverwork is made by a special class of craftsmen. They make objects in silver that are often covered with a fine layer of gold, and they make jewellery in both silver and gold. The silver is beaten, then embossed or engraved with good luck symbols.

The favourite Bhutanese stones are coral and agate etched with white lines, called *zi*. These two stones bring fabulous prices, higher even than gold, particularly the *zi* which the Bhutanese (and Tibetans) believe are found in the earth just as they are. In fact, the *zi* are agates that were etched by man centuries ago, but the technique is said to have been lost. The necklaces of *zi* and enormous coral beads which women wear on festival days are not for sale as they are family heirlooms.

Wood Wooden sculptures are usually made of pine or walnut. Woodwork, wooden bowls and receptacles—mainly from the Tashi Yangtse region of Eastern Bhutan—are turned on foot-powered treadle lathes. Bowls lined with silver are used only for butter-tea or alcohol. Wooden receptacles are used as serving dishes for food and also as plates by the heads of the household.

Some bowls and all receptacles are lacquered black or red with a substance that is extracted from the tree *Rhus succedanea*. This is the same substance that the Japanese use for lacquer, but in Bhutan the finishes are less sophisticated.

Bamboo and Rattan Bamboo and rattan wares are mostly made by peasants in the areas around the old region of Khyeng (see page 192). Some objects are made of bamboo or rattan cut into thin strips,

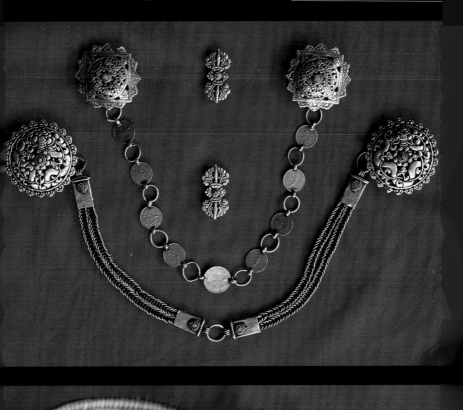

braided and sometimes coloured to form geometric designs or left natural. Other objects are made of much bigger laths sewn together with bamboo cord. These make totally sealed, waterproof receptacles such as the tall, cylindrical churns for butter and butter-tea, and smaller boxes for spices, salt or cheese. Still other kinds of bamboo are used for making bows and arrows.

Paper Bhutanese paper is made entirely by hand from special barks, used alone or, more often, mixed together in order to obtain the best qualities.

For methods of making paper, see page 113.

Religion

Bhutan is the only country in the world to have adopted Mahayana Buddhism in its Tantric form as its official religion. Certain valleys of Bhutan were converted to Tantric Buddhism in the eighth century; a second conversion took place in the 12th century, this time encompassing the whole country.

Tantric Buddhism

This form of the religion emerged as the last phase in the long evolution of Buddhism. In the West it is also known as the Diamond Vehicle (Vajrayana). The word 'Tantrism' comes from *Tantras*, the name of a body of esoteric texts which appeared roughly between the third and the tenth century. These are divided into four groups that proceed from the simplest to the most complex: *tantras* of action, *tantras* of behaviour, *tantras* of yoga, and finally *tantras* 'without any superiors'. In other earlier forms of Buddhism, the *Tantras* of course do not exist.

Tantric Buddhism disappeared from India, where it had begun, at the time of Muslim invasions early in the 13th century. It continued to exist only in Tibet, Ladakh, Mongolia, northern Nepal, Bhutan and Japan.

The Basic Ideas

Tantric Buddhist concepts have been explained in many books and, rather than trying to give a detailed explanation here, an effort will be made simply to place the religion in its Bhutanese context.

Tantric Buddhism is based on the same fundamental beliefs as other forms of Buddhism: that the consequences of actions in previous lives, or *karma*, force all beings to reincarnate. All human effort should aim towards Enlightenment, which means release from the cycle of incarnations into the state of *Nirvana*, annihilation of the suffering which accompanies all existence. This state of non-suffering leads to the idea of the Absolute, or the Void, a state in which there is no distinction between a subject and the object of its thoughts. Indeed, the sensory world of 'things' has only a phenomenological existence and possesses no true reality except on the plane of Relative Truth. The phenomena have no intrinsic being despite the illusion of reality that they project and do not exist on the plane of Absolute Truth.

Nevertheless, Mahayana Buddhism, and therefore Tantric Buddhism, recognizes a pantheon of symbolic deities and *bodhisattvas*, or 'Buddhas-to-be'. These enlightened beings have attained the option of Nirvana but they voluntarily decline it and reincarnate in the world of humans in order to help others.

The distinguishing characteristics of Tantric Buddhism are as follows: The Buddha's words are contained not only in the scriptures, or *Sutras*, and the texts which lay down rules of monastic discipline (*Vinaya*), but also in the *Tantras*, esoteric writings whose meaning can only be understood through the explanations of a religious master, or lama — a source of great power for the latter.

Different approaches can be used to attain the Void. These include: sublimation, not suppression, of the passions in order to make use of them; a complex system of symbols in which all the deities are seen to represent thought forms with no intrinsic reality; and rituals and religious practices, which are given prominence. These include the reciting of *mantras*, verbal formulae with precise objectives; prostrations; and the creation of *mandalas*, cosmic diagrams which the faithful use as an aid to meditation (see page 77).

Throughout Tibet and adjacent regions including Bhutan, Tantric Buddhism evolved in a singular way which is known in the West as Tibetan Buddhism or Lamaism. It assimilated certain elements of a pre-Buddhist, shamanic religion, notably the worship of mountains, lakes and indigenous deities which often appear warlike. This syncretism is particularly evident in religious ceremonies and popular beliefs.

A human being is believed to possess four ethereal entities, three of which derive from the pre-Buddhist religion and the last from Buddhism. They are the *la*, which is a kind of soul, the *sog*, or life principle, the *tshe*, or life span (these three disappear at the time of death), and the *namshe*, the conscious principle which transmigrates when the human body dies.

The divinities which appear to be terrifying are merely emanations from peaceful deities which assume a wrathful form to subdue evil spirits hostile to Buddhism; they only frighten the ignorant who do not recognize their true nature. Guru Rinpoche would have said that 'those who cannot be subdued by peaceful means must be dealt with by terrifying means.'

The nudity of most of these deities implies that the conventions of this world have no importance on higher planes. The various arms of the divinities hold attributes that are symbolic in nature, and the persons being crushed by the fearsome deities are either spirits hostile to Buddhism or primordial negative concepts such as ignorance, jealousy and anger.

Numerous divinities are seen in sexual union with their female counterparts. In Tantric Buddhism, the male principle represents knowledge or the means of attaining an objective, whereas the female principle represents wisdom. Without wisdom, knowledge leads nowhere. Similarly, without knowledge, wisdom is useless for attaining the sublime state of Enlightenment in which the world of relative truth is extinguished. The union of knowledge and wisdom permits the attainment of this state.

Rituals [1]

Rituals, on the one hand, help to neutralize negative conditions and to optimize positive conditions, and, on the other hand, to attain a state in which one can bring well-being to all living things. There are three categories of rituals: those performed with precise actions in view, those addressed to divinities existing outside the four groups of Tantras, and those addressed to the tutelary deities of the Tantra groups.

The first category has four subdivisions denoting the types of action to be accomplished: rituals of peaceful action (to bring rain or to cure physical and mental illnesses); rituals of prosperity (to increase financial or mental riches); rituals of submission (to subdue one's own spirit); and rituals of violent action (to overcome hostile forces).

A ritual always begins with an invitation to the divinity, followed by a confession of transgressions and negative actions. Next come offerings and prayers aimed at obtaining what one desires. The ritual ends with an invocation to the deity that it withdraw into the appropriate symbolic prop which might be, for instance, a statue, a painting or a mandala.

Ritual Objects

Certain ritual objects are the attributes of particular deities and these are also used during religious ceremonies. The most important is the 'diamond-thunderbolt', *dorje* (in Sanskrit called *vajra*, the root of the term *Vajrayana* or 'Diamond Vehicle' which is another name for Tantric Buddhism). The diamond-thunderbolt looks like a small dumb-bell. Four or eight prongs branch off from the middle of the central axis and join again at the extremities. Diamond and thunderbolt both represent purity and indestructibility; hence the Buddha-Spirit, too. The diamond-thunderbolt also symbolizes the knowledge necessary for attaining Enlightenment and therefore the male element. It is often used in rituals in combination with a bell, (*drilbu*), which stands for wisdom and therefore the female element.

The ritual dagger, *phurpa* (in Sanskrit *kila*), was used for Tantric rituals in India as early as the seventh and eighth centuries and it embodies the deity Phurpa. It has a triangular blade and its hilt is shaped like the head of an animal or deity. It is used primarily for sacrificing demons and thus liberating them from the evil sheath of their bodies, allowing their spirits to obtain a better rebirth. The *phurpa* is also used for rituals of purification and the protection of places.

There are other objects peculiar to Tibetan Buddhism, of which *tormas* are special. These are sacrificial cakes made of rice dough and butter, moulded in different shapes and colours. Each deity and each ritual has its own special *torma* and every ceremony is an occasion for making these 'cakes', which are then placed on the altar. *Tormas* replace the human or animal offerings that were made in the pre-Buddhist religion.

Constructions of coloured thread, *doe*, that one sometimes sees placed beside the road or at crossroads, are offered to harmful spirits to serve as their palaces. This palace is a substitute, or a ransom, offered to prevent such a spirit from laying siege to a human being or an animal, causing illness or death.

Seven bowls are placed upon altars and filled with water each morning. They represent the seven offerings which must be made to Buddha and the deities: food, drink, water for washing, flowers and incense to please the senses, a butter-lamp for light and perfume.

Religious Schools

The importance accorded to the utterances of a spiritual master, and therefore to his commentaries on religious texts, has given rise to multiple religious schools which nonetheless subscribe to the same basic doctrinal principles. They differ, however, in their interpretation of the doctrine, in the importance they give to intellectual knowledge as against religious practice, in their attachment to particular texts rather than others, and in the way they perform rituals.

The religious schools that exist in Bhutan today are the official Drukpa, 'Followers of the Oral Transmission', a branch of the major Kagyupa sect, and the Nyingmapa, or 'Elders', which was founded by Guru Rinpoche (see page 53).

This period, lasting from the end of the 10th century to the end of the 12th century, saw the emergence of the three major schools of Tantric Buddhism in Tibet: the Kadampa, the Sakyapa and the Kagyupa, the latter subdividing into numerous branches. The Drukpa school traces its origin to the Phagmogrupa, one of the four major branches of the Kagyupa sect.

The Drukpa school was founded in Tibet by the religious master Tsangpa Gyare Yeshe Dorje (1161–1211) and spread to Bhutan during the early 13th century. Tradition has it that, shortly before his death, Tsangpa Gyare prophesied to the nephew who was going to succeed him that a young man would arrive from Eastern Tibet. Once this man had received all of the Drukpa teachings, he should be sent to convert Western Bhutan. The young man was Phajo Drugom Shigpo who, in 1222, introduced the Drukpa teachings in Western Bhutan from where they spread. However, it was the arrival of Shabdrung Ngawang Namgyel that brought it to its political and religious peak at the time of the unification of Bhutan, producing the country that exists today (see History, page 56). The Drukpa sect is headed by the Je Khenpo, the most important religious authority.

The Religion in Practice

The religion as it is practised at the popular level consists of profound worship of the Buddha, Guru Rinpoche and all the deities of the Tantric pantheon, along with the indigenous gods. This worship extends also to religious masters and monks.

Certain spiritual masters are reincarnations of high lamas, *tulkus*, who are addressed by the title of *Rinpoche*, or 'Great Precious One'. The idea of the *tulku* or 'Body of Appearance' originates in the Mahayana Buddhist theory of the Three Bodies of the Buddha: the Body of Essence, the Body of Enjoyment and the Body of Appearance. However, Tibetan Tantric Buddhism is the only branch of Buddhism that pushes this doctrine to its extreme in declaring that the Buddha's Body of Appearance can take human form.

Rituals are performed on all occasions: birth, marriage, death, official functions, household ceremonies, departure for a trip, illness, to name a few. Ritual or religious ceremony is referred to in Bhutan by different words: *rimro* or *chogu* are the Dzongkha terms; the word *puja* is often used conversationally in other languages — this Sanskrit word means the same as *rimro* or *chogu*, but it may also refer to Hindu rituals in Southern Bhutan.

Bhutanese piety takes many forms: daily prayers before the household altar; offerings of butter-lamps; visits to high lamas and to temples or monasteries on auspicious dates in the Buddhist calendar; gifts in kind or money to monks, lamas or religious institutions; the gift of a child to the monastic community; the worship of relics; contributions of all sorts towards the construction or repair of religious monuments, banners or statues; sponsorship of readings from the holy scriptures; pilgrimages to holy places; participation in *wang* (a collective blessing), or *lung* (a collective initiation by a great master into one special text or a whole cycle of texts); putting up prayer flags; reciting prayers with a rosary or prayer wheel; taking part in religious festivals.

The Bhutanese generally do not question their religion. They are Buddhists by birth and they adopt the customs followed in their own families. Their duty is to offer material assistance to monks and others who are dedicated to the religious life, and to gain merit in a future lifetime by performing pious acts. The duty of monks, in return, is to give laymen spiritual support and help in performing acts of piety correctly. Except for young people brought up abroad, who

ask questions and desire to understand their religion in a more intellectual way, the overwhelming majority of Bhutan's population shows no evident need for explanation or rationalization of their religion.

Festivals, Dance and Music

Secular Festivals

National Day commemorates the establishment of the monarchy on 17 December 1907. H M the King's Birthday (11 November) and Coronation Day (2 June) are two other important secular festivals. National Day and the King's Birthday are celebrated in all districts with parades of schoolchildren, and dances which are often performed by the children too.

In addition, various 'New Years' are celebrated at different times in different regions. Although the official lunar New Year (*Gyelpo Losar*), which corresponds with the new moon in February, is a holiday, it is not an occasion for any particular public celebrations other than archery contests.

The other 'New Years' are times for merry-making among friends and relatives and, among the Drukpas, a time for archery tournaments. The Nepalese New Year is celebrated in the south of the country at the new moon in April; *Lomba* takes place in Paro and Ha on the last day of the tenth lunar month and the first two days of the eleventh lunar month (end of November or beginning of December), which corresponds with the old agricultural New Year (*Sonam Losar*); and New Year in the Eastern regions (*Nyinlo*) corresponds with the winter solstice at the beginning of January.

These 'New Years' are, in fact, halfway between secular and religious festivals because, although they do not celebrate any special religious events, ceremonies dedicated to certain indigenous deities are performed on those days.

Religious Festivals

Religious festivals are very numerous and have different names according to their types, the best known being the *Tshechus*,[2] which are festivals in honour of Guru Rinpoche, commemorating one of his great deeds. These great deeds are all believed to have taken place on the tenth day of the month, which is the meaning of the word

'Tshechu', even though all Tshechus do not, in practice, take place on tenth days. All the district dzongs and a large number of villages, especially in the east, have an annual Tshechu which attracts peasants from the surrounding countryside.

Tshechus are celebrated for several days, between three and five according to the location, and are the occasion for dances that are clearly defined in religious content. They can be performed by monks, laymen or *gomchens,* and the repertory is the same practically everywhere. Certain Tshechus end with the worship of a huge appliqué *thangka* representing Guru Rinpoche and his Eight Manifestations. Such a thangka is called *thongdroel,* which means that simply by viewing it, people can be delivered from the cycle of reincarnations. Some Tshechus also have a *wang,* a collective verbal blessing given by a high monk. Coloured threads are then distributed and people tie them around their necks as witness to the blessing. Sometimes the *wang* is called *mewang,* meaning 'blessing by fire', as the participants jump over a fire which burns away their impurities.

In a few important dzongs — Thimphu, Punakha, Paro, Tongsa, Wangdi Phodrang — two large festivals take place each year: a **Dromchoe,** which generally includes dances and is dedicated to Yeshe Gompo (Mahakala) or Palden Lhamo, the two main protective deities of the Drukpas, and a *Tshechu* dedicated to Guru Rinpoche. The *Dromchoe* at Punakha takes place in the first month of the lunar year and ends with a *Serda,* a magnificent procession which re-enacts an episode of the war against the Tibetans in the 17th century.

Atsaras are clowns whose expressive masks and postures are an indispensable element in any religious festival: they confront the monks, toss out salacious jokes, and distract the crowd with their antics when the religious dances begin to grow tedious. Believed to represent the *acaryas,* religious masters of India, they are the only people permitted to mock religion in a society where sacred matters are treated with the highest respect. For a few days these popular entertainers are allowed the freedom to express a formulaic challenge within an established framework that does not, however, upset the social and religious order.

Some religious festivals include only a few dances and consist mostly of readings from a particular text. On these occasions, villagers assemble in the temple and participate in the prayers while at the same time drinking strong alcoholic beverages. Each village

takes pride in its annual religious festival, whether it includes dances or simply prayers, and any villager who has gone to live in the city is expected to come back home for it. He will then sponsor a large part of the festival.

For the Bhutanese, religious festivals offer an opportunity to become immersed in the meaning of their religion and to gain much merit. They are also occasions for seeing people, and for being seen; for social exchanges, and for flaunting success. People bring out their finest clothes, their most beautiful jewels; they take out picnics rich with meat and abundant alcohol. Men and women joke and flirt. An atmosphere of convivial, slightly ribald good humour prevails.

Ceremonial Scarves

The large scarves (*kabne*) that men drape around their bodies — for official occasions or to go to a dzong — indicate a person's rank.

A white scarf with fringes is for commoners. A white scarf with fringes and a red band running lengthwise down the middle, with one, two or three red stripes across it, is worn by an assistant district administrator (*Dzongrab, Dungpa*). A white scarf with fringes and two broad, red, vertical borders is called a *khamar* and is worn by village chiefs, the *Gups*.

A red scarf without fringes is worn by a *Dasho*. This title means 'the best'. It is not hereditary but is conferred by the King on people of his choice as a reward for service.

A dark blue scarf shows that a person is a Representative of the People, elected by the Royal Advisory Council.

An orange scarf without fringes is worn by Vice-Ministers; Ministers wear the same scarf, but with part of it folded on the left shoulder.

The King wears a saffron yellow scarf, as does the Je Khenpo, the Head Abbot of the country.

All high-ranking officials wear a sword. Certain scarves are conferred by the King, while those of lesser rank are given by the Minister of Home Affairs. The personnel of the Royal Body Guard, the Armed Forces and the Police wear narrow scarves of stiff material.

Women of all ranks wear a red striped scarf with fringes on their left shoulder, folded in three lengthwise and then doubled over. This scarf is properly called a *rachu* but the term *kabne* is often applied to it.

Religious Dances and Music

Religious dances are called *cham* and there are a large number of them. Dancers wear spectacular costumes made of yellow silk or rich brocade, often decorated with ornaments of carved bone. For certain dances they wear masks which may represent animals, fearsome deities, skulls, manifestations of Guru Rinpoche or just plain human beings. The masks are so heavy that dancers protect themselves from injury by binding their heads in strips of cloth which support the mask. The dancers then see out through the opening of the mouth.

Dances can be grouped into three broad categories: instructive or didactic dances which are dramas with a moral (the Dance of the Princes and Princesses, the Dance of the Stag and the Hunting Dogs, the Dance of the Judgement of the Dead); dances that purify and protect a place from demonic spirits (the Dance of the Masters of the Cremation Grounds, the Dance of the Stags, the Dance of the Fearsome Gods, the Dance of the Black Hats, the Dance of the *Ging* and the *Tsholing*, the dances of the *Ging* with sticks and the *Ging* with swords); and dances that proclaim the victory of Buddhism and the glory of Guru Rinpoche (all dances with drums, the Dance of the Heroes, the Dance of Celestial Beings, the Dance of the Eight Manifestations of Guru Rinpoche).

The most famous dances are the following:

The Dance of the Black Hats (*Shanag*) A spectacular dance in which dancers representing Tantrists with supernatural powers take possession of the dancing area to drive out evil spirits and purify the ground with their footsteps. This dance also tells the story of the assassination of the anti-Buddhist Tibetan king, Langdarma, in the year AD 842 by a monk, Pelkyi Dorje, who had hidden his bow and arrows in the voluminous sleeves of his garment. Beating drums as they dance, the 'Black Hat' dancers proclaim their victory over the evil spirits.

The Dance of the Drummers from Dametsi (*Dametsi Ngacham*) This is the best-known dance of all, composed in the 16th century at Dametsi Monastery in Eastern Bhutan by a saint who had a vision of Guru Rinpoche's heaven. Twelve men wearing yellow skirts and animal masks beat drums as they dance; they represent Guru Rinpoche's entourage and they are celebrating the victory of the religion.

The Dance of the Masters of the Cremation Grounds (*Durdag*) This dance requires some measure of understanding of Tantric symbolism. Two skeletons guard the eight cremation grounds which are situated on the edges of the cosmic diagram where Tantric deities dwell. Their mission is to protect the cosmic diagram from demonic influences.

The Dance of the Fearsome Gods (*Tungam*) Dancers dressed in brocade and wearing masks of terrifying gods represent the entourage of one aspect of Guru Rinpoche, Guru Dorje Droloe, who leads the dance. Armed with ritual daggers (*phurpa*), the dancers execute and redeem an evil spirit by liberating its conscious principle from its body.

The Lute Dance (*Dranyen Cham*) This dance celebrates the founding and spread of the Drukpa school.

Religious Song (*Choeshe*) Very similar to the preceding dance and performed in the same costume, this dance and the song which accompanies it commemorate the beginning of a pilgrimage to Mount Tsari in Tibet by the founder of the Drukpa school, Tsangpa Gyare.

The Dance of the Four Stags (*Shacham*) This dance commemorates the vanquishing of the God of the Wind by Guru Rinpoche who commandeers the god's stag as his own mount.

The Dance of the Judgement of the Dead (*Raksha Marcham*) This dance is one of the most interesting of the *Tshechu* and it is extremely didactic. It is divided into two parts.

First comes a long dance by the *Rakshas* who are aides to the God of the Dead. They wear yellow skirts and animal masks. Then the God of the Dead — Shinje Choekyi Gyelpo — enters together with his attendants, the white god and the black demon who live with all beings and bear witness to their actions. Next begins the judgement proper. The first to enter is a sinner dressed all in black with a black mask, holding a basket containing a piece of meat that symbolizes his sins. The God of the Dead listens to his tale, then has his actions weighed on a scale. The good actions are symbolized by white pebbles, the bad ones by black pebbles. The white god tries to save the sinner by emphasizing his good actions, whereas the black demon then describes the man's wicked actions in detail. In the end, the sinner is sent to hell to the great joy of the black demon who accompanies him on the road to hell, symbolized by a length of black cloth.

A general dance ensues and then a virtuous man enters. As a sign of his piety, he is dressed in white, with a white face, and he holds a prayer flag. The same judgement scene as before unfolds and the virtuous man is sent to paradise on a road which is symbolized by a length of white cloth. The black demon tries to seize him at the last moment but the white god saves him and he is welcomed by celestial beings.

The Dance of the Princes and Princesses (*Pholey Moley*) This is certainly one of the Bhutanese public's best-loved dances which is also a little lewd!

The written story of King Norzang concerns the king's love for his favourite queen, Yidrogma, which provokes the jealousy of the other queens. The latter arrange things so that the king goes off to war, and they then force Yidrogma to flee to her father in fear of her life. But when the king returns from battle he soon understands the stratagems of the other queens and begs Yidrogma to come back and live with him, which she finally consents to do.

The popular version of the original story is quite different: two princes go off to war, leaving their wives in the charge of a couple of old servants. As soon as the princes are out of sight, the princesses and the maidservant start romping with the *atsaras*. When the princes return they are furious and cut off the noses of their wives as punishment. The old servant also cuts off his wife's nose. Then the princes allow themselves to weaken and they call for a doctor to sew back the noses. Although the doctor gladly sews back the noses of the beautiful princesses, he is far less enthusiastic about sewing on that of the maidservant, who smells awful. In the end all's well that ends well and everyone is reconciled.

The Dance of the Stag and the Hunting Dogs (*Shawa Shachhi*) This dance depicts the conversion to Buddhism of a hunter named Gonpo Dorje by the great saint Milarepa (1040–1123). More like a theatrical play than any of the other dances, it is very long and is usually performed in two parts, each of which concludes one day of *Tshechu*.

The story goes that while the saint Milarepa was meditating in a cave, he heard shouting and barking. He came out of his retreat and saw a stag covered with sweat and trembling with fear. Milarepa calmed it by singing a religious hymn and took it under his protection. Soon afterwards two dogs appeared which had been chasing the stag, and Milarepa won them over with one of his songs. The hunter arrived unexpectedly, looking for his dogs, and when he saw them lying down with the stag at Milarepa's feet, he flew into a rage and shot a poisoned arrow at the saint. The saint used his

superhuman powers to snap the hunter's bow, while the arrow, instead of hitting him, returned to the astonished hunter. Milarepa then intoned a song that succeeded in convincing the hunter to give up hunting and take up Buddhism.

The first part of this dance has a comic tone, starting with the hunter's servant who jokes with the *atsaras*. The hunter, crowned with leaves and carrying his bow, then arrives with his two dogs. He performs non-Buddhist rituals aimed at bringing him good luck on the hunt, while his servant and the *atsaras* clown around him.

The second part is more dignified and religious. Milarepa appears clad all in white except for his characteristic red hat. He holds a pilgrim's staff in his hand and with his songs he converts first the dogs and then the hunter. The conversion is symbolized by a rope over which the hunter and the dogs must jump.

The Dance of the Ging and the Tsholing (*Ging dang Tsholing*) It is said that this dance was performed for the first time in Samye Monastery in Tibet, in the eighth century, by Guru Rinpoche himself. The *Tsholing*, terrifying deities who are seen as protectors of the religion, purify the ground of demonic influences. The *Ging*, who make up Guru Rinpoche's retinue, then chase away the *Tsholing* in order to take possession of the area and proclaim victory for the religion by beating drums. They tap the public on the head to drive out impurities, and the public whistles to keep demons far away.

The Dance of the Eight Manifestations of Guru Rinpoche (*Guru Tshen Gye*) The Eight Aspects under which Guru Rinpoche manifested himself on various occasions appear in a procession with the principal aspect of Guru Rinpoche shaded by a parasol. Certain other aspects are accompanied by their retinues and small celestial beings. In order of appearance they are:

Dorje Droloe, 'Liberated Diamond-Thunderbolt', who has a terrifying dark red mask and a garland of skulls around his body, holds a diamond-thunderbolt (*dorje*) and a ritual dagger (*phurpa*). He earned this name after vanquishing evil spirits who were creating obstacles to Buddhism at Taktsang in Paro and Singye Dzong in Kurtoe. Dorje Droloe is followed by his entourage of fearsome deities.

Tshokye Dorje, 'Diamond-Thunderbolt Born from a Lake', who is dressed in blue brocade and wears a peaceful blue mask, carries in his hands a diamond-thunderbolt and a small bell. His name derives from his miraculous birth in a blue lotus on Lake Dhanakosha.

Loden Chogse, 'He Who Wishes to Acquire Supreme Knowledge', who wears a robe of red brocade and a white mask with a knot of hair and a crown, holds in his hands a little drum and a bowl. He got this name after he had listened to the teachings of the *Vajrayana* and mastered the sciences inculcated by the Indian masters; tutelary deities then appeared to him.

Padmasambhava, 'Born of the Lotus', who wears a monk's robe of dark red and yellow, wears a white mask with a pointed red hat, a so-called pundit's hat. He got his name after he used his supernatural powers to transform the wood-pile (on which the king of Zahor wanted to burn him alive) into a lake.

Guru Rinpoche, 'Most Precious Master', is the chief aspect, yet he is not listed as one of the Eight Aspects. He wears a mask of gilded copper crowned by his characteristic hat and is attended by two monks while a third shades him with a parasol.

Shakya Sengye, 'Lion of the Shakya Family', who has a red and yellow monk's robe and wears a mask resembling Buddha's face with a hairstyle of tight blue curls, holds a begging bowl in his hands. He was called by this name when, after having renounced his kingdom, he went to meditate and study in the cave of Maratika in Nepal with the master Prabahati.

Pema Gyelpo, 'Lotus-King', who wears a robe of red brocade and a pinkish-orange mask with a beard, holds in his hands a mirror and a small drum. He got this name when he returned to his native kingdom of Ugyen (Oddhyana); at that moment the chiefs of the country wanted to burn him but could not succeed in doing so. Seeing this as a sign of the spiritual realization of Guru Rinpoche, they converted to Buddhism and offered him the kingdom.

Nyima Oezer, 'Sunbeam', who is dressed in yellow brocade, wears a yellow mask with a beard of blue hair and holds a trident in his hand. He got this name when, as he was preaching in the cremation grounds, he conquered evil spirits and made them promise to protect the Buddhist doctrine ever afterwards.

Sengye Drathok, 'He with the Voice of a Lion', is clad in blue brocade; his blue mask crowned with five skulls is terrifying. He was called by this name after the power of his words vanquished 500 heretical masters who had tried to destroy the doctrine of Buddhism.

The principal aspect of Guru Rinpoche is seated, whereas each of

The Art of Books

Most historical writing in Bhutan has been religious. A religious book is sacred because it represents the speech of Buddha, and must be treated with respect, for blessings are frequently received from it. It is also extremely beneficial to own religious books at home. The great importance given to books is reflected in the care that goes into writing and making them.[3]

Paper is made from the inner bark of two shrubs, *Daphne* and *Edgeworthia*, that grow in abundance in Bhutan. The bark is reduced to pulp and mixed with ashes while it goes through a long cooking process. The pulp is then beaten and two methods are used for obtaining the finished sheets.

One method, widely used throughout the Himalayas, produces paper called *resho*, 'cotton paper'. The process begins with the pouring of the pulp on to a cotton screen; it is then spread over the cotton surface while it is floating in water. This manoeuvre requires dexterity and practice. The screen and the pulp are then left to dry, which takes half a day, before the sheet of paper can be taken off.

The second method is only used in Bhutan and produces a kind of paper called *tsasho*, 'bamboo paper'. A screen made from slim bamboo sticks is lowered into a vat of pulp; the paper-maker then lifts it out and spreads the pulp over the surface of the screen while it is out of the water. The screen is subsequently turned over, and the sheet that has formed on it drops off and is put on a growing pile of freshly made paper. At the end of the day, a stone is placed on the pile to help the water drain out of it during the night. The next day, the paper-maker peels the sheets off one by one and sticks them directly on to the earthen walls of a hut built for this purpose. By the end of the day, the sheets are dry and fall off the wall.

Bhutanese paper is of excellent quality and impervious to insects. Unfortunately, insects love the ink, which is made from soot, herbs, yak-blood and animal-based glue.

The sheets of paper are cut to the size of book pages and the text is then either written by a calligrapher or printed by xylography. Xylography entails carving the text in reverse on a wooden board, coating the plank with ink and then pressing a sheet of paper on to it with a roller; the printed text appears on the page the right way around. Certain texts are written in calligraphy with ink made from gold dust and illuminated like medieval manuscripts in Europe.

When the printing or calligraphy of a whole text is completed, the pages are not bound but simply pressed between two wooden boards. The upper board, which makes the cover, may be a work of art in itself because it is often carved with religious subjects and perhaps covered with a sheet of wrought, gilded copper.

It is possible to see some of these books, printing boards and paper at the National Library in Thimphu. Established in 1969, the library was moved in 1984 to a new building constructed in traditional style. It contains about 6,100 Tibetan and Bhutanese books, both manuscripts and xylographs, and a collection of 9,000 printing boards.

the other aspects, with the exception of Padmasambhava, dances before going to join the principal aspect. Then a public blessing takes place and the fervour of the people is fully demonstrated: the faithful press forward to receive a thread of blessing, not from a monk who represents Guru Rinpoche but from Guru Rinpoche himself, incarnated as a human being. The dance area is transformed into a heaven, and celestial beings adorned with bone ornaments come to dance and sing the praises of Guru Rinpoche. The dance concludes with a final procession and the exit of all the aspects of Guru Rinpoche. It is the culmination of a *Tshechu* because it is the most religiously important.

Religious Music

Like the dances, religious music reflects a strong Tibetan influence. The instruments are long trumps (*dungchen*), oboe (*gyaling*), a double-sided drum (*nga*) held in a frame and beaten with a curved drumstick, cymbals with a vertical movement (*rolmo*) or horizontal movement (*silnyen*), a trumpet made from a femur (*kangling*), and a conch shell. In addition there is the *damalu*, a small, double-faced, hand-held drum that is beaten with hard pellets attached by strings, and the small bell (*drilbu*). Music gives rhythm to the dances and religious ceremonies, and it punctuates the singing or recitation of the texts.

Secular Dances and Music

These dances are performed by both sexes, either separately or together, and can be divided into two groups: dances from Southern Bhutan which are influenced by Nepalese culture, and those of the rest of the country which are influenced by Tibetan culture. Generally, dancers accompany themselves by singing; musical instruments being used only on the most official occasions. A flute, drums and, more recently, a harmonium and guitar make up the orchestra for the music of Southern Bhutan. In the north, the orchestra is a flute (*lim*), a seven-stringed lute (*dranyen*), a two-stringed viol played with a bow (*piwang*), and more rarely, a trapezoidal, tabletop zither played with two hammers.[4]

While dances from the southern borderland usually have a lively rhythm, dances in the rest of the country have a much slower rhythm which often picks up speed as the dance progresses, the steps sliding and tapping. The musical scale here is pentatonic. Many of the songs, even folksongs, have a religious base. There also exist mystical songs — composed by saints, prayers and biographies of saints sung by wandering monks, and the great epic cycle of King Gesar. All these are in classical Tibetan.

Songs associated with daily life, on the other hand, are in the vernacular languages and are much freer, even allowing a certain amount of improvization.[5] Songs ring out at times such as rice-planting, ploughing and harvesting, when women pound earth for building the walls of a house or when they weave with the rhythm of the shuttles, when a carpenter fits his timbers or a herdsman drives his animals to pasture, when a village makes merry at a wedding or when muleteers set off along precipitous paths.

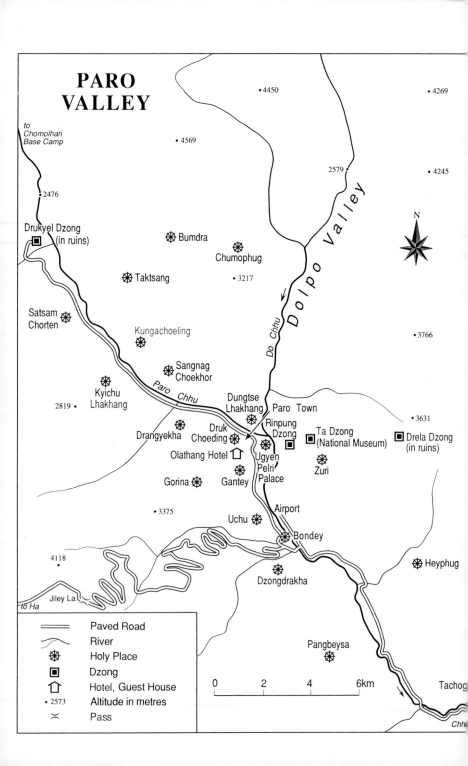

Places to Visit

Although the interiors of temples, monasteries and dzongs are still forbidden to foreign travellers at the present time, short descriptions of all these sites will nonetheless be given.

Western Bhutan

The Paro Valley

The first thing you will notice in the Paro valley is the transparent purity of the air and the absence of noise.

The Paro valley has kept its bucolic nature in spite of the airport and the existence of development projects. Fields, brown or green depending on the season, cover most of the valley floor, while hamlets and isolated farms dot the landscape. The houses of the Paro valley are considered to be among the most beautiful in the country; they are the only ones with rows of windows on three levels, and the prosperity of the valley is evident from their size.

Starting as an arid gorge at Chhuzom ('the confluence'), the valley opens up little by little, reaching its widest point before the airport. Then it divides in two near the dzong and Paro village: one valley called Dopchari runs northwards for about 15 kilometres (nine miles), while the main valley with the paved road continues northwest. The road terminates at Drukyel Dzong, 16 kilometres (ten miles) from Paro. The end of the valley appears to be blocked by the dzong but in fact it continues, growing steadily narrower, for about a dozen more kilometres (about seven and a half miles).

The Paro valley is enchanting. The road is lined by willow trees following a mountain stream; the gaily decorated houses have shingled roofs; peasants lead horses adorned with bright woollen pompoms; sturdy young women work in the rice fields with their skirts tucked up to their knees, easing their hard labour by singing or joking with passers-by. A walk on foot across the valley is without doubt the best way to appreciate its beauty.

Paro is believed to be one of the first valleys to have received the imprint of Buddhism, and two temples bear witness to the glorious introduction of the religion: Kyichu and Taktsang.

Kyichu Lhakhang

Kyichu Lhakhang is composed of twin temples which are somewhat set back on the left of the road to Taktsang and Drukyel Dzong. Built on a promontory and surrounded by a low wall, the two temples are visible from the road through a cluster of prayer flags.

According to Bhutanese tradition, the first temple at Kyichu was built by the Buddhist Tibetan king, Songtsen Gampo, in the seventh century. The story goes that a giant demoness lay across the whole area of Tibet and the Himalayas and was preventing the spread of Buddhism. To overcome her, King Songtsen Gampo decided to build 108 temples which would be placed on all the points of her body. Of these 108 temples, 12 were built in accordance with precise plans. Thus it happened that in about the year AD 638 the temple of the Jokhang in Lhasa was built over the very heart of the demoness. Kyichu Lhakhang was built on her left foot and belongs to a group of four temples categorized as 'subjugating regions beyond the frontiers'. After this initial construction which put the Paro valley on the Buddhist map, the temple of Kyichu was visited by Guru Rinpoche, who came there to meditate.

The history of Kyichu Lhakhang remains unclear until the beginning of the 13th century, at which time it is known that it was under the administration of the Lhapa school. It can be assumed that the temple came under the protection of the Drukpas at the end of the 13th century when the Drukpas defeated the Lhapas.

In 1839, the temple was restored on the orders of the 25th Je Khenpo, Sherab Gyeltsen, who also donated the superb statue of Avalokiteshvara with a thousand hands and a thousand eyes, which is located in the sanctuary.

In 1968, H M Ashi Kesang, the Queen Mother of Bhutan, arranged for a second temple to be built alongside the first one, in the same style. It is so skilfully constructed that it is impossible to discern any difference between the two.

At the entrance to the small courtyard leading to the two temples, a big prayer wheel is turned by an old woman and the walls are decorated with paintings of the Guardians of the Four Directions, a water deity, and Genyen Dorje Dradul, a Protector of Buddhism, mounted on a red horse. An orange tree grows in the little courtyard. The ancient temple stands opposite the entrance with the modern temple on the right.

The Ancient Temple is deeply venerated for its antiquity and for the role it has played. Turquoise and coral that have been donated by the faithful are set into the floor at the place where prostrations are performed. The paintings covering the walls on all sides of the sanctuary show the Twelve Acts of Buddha and his Previous Lives.

On the left side of the window is a painting of three personages: at the top is Guru Rinpoche, below him is Shabdrung Ngawang Namgyel with the First Desi of Bhutan; at the bottom is the 25th Je Khenpo, Sherab Gyeltshen, who restored the temple. Immediately to the right of the window is a painting of Buddha and the Sixteen *Arhats*, the first persons to attain the state of Buddhahood. At the corner of the wall above is the goddess Tsheringma, mounted on a white lion, while below is the Protector of Buddhism, Genyen Dorje Dradul, riding a red horse.

There are many statues attesting to the reverence in which this temple is held, and nearly all of them are statues of Avalokiteshvara in his form with a thousand hands and a thousand eyes. There is also a statue of the Tibetan king, Songtsen Gampo, recognizable by the white hair styled in a knot, and a statue of Amitayus, sitting in a posture of meditation with a vase of long life in his hands.

The sanctuary is closed, but it is possible to catch a glimpse of the Eight Bodhisattvas and most especially one of the holiest statues of Bhutan, the statue of the Jowo, Buddha as a prince at the age of eight years, which is similar to the one in the Jokhang Temple in Lhasa.

The New Temple is dedicated to Guru Rinpoche and to the secret teachings called *Kagye* which he transmitted to his disciples and which constitute part of the earliest, fundamental teachings of the Nyingmapa school.

The Way to Taktsang Lhakhang

Beyond Kyichu Lhakhang, the road continues downward into the valley and after about five kilometres (three miles) you will see the Taktsang Lhakhang complex on the right, at 2,950 metres (9,678 feet) above sea level. The buildings cling to the black rock, overhanging the valley below by 800 metres (over 2,600 feet). The fact that the access path to the complex of temples called Taktsang Pelphug is scarcely visible makes its location all the more impressive.

For people unaccustomed to the altitude it takes about three hours at an average walking speed to reach the temples. After crossing the river, the way rises gently through a forest and comes to a hamlet where prayer wheels are turned by water and the sound of tinkling bells fills the air.

Some 100 metres (328 feet) beyond, the path crosses a meadow on
the other side of which the real climb begins, up through a forest of
oak and rhododendron. You come to the first level ground at a place
where there is a group of prayer flags. On the right, a short route
about 100 metres (328 feet) long leads to the Taktsang tea house, a
log cabin that can be seen through the trees from the prayer flags. The
view over the temples from this tea house is extraordinary, and the
effort of climbing up to it is amply rewarded.

After a refreshing drink, the climb continues very steeply; the
forest now takes on a ghostly quality as some of the trees have been
attacked by disease and are festooned with Spanish moss. The path
skirts around a field below a house; this is the only flat stretch of the
journey and it is all too short! This brings you to a second group of
prayer flags, and it becomes clear that you are now well above the
main complex of Taktsang. The view from the overhang is dizzying.

The way down begins along the face of the cliff and for several
metres it can appear somewhat hair-raising, although the path is well
defined and there is no danger whatever of falling off. The path then
gets wider but continues downwards to a bridge spanning a ravine
between two outcrops of rock. Taktsang now stands above you. A
small house perched in a hollow of the rock is used as a meditation
house. Close by flows a sacred spring which is said to have gushed
forth miraculously when Yeshe Tsogyel, one of Guru Rinpoche's
consorts, threw her rosary against the rock. This humid spot is always
in the shade so it is very cold and it is not unusual to find patches of
ice there, even as late as June. From here on, a long flight of steps
along the rock face leads by way of one last, short, steep stretch that
kills your legs, to the entrance of the complex of Taktsang.

A final staircase inside the entrance leads up to a landing. The
narrowness of the place makes the whole ground plan somewhat
complicated, but the three main temples are all situated in the same
building.

Taktsang Lhakhang

Taktsang is one of the most venerated pilgrim sites of the Himalayan
world and it contains 13 holy places. However, most people only visit
the one called Taktsang Pelphug.

Taktsang, the 'tiger's lair', gets its name from the story of its
foundation. In the eighth century, Guru Rinpoche came to Taktsang in

a miraculous manner, flying on the back of a tigress from Khenpajong in the region of Kurtoe. According to Bhutanese tradition, the tigress was a form taken by one of the Master's consorts for the occasion. Guru Rinpoche meditated for three months in a cave at Taktsang and converted the Paro valley to Buddhism. In his terrifying form of Dorje Droloe, Guru Rinpoche used the religious cycle of the Kagye to subjugate the Eight Categories of Evil Spirits during his stay at Taktsang.

Guru Rinpoche then returned to Tibet and transmitted the teachings of the Kagye cycle to his disciples, particularly to Langchen Pelkyi Singye who, in his turn, came to Taktsang to meditate in the year 853, following in the footsteps of his master. He gave his name of Pelphug to the cave, 'Pelkyi's cave'. He then went on to Nepal where he died. His body was brought back miraculously to Taktsang by the grace of the deity Dorje Legpa and is now sealed inside the chorten standing in the room on the left at the top of the entrance stairway. The chorten was restored in 1982–3.

Many Tibetan saints came to meditate in this intensely spiritual place, notably Milarepa (1040–1123), Phadampa Sangye (died 1117), the famous Tibetan yogin Machig Labdoenma (1055–1145 or 1153) and Thangton Gyelpo (1385–1464).

The first sanctuary to be built at Taktsang Pelphug probably dates back to the 14th century. Sonam Gyeltshen, a Nyingmapa lama of the Kathogpa branch, came from Tibet and constructed the first sanctuary at Taktsang. The paintings which can still be dimly discerned on the rock above the principal building seem to bear witness to this earlier structure which no longer exists today.

Taktsang remained under the authority of Kathogpa lamas up until the 17th century, but in 1645 the whole site was offered to Shabdrung Ngawang Namgyel when he visited the locality with his Nyingmapa master, Rinzing Nyingpo. The Shabdrung immediately expressed his desire to put up a new building, but at that time he was involved in the construction of the Paro Dzong and he died before he was able to carry out his aim. It was the Fourth Desi, Tenzing Rabgye, who fulfilled the Shabdrung's wish and arranged in 1692 for the the construction of the buildings that we see today.

The edifice was apparently restored in 1861–5 at the time of the 34th Je Khenpo, Sheldrup Oezer, whose portrait can be seen in one of the temples. The most recent restoration took place in 1982. Three important temples are located in the building on the right-hand side of the entrance stairway, the foremost of which contains the cave where Guru Rinpoche and Langchen Pelkyi Singye meditated. To reach it, you have to go down several steps; the view from the temple is vertiginous since it perches 800 metres (over 2,600 feet) above the Paro valley.

The diminutive size of the **first temple** should in no way detract from the fact that this is the most profoundly sacred spot of Taktsang. On the rock which forms the left-hand wall there is a picture of Zangdopelri, the heaven of Guru Rinpoche. The meditation cave itself is concealed behind a carved wooden grille that is only opened once a year. A large image of Guru Rinpoche, in his terrifying form of Dorje Droloe standing on the tigress, guards the cave. The right-hand wall with a window in it is covered with paintings illustrating another cycle of secret teachings that were given by Guru Rinpoche, the Phurpa cycle (*Vajrakila* in Sanskrit), the deity of the Magic Dagger.

The medium-sized **second temple**, immediately above the first, is reached by climbing the stairs again. It is dedicated to Guru Rinpoche and contains elegant paintings. Under the projecting roof in front of the entrance there is a large painting of Pelkyi Singye, the disciple of Guru Rinpoche whose remains are preserved in the chorten, as mentioned above. He is surrounded by five aspects of Buddhism's formidable guardian deity, Pehar.

In the temple the main statue, to the left of the entrance, is of Guru Rinpoche and this image is particularly venerated. It is said that when it was being brought up to Taktsang the statue spoke, and the name of this temple — 'the temple of the Guru statue which speaks'— is taken from this event. On the altar there are two noteworthy statues, one is of the builder of the Taktsang complex, Tenzing Rabgye, the Fourth Desi of Bhutan (1638–96), and the other of Pelkyi Singye.

To the left of the altar is painted the Kagye cycle of teachings. On the wall opposite the entrance, a painting of exceptional refinement shows Guru Rinpoche with his two consorts and his Eight Different Manifestations. Below the picture of Guru Rinpoche is a portrait of the 34th Je Khenpo, Sheldrup Oezer (r. 1861– 5). To the right of this wall are depicted the divinities of the Gondu cycle of teachings. The Phurpa, the Kagye and the Gondu cycles of teachings are the three principal cycles of the Nyingmapa school and all three were first preached by Guru Rinpoche.

A painting of the historical Buddha appears to the left of the window, while the unifier of Bhutan, Shabdrung Ngawang Namgyel, is portrayed on the right. On the next wall is depicted Amitayus; he is coloured red, holding a vase of Long Life and is seen here in union with his consort. The last wall, just before the door, has pictures of the three great Buddhist kings of Tibet, Songtsen Gampo (seventh century), Trisong Detsen (eighth century) and Relpachen (ninth century).

The **third temple**, of large dimensions, is also consecrated to Guru Rinpoche as testified by the principal statue of the temple. The left wall portrays Guru Rinpoche and his Eight Different Manifestations. Be sure to notice also a very interesting little painting that shows Shabdrung Ngawang Namgyel subduing his enemies with the assistance of his protective deities. On the left and right of the window are depictions of the gods of the Gondu cycle, whereas most of the wall opposite the entrance is taken up by the deities of the Phurpa cycle. On the part of the wall closest to the altar there is a painting of Amitayus.

Up above the main building, but still in the same complex, there are three more temples. One contains a statue of Dorje Droloe standing on the tigress, the next is a temple to Amitayus, and the last is a temple dedicated to the god of wealth, Kubera/Vaisravana.

Three other complexes are situated above the Taktsang Pelphug complex. **Taktsang Ugyen Tsemo** was first built in 1408 then rebuilt after a fire in 1958, **Taktsang Oezergang** was constructed in 1646, and finally **Taktsang Zangdopelri** is dated 1853. These are also deeply venerated sites and receive many pilgrims.

Drukyel Dzong

If you continue to the end of the paved road you will come to Drukyel Dzong. In fine weather, the towering peak of **Mount Jhomolhari**, 7,314 metres (24,000 feet) high, appears as a backdrop. This mountain, which marks the frontier with Tibet, is sacred, as are all the mountains in Bhutan, and it is the dwelling place of the goddess Jhomo. It was first climbed in 1937, but the expedition made it clear that it had not actually set foot on the summit. Jhomolhari has never been climbed since and it is now a 'protected peak'.

Drukyel Dzong, with a delightful village nestling at its foot, is built on a rocky spur that blocks the Paro valley and protected it from invasions from the north. The dzong was built in 1647 by Shabdrung Ngawang Namgyel to commemorate his victory over the Tibetans in 1644. Drukyel Dzong means 'fortress of the victorious Drukpas'.

The dzong was enlarged in 1651 by the Shabdrung's half-brother, Tenzing Drugda, who was the Paro Penlop at the time. The remains of protected passages can still be seen, where the occupants could go to fetch water from a cistern, safe from enemy arrows.

In 1951, a butter-lamp fell over and started a terrible fire. Only the walls remained and Drukyel Dzong became no more than a dramatic silhouette falling into ruins. In 1985, in order to save the dzong from total ruin, a shingled roof was put on, giving it the same appearance as in the first photograph of it, published in 1914 in the *National Geographic Magazine*.

Skirting the dzong, a road heads towards the end of the valley and points towards the base camp of Jhomolhari, three days' further walk. A short incline leads up to the dzong, but the visit will only bring a sigh of nostalgia as you consider the glorious past of this sentinel. It is dangerous to climb on the ramparts or to go inside the central tower because the stones are loose.

One of the targets for the local archery field is located very close to the path leading to the dzong. It is not particularly noticeable and, given the distance between the two targets, you may not be aware when an archery tournament is taking place so keep a sharp look-out.

Dungtse Lhakhang

This temple is remarkable primarily because it is in the form of a chorten, the only one in Bhutan except for the Memorial Chorten in Thimphu. It is situated on the edge of a hill that thrusts forward between the principal Paro valley and the Dopchari valley, across the bridge of Paro village, on the road to the National Museum.

Dungtse Lhakhang was built in 1421 by the famous Tibetan lama, Thangton Gyelpo (1385–1464), also known by the name of Chagzampa, 'the builder of iron bridges' or Drubthob, 'the Realized One'. Thangton Gyelpo had come to Bhutan to search for iron ore and built eight bridges there before he returned to Tibet. In Paro, a demoness was terrorizing the valley and this very hill turned out to be her head. Thangton Gyelpo built a temple in the form of a chorten to overpower her, as chortens often play the part of a nail which immobilizes a demon at the same time as proclaiming the victory of Buddhism.

In 1841, the 25th Je Khenpo, Sherab Gyeltsen (r. 1836–9), decided to restore the temple and all the villages contributed to the effort. The names of the donors are inscribed on the tree-trunks which form the

Bhutanese Medicine

One of the ancient names for Bhutan was 'the Land of Medicinal Herbs', for Bhutan exported many herbs to Tibet.

Bhutanese medicine has been influenced by traditional Indian Ayurvedic medicine from which it borrowed the theory of Three Humours (bile, phlegm and wind), and by Chinese medicine which taught the reading of pulses. Like both of these, it has a rich pharmacopoeia with preparations based on vegetable, animal and mineral substances.

Bhutanese medicine is similar to the traditional medicine formerly practised in Tibet, where Bhutanese doctors used to receive their training.

The origin of this medicine goes back to the seventh, and particularly the eighth, century when the first Indian and Chinese works were translated into Tibetan. The first great Tibetan doctor, Yuthog the Elder, lived during that period and one of his descendants, Yuthog the Younger, was equally famous in the 11th century.

There are about 300 medical treatises in Tibetan, of which the most important are the *Quadruple Treatise: Gyuzhi* and the *Vaidurya Ngonpo*. All teachings in the 'science of treatment' (*Sorig*) go back, according to Buddhist tradition, to the Medicine Buddha (*Menlha*). Medical science went through a remarkable development in the 17th century when the first medical school was founded in Lhasa and the *Quadruple Treatise* was revised by the Regent, Sangye Gyatso, into the form that we know today.

Diagnosis begins with an examination of the 12 pulses, the tongue and urine, and questions to the patient. Illnesses develop with the increase, decrease or destabilization of the humours caused by bad food, the weather, evil spirits, the weight of previous actions, *karma*, or way of life. Remedies, in general, consist of a diet that varies with the nature of the illness, and medicines, which may be aided by acupuncture and moxibustion.

Physical treatment is accompanied by religious treatments aimed at subjugating evil spirits and ameliorating bad *karma*.

Traditional medicine has always been regarded as important in Bhutan, and a dispensary, which doubles as a training centre, was opened at Dechenchoeling in 1967. In 1979, a traditional medical hospital with a laboratory for making medicines was opened in Thimphu, subsidized by the World Health Organization. This hospital can be visited (see page 27). Four dispensaries were also set up in the rest of the country. In 1988, a project for cataloguing plants and establishing a training centre for doctors was begun with the help of an Italian non-governmental organization.

columns of the ground floor. The paintings were redone at this period.

Dungtse Lhakhang possesses one of the most extraordinary collections of paintings in Bhutan or even in the Himalayan world. Bring a torch (flashlight) as the lighting inside can be dim. They are remarkable as much for the artistic quality of the work as for the quantity of deities who are depicted and arranged according to a very precise religious order. The collection provides a priceless example of the iconography of one religious school, the Drukpa Kagyupas, at a given time. The number of images is so great that it is impossible to give a detailed description of the whole temple. It will have to suffice here to point out the most important images and the guiding principle behind the arrangement of the paintings.

This temple is conceived as a mandala (see page 77) with the different storeys corresponding to different levels of initiation, leading progressively upwards towards the heart of the mandala.

The ground floor contains the Five Buddhas of Meditation, also different forms of Avalokiteshvara, Guru Rinpoche, various historical characters including Thangton Gyelpo — the founder of the temple, as well as various forms of Kubera/Vaisravana and some protective deities. The second storey, corresponding to a higher degree of initiation, shows the forms of Mahakala displayed on the outer wall. On the interior wall can be seen visions of the *Bardo*, the intermediary state that exists between death and another rebirth.

The images on the third floor belong to the highest Tantric cycles. The great deities of these cycles are represented on the exterior wall: Guyasamaja, Vajrabhairava, Cakrasamvara, Hevajra, Kalacakra, Vajravarahi, Hayagriva. On the inside wall are depicted the Eighty-Four Indian Saints, the Mahasiddhas, who, although their occupations did not dispose them to a religious life, were the first to receive the Tantric teachings, which enabled them to attain the state of Buddhahood in their lifetime. Also shown are the Tibetan saints who obtained these teachings from the Mahasiddhas and who are at the origin of the Kagyupa school: Marpa, Milarepa, Gampopa. At their side is Tsangpa Gyare, who founded the Drukpa Kagyupa school in the 12th century. Particularly worth noting on this floor, in an alcove, is a magnificent statue of Milarepa, the 12th-century Tibetan poet–saint.

The National Museum (Ta Dzong)

The National Museum is located just above Paro Dzong, but the paved road passes first in front of Dungtse Lhakhang and then climbs for five more kilometres (three miles) up the hill to reach the museum. The museum is in fact housed in Paro Dzong's ancient watchtower, the Ta Dzong. This tower was built around 1651—the date is not certain—by Tenzing Drugda, the half-brother of Shabdrung Ngawang Namgyel, while he was the Penlop of Paro.

It was in this tower that Ugyen Wangchuck, the future First King of Bhutan, was imprisoned in 1872 when he came to put down a revolt. By the 1950s, the Ta Dzong had fallen into a badly dilapidated condition. In 1965, the Third King, Jigme Dorji Wangchuck, conceived the idea of restoring the Ta Dzong as a place to house the National Museum. This was inaugurated in 1968.

The museum is open from Tuesday to Saturday 9 am – 4 pm; on Sundays 11 am – 4 pm. It is closed on Mondays. Bring a torch (flashlight) as the electricity sometimes fades out. It can also be very cold in the galleries. The museum is considered to be a temple because of the number of religious objects it contains, and this is why you must proceed in a clockwise direction. A guard will point out the way.

Iron chains lie on the parapets by the footbridge leading to the museum. These chains, which have all been collected from different parts of Bhutan, are the remains of the iron bridges constructed by Thangton Gyelpo in the 15th century (see page 144).

The Collection The National Museum not only contains works of art but also handcrafted objects of daily life, stuffed animals, costumes, armour and even stamps. You can thus get an idea of the cultural and ecological richness of Bhutan in a very short time. Moreover, the massive exterior architecture and the beautiful interior decoration are worthwhile in themselves.

The **first gallery** after you enter contains a collection of costumes and traditional fabrics, as well as masks, hats, splendid harnesses and saddles of chased silver, and ancient books.

A small staircase on the left leads up to a **gallery of thangkas**; this is constructed as a balcony overhanging the first gallery. The thangkas are of great artistic interest and offer a good introduction to the complexities of Bhutanese iconography. There is a magnificent thangka embroidered in a way rarely used in Bhutan. It was imported from China through

Tibet. Also to be seen is an impressive piece of appliqué cloth which demonstrates the skill acquired by the Bhutanese in this particular technique. Equally interesting are the giant constructions of thread which are palaces for evil spirits. There are good examples of *tormas* here too (see page 266).

In the centre of this gallery, a staircase leads to the **stamp gallery** located at the top of the building. All the famous Bhutanese stamps are on display here: three-dimensional stamps, disc-stamps, stamps made of silk, stamps of the coronation in relief, not to mention the triangular stamp with the yeti. On this floor there is also a chapel with a 'tree of life' showing the different schools of Tibetan Tantric Buddhism.

Descending the staircase again to the level of the thangka gallery, you will find a **room of statues and engraved slates** directly underneath the chapel. The exceptionally fine statues and slates are displayed individually in alcoves that are enclosed in the same trilobed framework as the windows of houses. Leaving this room you can then complete the tour of the thangka gallery. Be sure to notice the beautiful ritual objects and musical instruments that are kept behind glass.

Returning to the first gallery, you will now go down several steps leading to a **gallery of silverwork and armour**. Two types of weaving loom are exhibited in the passage: a vertical back strap loom and a horizontal pedal loom.

The windows of the silverwork and armour gallery offer a superb view of the entire architectural structure of the Paro Dzong. In the showcases against the left-hand wall are exhibits of armour, helmets and shields made of bamboo and rhinoceros hide as well as lances and bows. Beyond the door that leads to the Third King's large collection of guns (about 180) there is a spectacular display of lacquered wooden receptacles. On the shelves to the right, boxes for betel nut, portable reliquaries, ancient clasps and pins for dresses are all examples of skilful Bhutanese silverwork. Necklaces made of enormous coral beads and etched agate show which stones are the most favoured by Bhutanese women. An ancient seven-stringed lute, a *dranyen*, has delicate decorations; it is just to the right of the door leading to a gallery of copper and silver utensils.

This **circular gallery**, on the same floor, displays objects made of copper and silver such as jugs for water or milk and particularly marvellous teapots with massive outlines and magnificent decorations.

The **animal gallery** on the floor below contains an exhibition of

Bhutan's most famous animals: takin, Himalayan bear with its white collar, blue sheep, musk deer, snow leopard, trophies of the *mithun* — the mighty indigenous buffalo, the amazing hornbill and spectacular Bhutanese butterflies. The circular gallery contains traditional receptacles and utensils made of wood. On the floor below, you can look at utilitarian objects made of bamboo and clay, and alcohol containers made of horn decorated with chased silver. The bamboo work is nearly all made in the Khyeng region of south central Bhutan and the articles are used as part of daily life.

On the last floor, where the exit is located, there is a **display of gigantic metal pots** that were used to cook food for monastic communities or men-at-arms. On either side of a little sanctuary to the water deity there are two small rooms that were formerly used as prisons but where only a few harquebuses hang today.

From the Museum you can go down to the dzong by way of a short, very steep path — for this you need sturdy shoes.

Paro Dzong

The full name of Paro Dzong is Rinpung Dzong, which means 'the fortress of the heap of jewels'.

In the 15th century, two brothers named Gyelchok and Gyelzom lived in the Paro valley; they were descendants of Phajo Drugom Shigpo, the founder of the Drukpa Kagyupa school in Bhutan. While Gyelzom established himself at Gantakha Monastery, his brother Gyelchok went off to Tibet to study theology with the great masters of that time. When he came back to Paro, he cut a very sorry figure after all the years he had spent studying without earning any money. His brother, Gyelzom, refused to receive him, telling him that there were no beggars in their family.

Gyelchok went away to live beside the river at Humrelkha, a place which took its name from the guardian deity of Paro, Humrel Gompo. There he constructed a little building that would later become the Paro Dzong. Gyelchok's descendants are well known through history as the 'Lords of Humrel' and they controlled a large part of the valley.

In 1645, the Lords of Humrel gave their little fort to Shabdrung Ngawang Namgyel, thus recognizing his religious and political authority. The Shabdrung immediately began construction of a much more commanding fortress and the dzong was consecrated in 1646. In October 1907, the dzong burnt almost to the ground but it was

immediately rebuilt to the same design by the Paro Penlop, Dawa Penjor, with money raised by a special tax levied throughout Bhutan.

Today the dzong is the administrative seat of the district of Paro and it also contains a state monastic community of about 200 members. It is approached by a gently sloping flagstone road and a beautiful wooden bridge roofed with shingles and abutted by two guard houses.

Inside the Dzong The **first courtyard** of the dzong is lined with administrative offices. The entrance is guarded by two traditional effigies standing on either side of the gate: a Mongol holding a tiger on a leash and a man holding a black yak.

The **central tower** of the dzong, the *utse,* is one of the most beautiful in Bhutan with its superb woodwork. The central tower includes a temple dedicated to the line of Drukpa Kagyupa lamas, a temple of Hayagriva, another one dedicated to the great Tantric deities, a temple of the Eight Kinds of Chortens and a temple of the Taras.

Beneath the gallery that runs along the courtyard are classical paintings of the Mongol holding his chained tiger, the Old Man of Long Life and the Four Friends. The latter are characters in a fable that recounts how a bird, a rabbit, a monkey and an elephant combined their efforts to grow a fruit tree and enjoy its fruit. The bird brought the seed, the rabbit watered it and the monkey supplied natural fertilizer while the elephant provided shade and protected it from harm. This fable, with its moral of co-operation and unity, is very popular and is represented in many places.

The Old Man of Long Life, originally a Chinese Taoist theme, has become, in Buddhism, the example of the longevity that can be achieved by careful practice of the religion. Immortality is symbolized by the stream, the mountains and the trees. The deer hark back to the First Sermon which Buddha preached in the Deer Park. This representation also emphasizes that men and animals can live in harmony within nature if they will respect certain rules of conduct. The paintings of deer and birds are noteworthy for their artistic quality and the rareness of their composition.

A flight of stone steps leads to a **second courtyard** on a lower level which belongs to the clergy. On the left side of the courtyard is a large hall, **the Kunre,** where the monks study and eat. Here the main statue is of the Buddha in his Jowo form. Paintings of Guru Rinpoche, the Buddhas of the Three Ages, Shabdrung Ngawang Namgyel and other divinities cover its walls.

Beneath the gallery that gives access to the Kunre can be seen extraordinary cosmic mandalas, representing the universe as seen by two different philosophic streams. The significance of these images in Buddhist cosmology is as great as the beauty of these works of art.

The two mandalas on the left portray the cosmos as seen through the teachings of the *Kalacakra*, 'the Wheel of Time', a Tantra that was taught in the tenth century. The first mandala shows the cosmos seen from above, divided into four concentric circles, each representing an element: air (yellow); fire (red); water (blue); earth (dark blue). Four continents are laid out at the edge of the ocean and the earth, each with two sub-continents of its own. Next come 18 slender concentric circles which represent the combination of earth–ocean–mountain six times. The central part, divided into five sections, is Mount Sumeru, the central pillar of the world. The 12 brightly coloured circles represent the 12 months of the year. The next mandala repeats the same theme, but here Mount Sumeru is seen in perspective; another difference is that the earth element and the 12 months are omitted.

The mandala on the right is painted according to the cosmology of the *Abhidharmakosha*, a text written in the fifth century by the Indian scholar Vasubandhu. In the centre rises Mount Sumeru with its different levels where the gods dwell. Mount Sumeru is surrounded by seven ranges of golden mountains. The continents, each with a different shape and its two subsidiary continents, float on the ocean. The various colours of the ocean are caused by reflection of the minerals which make up the composition of Mount Sumeru: white conch, blue turquoise, red coral and yellow gold. A chain of iron mountains closes the universe which, in both cases, is flat and not round.

Underneath the gallery on the right side of the courtyard are painted different episodes from the life of Milarepa. The room on that side is the monks' assembly hall. The paintings on the walls show the former lives of the Buddha.

Paro Village

The lane which goes from the dzong's bridge to the village of Paro is punctuated by enormous chortens. On the right, the royal palace of Ugyen Pelri is barely discernible. It was built in around 1930 by the Penlop of Paro, Tshering Penjor. On the left of the lane is the rural archery field.

On arriving at Paro village, the **temple of Druk Choeding** lies by the road, slightly to the left; it was built in 1525 by Ngawang Choegyel, the great-great-grandfather of Shabdrung Ngawang Namgyel. The latter lived there when he arrived in the Paro valley in 1616.

Paro village is new, having only been constructed in 1985. As so often in Bhutan, there was no village near the dzong, and what might be called an urban centre is a recent creation. Houses built in traditional style and painted with coloured designs line the main street. Small shops occupy the ground levels and provide the basic necessities that one would expect to find in a mountain village: pots and pans, hardware, flour, butter, oil, sugar, salt, lentils and a few tinned goods. With its main street straight and windswept, its caravan drivers leading their horses, its occasional idlers leaning against the store-fronts, Paro strangely resembles a village of the old American West.

Just above the crossroads leading to the Olathang Hotel, a beautiful residence catches the eye. It is the Gantey residence, privately owned today, but which has an excellent view of the dzong. It was built at the end of the last century to be the home of the Paro Penlops. Women were not permitted to stay overnight in the dzongs, so the families of the Penlops were housed outside.

Hotels and Restaurants

A small restaurant on the square, the Camall, serves Bhutanese, Indian and Chinese food at moderate prices in an uninspired but clean setting.

The Olathang Hotel, where tourists stay, is hidden in a pine forest three kilometres (two miles) from the village. With its lovely surroundings and superb architecture, it is an ideal place for a rest but the hotel is freezing in winter, like most hotels in Bhutan. Visitors can choose between rooms inside the main hotel building or charming little individual cottages which were built at the time of the coronation in 1974. A double room costs about 400 Nu.

Tachogang Lhakhang

Tachogang Lhakhang, 'temple of the hill of the excellent horse', rises in austere surroundings on the left bank of the river, a few kilometres before Chhuzom at the confluence of the Paro and Thimphu rivers. This private temple was founded by the Tibetan saint, Thangton Gyelpo (1385–1464), who also built Dungtse Lhakhang. While he was meditating here, Thangton Gyelpo had a vision of the excellent horse

Balaha – an emanation of Avalokiteshvara. He decided thereupon to build a temple at this spot in addition to one of his famous iron bridges (later carried away by floods in 1969). The exact date of the temple's construction is not certain, but it was probably around the year 1420. Monkeys can sometimes be seen running through the fields that surround the building.

Chhuzom

Chhuzom is now a very congested junction where the roads from Ha, Paro, Thimphu and Phuntsholing meet. On the left bank of the Paro River, at the place where it meets the Thimphu River, three chortens have been constructed. They protect the site from the influence of any evil spirits. Built at different times, they reflect the three styles of architecture commonly found in Bhutan: Nepalese, Tibetan and Bhutanese. The Bhutanese one was built at the beginning of the 1980s.

The Paro–Thimphu Road

The road to Thimphu follows the valley of the Thimphu River through an arid landscape. A few houses here and there cling to the slopes. The valley widens somewhat near the village of Khasadrapchu where the side valley of Gidakom opens into it. A small hydroelectric plant has been installed here and it provides part of the electricity for Thimphu.

After Khasadrapchu, the valley turns back into a gorge before it widens out for a second time at Namseling, about a dozen kilometres (seven miles) from Thimphu. Namseling is a very lovely spot with a forest of conifers covering a gentle slope and a large village surrounded by rice fields below the road.

After Namseling, the suburbs of Thimphu begin to appear. The state veterinary farm of Wangchutaba (or Serbithang) perches on the heights, and two large images of the Guardians of the East and the North come into sight at a bend in the road. The way then passes through a camp of the Dantak, an Indian organization that takes care of the upkeep of certain routes. The city of Thimphu now comes into view in a cross-valley that runs north–south. After the road crosses a bridge and bears off towards the north, you can see Simtokha Dzong on the left. The road now cuts through Lungtenphug, a Bhutanese army camp, and you will get your first glimpse of a traffic policeman with his elegant gestures, a special characteristic that Bhutan should certainly try to preserve.

The distance from Paro to Thimphu is 55 kilometres (34 miles), a drive of one and a half hours. The altitude is 2,350 metres (7,700 feet) at the Thimphu bridge, 2,450 metres (about 8,000 feet) at Motithang.

Thimphu

The entry into Thimphu, three kilometres (nearly two miles) beyond the first policeman, is over a bridge festooned with prayer flags. The bridge is named **Lungten Zampa**, which means 'the bridge of the prophecy'. In accordance with a prophecy, Phajo Drugom Shigpo, the founder of the Drukpa school in Bhutan, and his future wife, a young country girl, spent their first night in a cavern beneath this bridge. Their sons would contribute to the spread of the Drukpa school in Western Bhutan.

It is interesting to note, as you pass beyond the bridge and the first roundabout, that even the petrol pump on the right is built in traditional style. By royal decree, all buildings in Bhutan must keep the traditional style and this certainly helps to give a distinctive character to the new urban centres. The petrol pump can still be operated by hand in case the electricity is cut off; its electrification only dates from 1986.

Thimphu is surely the only capital in the world where there are no traffic lights, only three roundabouts, and the police-boxes are decorated with dragons. The policemen direct the traffic with highly elegant gestures and salute people that they know with a broad smile. It is very rare for them to castigate a motorist who disregards the law or a visitor who becomes so fascinated by their dance-like movements that he forgets what the gestures are telling him to do.

Thimphu has a population of about 15,000, composed mainly of civil servants and shopkeepers. Some families are still engaged in purely agricultural activities but they are becoming rarer. Although it is ancient to the Bhutanese, by international standards Thimphu's emergence as a city is fairly recent. It was established as the permanent capital in 1952–3, but at that time it was hardly more than a dzong surrounded by some huts. The houses of the peasants were scattered throughout the valley in hamlets whose names still exist as districts in modern Thimphu: Kawajangsa, Chamzato, Motithang, Changangkha, Changlimithang, Langchupakha. Dechenchoeling Palace, seven kilometres (nearly four and a half miles) north of the city, was built in 1952–3.

It was only in the late 1960s and early 1970s that Thimphu began to take on the form that we see today. The 1980s brought a real-estate boom fuelled by private initiative. Unlike many modern cities, Thimphu has kept a strong national character in its architecture, and this is due to guidelines from the government.

Street names are a recent innovation, so it is useless to ask a passerby how to find such and such a street. It is better to buy a map of Thimphu or ask for the name of the place you want to reach.

The Centre of Thimphu

There is only one main street in Thimphu, **Norzim Lam**, which is lined with shops of all descriptions. It is split into two levels for about 300 metres (984 feet). Each level is one-way for motorists, without any signs to indicate that this is the case.

From the petrol pump to the second roundabout, the upper part of the street is completely given over to small shops. There you will find the best dry cleaner in the city, Kunzang Dry Cleaners, as well as grocery shops No. 7 and No. 8. No. 7 carries many imported goods from India and sometimes has Bumthang cheese and honey, while No. 8 sells typically Bhutanese products and a few vegetables.

To the left of the second roundabout, the Swiss Bakery opens on to a small raised space. Owned by a Swiss who has become Bhutanese, the Swiss Bakery is one of the bright spots of sociability in Thimphu. It is open every day except Thursday from 8 am to 6.30 pm and serves as a tea-room where you can get a quick snack like a sandwich or an omelette at any time of the day. The French 'baguettes' and wholewheat bread, which are made on the premises, are very good.

The medium-range Taktsang Hotel and the Shangrila Travel Agency are situated between the Swiss Bakery and the roundabout. On Chorten Lam, the street opposite the Swiss Bakery, there is the Hotel-Restaurant 89 which specializes in Italian and Bhutanese food. It is very clean and its prices are reasonable. The drawback is that the service is extremely slow. It is advisable to order in advance.

The lower part of the street is parallel to the upper and this is where three fully adequate hotels have their quarters: the Druk Hotel, the Jhomolhari and the Druk Sherig. The Jhomolhari and the Druk have good restaurants which serve very good Indian dishes such as tandooris, as well as Chinese and Western specialities. They are gathering places for high officials and the development experts who pass as Thimphu's foreign community. The Druk Sherig, which only serves lunch and dinner to order, is the cleanest of the three hotels and has by far the best service. The staff are friendly, the décor is charming and the Bhutanese specialities are very well cooked.

The offices of the airline company, Druk Air, are on a part of the street that is being transformed into a square where a clock decorated with dragons has been put up. The travel agency, Tashi Tours, is situated next to Druk Air.

A big shop named Tashi is underneath the Druk Hotel. There you can find a stationery shop, a grocery that carries bottled mineral water, a drugstore, a shoe shop and a shop selling imported, so-called luxury goods.

Along this same lower street going up towards the second roundabout, the shop on the right, called Karma Garchen Tsongkhang, sells a few groceries but mainly small religious objects and *katas*, white ceremonial scarves. Yongdu sells imported goods, as does Onsang at the corner of Gatoen Lam, a small street that goes up at a gentle slope on the right.

In **Gatoen Lam**, at the other end of the building where Onsang is situated, is a tiny restaurant called Benez. Its prices are low, it serves Chinese and Indian food at all hours, and it is the headquarters for affluent Bhutanese youth and foreign volunteers of every complexion. The owner is a former Dasho, who has retired and now runs his restaurant assisted by his wife's firm hand and cheerful smile. Opposite Benez, in a new grey building, The Larder sells frozen sausages and bacon and ice cream. On the top floor is hidden The Rendez-Vous, a small restaurant with a short menu but excellent food — the chef was trained in the Hong Kong Holiday Inn and in Singapore. The set lunch is gigantic and enough for two. To date it is the 'in' place of Thimphu. The little street ends at a football field and a flight of steps leading to a squash court, tennis court and beyond them the river and the weekly marketplace.

After the second roundabout and back on Norzim Lam, the street rises northward as a single road with two-way traffic. On the left-hand side the shops worth noting are the handicrafts shop Pelijorkhang, a drugstore called the Druk Medical Store, the Sangye Department Store which sells calendars and modern religious objects, the fabric shop Gyeltsen Tsongkhang, the Chundu Travel Agency and New Ideas, one of the biggest video-rental stores in town. There is also the National Library shop, the Municipal Library and an imported wine and liquor store that is reserved for residents only. As on the lower part of the street, there are a multitude of little shops which all sell the same things.

Personal Names

Bhutanese personal names are singularly complicated, not only by the way they are written but by a number of other factors as well.

In Bhutan there are only about 50 personal names in existence. The same names appear over and over again, but this does not mean that the people bearing them are in any way related to each other. There are no family names except for the Royal Family of Dorje and the Royal Dynasty of the Wangchucks. There are a great many other Dorjes and Wangchucks, but they are unrelated to the Royal Family or the Royal Dynasty.

Among the commonest names are: Chime, Chencho, Choeden, Choekyi, Dago, Dawa, Dechen, Dekyi, Dorje, Drolma, Gyamtsho, Gyeltsen, Jamyang, Jigme, Jinba, Karma, Kezang, Khandro, Kunley, Kunzang, Lhendrup, Nima, Pema, Penjor, Phub or Phurpa, Phuntsho, Rinzing, Sangye, Singye, Sonam, Tashi, Tenzing, Thinley, Tobgye, Tshering, Tshokyi, Wangchuck, Wangdi, Wangmo, Yangkyi, Yeshe, Yoedoen, Yonten and Zangmo.

To make things more difficult, a great majority of the names can be given without distinction to boys and girls. However, there are a few names that are typically feminine: Choeden, Choekyi, Dekyi, Drolma (Dem in spoken Dzongkha), Tshokyi, Wangmo (Om in spoken Dzongkha), Yangkyi, Yoedoen and Zangmo (Zam in spoken Dzongkha).

People are always called by two names, which can be given at will as first or second names (for example: Karma Dorje or Dorje Wangdi). It happens while travelling abroad that somebody says: 'I know a Bhutanese whose name is Dorje (or Wangdi or Yeshe)' but that is like saying 'I know somebody named Smith' in England. Some Bhutanese differentiate themselves from others with the same name by adding the name of their village or office as a prefix to their name.

To complicate things even further, a woman does not take her husband's name but keeps her own, and the children have names that are totally different from their parents and different from each other. This means that a man called Tenzing Dorje and his wife Phuntsho Choeden may have a son named Nyima Wangdi and a daughter Kezang Wangmo.

Nicknames are common and it is not unusual to meet someone whose nickname has, by continued use, come to replace his original name, even if it is something like 'idiot' or 'animal'.

Once again, when it comes to personal names it is all a question of everyday use, memorization and practice!

So where do the names come from? Names are not chosen by the family but given by a monk a few weeks after birth. The name almost always has some meaning or a religious connotation: Dechen means 'Supreme Happiness' and refers to the name for Heaven; Tashi means 'Good Auspices or Good Luck'; Sonam means 'Religious Merit'; Chime is 'Immortality'; and Tenzing is 'Holder of the Faith'.

Names in Southern Bhutan work by a completely different system, coming out of a society that is strongly influenced by Hinduism. Here family names, or rather names of castes or tribes, do exist and are transmitted to the male children, while women take their husband's name.

First names, or two first names in the case of men, are likely be the names of Hindu deities: Devi, Lakshmi, Shiva, Vishnu. Last names designate the caste (or sub-caste) or the tribe to which a person belongs. For instance: Basnet, Chetri, Katwal are names for the Kshatriya caste; Adhikari, Bandhari, Sharma, Upadhya are Brahman names; Gurung, Limbu, Rai or Sherpa are tribal names. Here again the number of names is limited, so it is important to remember the initials that precede the last name in order to know which Sharma or Gurung is the one in question.

These little shops are worth a visit and the shopkeepers are not upset by visitors who merely come to look around. One of the best shops of this type is the last one just before the Hotel Jhomolhari as you head down towards the petrol pump. This shop has no name or signboard, but the owner's daughter who serves there is charming and friendly. You can find such things as baking soda and coarse tea leaves for making butter tea, noodles, beer, coffee, high-quality tea, flour, sugar, eggs and candy, all of which are neatly arranged on shelves or in big wooden boxes. Traditional scales form the centrepiece in the middle of the little grocery.

The right-hand side of the street has more administrative offices. A white building on the square almost immediately after the roundabout has two handicraft shops on the ground floor, Etometho and Tshering Drolkar, as well as an audio-video repair shop and a travel agency, Yu Druk Travels. Upstairs in this building is the Bhutan Tourism Corporation. The next building houses a cinema which shows mostly Indian films, and a tiny bookshop that also sells Indian and Western newspapers and magazines. A small street on the right of the main street, **Drentoen Lam,** leads to the Post Office where the philatelic office is located and to the UN building which contains the offices of UNDP, WFP, FAO and UNICEF.

Still keeping on the right side of the street, you come next to the police station, to the Bank of Bhutan and finally to the Emporium, the state handicraft store. The rest of the street on this side has not yet been constructed.

Another street, **Doebum Lam,** runs parallel to the main artery; it is basically a residential street, but a sports complex containing a swimming pool and basketball court, the Chamber of Commerce and the offices of the Development and Credit Bank are also situated there. These two streets, Norzim Lam and Doebum Lam, join on the north side near the third and last roundabout, where the only important building is the former Bhutan Hotel, now converted into the Royal Institute of Management for training civil servants. A new, very clean hotel, the Dechen Hotel, opened in September 1989 between Doebum Lam and the main street.

The Memorial Chorten Area
From the second roundabout, Chorten Lam leads, as its name indicates, to the Memorial Chorten about 200 metres (656 feet) up the street after

*(following pages) Thimphu valley, seat of the capital of Bhutan during the
monsoon period. In the foreground, the imposing Tashichleodzong
which houses the government*

151

passing Hotel 89 and the Indian military hospital on the left. The
Memorial Chorten is an impressive monument with its golden spires
shining in the sun, its bells tinkling in the wind and an endless
procession of elderly people circling around it.

The Memorial Chorten was built in 1974 in memory of the Third
King, H M Jigme Dorji Wangchuck, who died in 1972. There are no
mortal remains of the King inside the chorten and only a photograph
draped in ceremonial scarves on the ground floor serves as a discreet
reminder that the chorten was built to fulfil one of his wishes. The late
King had, in fact, decided to put into tangible form the three traditional
pillars of Buddhism, the Word, Body and Mind of Buddha. He had the
Commentaries of Buddha, the *Tanjur*, transcribed in letters of gold to
represent the Word of Buddha and had 1,000 statues made to represent
the Body of Buddha, but he died before he could complete the Mind of
Buddha, in the form of a chorten. His mother, the Royal Grandmother,
Ashi Phuntsho Choegron, put up the monument on his behalf and in his
memory.

The chorten is approached through a small garden with a gate
decorated both outside and inside with three slate carvings. On the
exterior are representations of Buddhism's three protective bodhisattvas:
Avalokiteshvara, the symbol of compassion; Manjushri, the symbol of
knowledge; and Vajrapani, the symbol of power. On the interior slates
are engraved the image of Shabdrung Ngawang Namgyel, the historical
Buddha and Guru Rinpoche. Over to the left, enormous prayer wheels
are kept turning by the faithful.

The chorten was conceived by Dungse Rinpoche, the son of the great
master, Dujom Rinpoche (1904–87), according to the Nyingmapa
tradition, and its special distinction is the fact that it is a chorten-chapel.
On the east side of the chorten, and visible from the outside, is a large
image of the historical Buddha.

The ceilings of the small porches that grace all four sides of the
chorten are painted on the south with the mandala of the Buddha
Ratnasambhava, on the west with that of Hayagriva, on the north with
the mandala of Phurpa and on the east with that of Vajrasattva. The
chorten is entered by a door on the north side. The abundance and size of
the statues may surprise you. Peaceable gods assume these forms
expressly to overcome the evil spirits that attack the Buddhist doctrine.

The ground floor is consecrated to the cycle of teachings of the deity
Phurpa, the next floor to the Kagye cycle, the teachings for subduing

eight kinds of harmful spirits, and the top floor to the cycle of teachings of the Lama Gondu. Together these form the three basic teachings of the Nyingmapa school. All three are revealed texts that were hidden by Guru Rinpoche in order that they be rediscovered at propitious moments by lamas called *tertons*, the 'discoverers of religious treasures'. This particular cycle of the Phurpa was rediscovered by a previous incarnation of Dujom Rinpoche, Trakthung Dujom Lingpa, in the 19th century. The text of the Kagye was discovered by Nyangrel Nyima Oezer in the 12th century and that of the Lama Gondu by Sangye Lingpa in the 14th century. An exterior gallery above the top floor makes it possible to circle the chorten at the level of its spires from where there is a splendid view over the city.

The Memorial Chorten is an excellent introduction to Tantric Buddhism in all its complexity but you should try to visit the site in the company of someone who understands its significance. This advice holds for all Tantric Buddhist temples, of course, but most especially for the Memorial Chorten where the teachings are esoteric and can be easily misinterpreted.

Continuing on from the chorten, the road called Gonphel Lam skirts an archery field used by the police on the left and arrives at the general hospital and a residential district. Shortly before the hospital, Menkhang Lam leads steeply up on the right to the Department of Education complex and a little further on, before coming back down to the hospital. There is an outstanding view of the chorten here, unspoiled by any electric wires!

Changlimithang Area and the Weekly Market

On the east side of the chorten, Dzogchen Lam is the wide street which goes down towards the petrol pump. It leads back to the first roundabout and Lungten Zampa Bridge, which is at the entrance of the city. On the far side of this bridge is located the bus station, on the city side. The avenue Choegyel Lam forms a delightful promenade right along the river.

On the left is a sports ground named Changlimithang. A decisive battle in Bhutanese history was fought here in 1885, and it gave virtual control of the whole country to the future First King, Ugyen Wangchuck. Football matches and archery competitions take place on the sports ground and archers practise here on practically every holiday. North of the sports ground, a billiard parlour and a banquet hall surrounded by forsythia make an attractive boundary to the tennis court.

The low building is the administrative and judiciary seat for the district of Thimphu. Just in front of it, a big square chorten indicates the spot where, formerly, people had to dismount from their steeds before approaching the dzong. Some 200 metres (656 feet) further on to the north is the square where the weekly market is held on Saturday and Sunday mornings. These are the only days when Thimphu's residents can buy fresh fruit and vegetables. The market is therefore the most important event of the week and should not be missed.

For years the market took place directly on the ground, in the open air, and merchants sometimes had to spend the night in the pouring rain. In 1986, platforms were built and, in 1989, covered market halls roofed with shingle were erected over the platforms and a building for meat was constructed on the north side of the market.

The weekly market certainly offers the best opportunity to see agricultural products and look at people. In winter, now that communications are easier, Bhutanese from remote provinces come to sell products such as yak butter, strings of cheese cubes, fermented cheese, bowls made of turned wood and, of course, fabrics. The products that are sold change with the seasons and migrations of people, the only imperative being that hot peppers must be available all year round!

There is no bargaining and the same price is charged for everybody. Religious men say prayers in front of their portable chapels, buyers examine betel leaves or blow into trumpets, the odour of dried fish mixes with that of the little cheeses, peasants who barely know how to count sell their rice or the products they have picked in the forest with full confidence in their clients, while a passer-by accidentally knocks people with the haunch of beef on his shoulder.

The Dzong Area

Continuing north along the river after the marketplace, you arrive via the old road at Tashichoedzong, Thimphu's dzong and the seat of government. However, the more common route nowadays is by way of Desi Lam which starts from the third roundabout at the end of Norzim Lam, the main street.

Just after the third roundabout are the last of the shops and a little bridge, beyond which it is forbidden to sound a car horn. Since the dzong is below the level of the road, nothing can be seen of it but its red roofs. Desi Lam, on the right, leads straight to it, passing the handsome white, shingle-roofed edifice of the High Court of Justice on the left and skirting the golf course where a few animals may still sometimes be seen grazing. Lamp-posts in Bhutanese style line the majestic avenue. The small buildings in front of the dzong are government offices which have been built to relieve the pressure of space within the dzong resulting from the development and expansion of the administration.

Tashichoedzong

Thimphu's dzong, named Tashichoedzong, delights the eye with its balanced proportions and air of majesty. Its history is very old, dating back to the 13th century, but the original dzong was not built on this flat land, which offers no strategic advantages.

Gyelwa Lhanangpa, the religious man who founded the Lhapa school, a branch of the Drigung Kagyupa school, built a dzong in the Thimphu valley in 1216 which was named Do Ngon Dzong, 'fortress of the blue stone'. The location of this fortress was excellent. It was situated on a spur to the northeast of the present dzong where today one can see a white building that houses the monastic school of Dechen Phodrang. A few years later, Gyelwa Lhanangpa took offence at the religious influence of Phajo Drugom Shigpo of the Drukpa Kagyupa school, and in the struggle that ensued the fortress was badly damaged.

It is not clear what role it played or to which religious group it belonged during the following centuries, but the dzong became the property of Shabdrung Ngawang Namgyel towards the end of the 1630s after he triumphed over the Five Groups of Lamas, which were headed by the Lhapas. In 1641, the construction of the new dzong was finished at the same spot and the Shabdrung named it Tashichoedzong, 'the fortress of the auspicious religion'. The fortress became the summer residence of the Shabdrung and the state clergy, while Punakha Dzong became their winter home.

The dzong suffered serious damage from fire in 1772. Zhidar, the Desi at that period, and Yonten Thaye, the Je Khenpo, then decided to rebuild the dzong at the bottom of the valley, in the place where it now stands. After this reconstruction, the dzong caught fire once again in 1869 and was restored in 1870 when Jigme Namgyel, the father of the future First King, was the Desi of Bhutan. Further repairs had to be undertaken after the earthquake of 1897.

After the Third King, H M Jigme Dorji Wangchuck, had made Thimphu his permanent capital, he started to enlarge Tashichoedzong in

1962 so that it could serve as the seat of government. The new dzong, which was constructed by traditional methods, was consecrated between 24 and 26 June 1969.

Inside the Dzong The dzong is entered by the first door on the east side. The high-relief sculptures in the **entranceway** represent the Guardians of the Four Directions. They are bracketed on the left by the bodhisattva Vajrapani, who is coloured black and shown brandishing a diamond-thunderbolt, and on the right by the great Drukpa tutelary deity Hayagriva, who is coloured red with a horse's head in his headdress. To the right of Hayagriva is the most popular saint of Bhutan, the 'divine madman' Drukpa Kunley (1455–1570) holding a bow and arrow and accompanied by his dog. At the end, on his right, is the easily recognized fable of the Four Friends (see page 139).

A great **staircase** leads into the interior of the dzong. You will be immediately struck by the national crest on the wall facing the steps as well as by the splendid carved pillars that support the ceiling. The

courtyard where you will emerge leaves an indelible impression. The majesty of the architecture, the beautiful proportions and the lavish decoration are enough to take your breath away. This is the **courtyard of the central administration** and all around it are the ministries and the Royal Chamber.

On the other side of the central tower, in which temples are located, is the **courtyard of the state clergy**. In the middle of this courtyard, the **Lhakhang Sarp** or 'new temple' was built in 1907. Its façade is decorated with mythical animals. An image of Guru Rinpoche 'Victorious in the Three Worlds' is the main statue on the upper floor. The coffered ceiling is covered with superb mandalas.

A large building with a porch occupies the north side of the courtyard. Large paintings of cosmic mandalas and a magnificent Wheel of Life decorate the porch on the ground floor. The mandalas represent the universe in the same way as those at Paro, but the artistic rendering is somewhat different. Inside, the ground floor houses a large assembly hall for the monks where the principal statue represents the historical Buddha. This statue is so tall that the Buddha's head reaches the level of the National Assembly chamber on the floor above.

The **Chamber of the National Assembly** is superbly decorated. Paintings of the highest quality illustrate different episodes from the life of Buddha, while on the ceiling a great mandala depicts the Buddha and and the Sixteen Arhats. The King's throne, intricately carved, stands in the middle of the Chamber. The National Assembly's sessions take place twice a year, but at other times the Chamber serves as a workshop for the tailors of the government and the clergy. It is then possible to admire their skilled work in appliqué and embroidery.

The Valley North of the Dzong

The door on the north side of the dzong gives access to a traditional cantilevered bridge with a shingled roof. Opposite the bridge, a large conference hall is under construction.

Behind the dzong are the lodgings of the Royal Bodyguard, then the rice fields begin. Picturesque hamlets dot the valley as far as the Indian Embassy complex. Four kilometres (two and a half miles) further north is **Dechenchoeling Palace** and, on the other side of the river, the village of Taba where the Forestry Institute is located. The government's gold- and silversmiths are installed at Dechenchoeling, but you need permission to visit their workshop.

Pangri Zampa Temple is situated just beyond Dechenchoeling. Two imposing structures are set in the middle of a meadow, not far from the river; this was the residence of Shabdrung Ngawang Namgyel when he arrived in Bhutan in 1616. The monastery was built during the first quarter of the 16th century — the exact date is not known — by Ngawang Choegyel, the great-great-grandfather of the Shabdrung and 14th hierarch of the Drukpas. A prayer wall covered with carved and painted stones, an unusually long one for Bhutan, and huge cypress trees combine to give this place an almost magical charm.

Beyond Dechenchoeling, the motor road ascends the valley for about 20 kilometres (12 miles) and comes to a dead end at the foot of a mountain. **Cheri Monastery** was built on this mountain in 1619. The covered bridge leading to the monastery is new, but it is built in traditional style with cantilevers and shingles. **Tango Monastery** is also close by, on the right, at the same level as Cheri but out of sight of the road. Tango dates from the 13th century but it was rebuilt in its present form in 1688. A path that starts on Cheri Mountain leads across gorges and mountain passes to the northern region of Lingshi.

A Stroll through Thimphu

Let us return now to the place where the road to the dzong begins. At the small bridge on Desi Lam do not take the avenue leading to the dzong but follow the road called Choephel Lam on the left. Just after the bridge, before proceeding along Choephel Lam, another road, Drophen Lam, leads to the satellite telecommunications centre, the Department of Agriculture, the Geological Survey and Land Survey Department and finally to the **Traditional Medicine Hospital** where visitors can watch the preparation of traditional medicines. This road is a dead end.

Back on Choephel Lam, you leave the High Court on the right and come to a small, red brick building which is the Golf Club. Just across the road there is a striking, tall white building in traditional style, roofed in shingle. This is the **National Library** where thousands of manuscripts and ancient xylographs are stored, as well as many wooden printing blocks. Hundreds of Western books and magazines can be consulted on subjects relating to Buddhism, the Himalayas and Bhutan.

From there, the rough road leads up to the **Painting School** situated just above the National Library. At this school, children learn the traditional techniques of drawing and painting. It is well worth a

visit, not only to see the skill of the children but also to observe the traditional teaching methods which are quite different from any practised in the West.

One kilometre (just over half a mile) further along Choephel Lam, after leaving the golf course and the dzong behind on the right, you will reach **Dechen Phodrang,** where Thimphu Dzong was situated up until 1772 and which subsequently became the residence of the Chief of Thimphu Dzong. The building today is occupied by the state monastic school and was reconstructed after a fire in 1895.

Back on the main road it is possible to take a long walk, starting at Ganden Lam on the right. The road climbs gently along the slope of the mountain to **Drubthob Monastery**, a small red building dating from the early 1980s. This monastery, situated just above the dzong and surrounded by prayer flags, protects the dzong from fire. Its name comes from the incarnation of the saint Drubthob Thangton Gyelpo who lived there and who had the idea of building it. It is inhabited at present by some nuns.

Ganden Lam carries on, and from the highest point the view over the dzong and the Thimphu valley is magnificent. One kilometre (half a mile) further on, you will arrive at a decorated gate which marks the entrance to the gardens of the Motithang Hotel.

Motithang Area

Known locally as Motithang, the 'meadow of pearls', this is the smart residential district of Thimphu. Its growth dates from the middle of the 1980s, although its beginnings can be linked to the construction of the Motithang Hotel in 1974, on the occasion of the coronation of H M Jigme Singye Wangchuck. At that time, the hotel was situated in a forest far from the main road. Today, the fields and fallow land that once lay between the hotel and the city have been replaced by nice houses surrounded by gardens. A few offices, including the Embassy of Bangladesh, have also been set up in this quarter. Nevertheless, the hotel is still close to the forest, and people say that it is unwise to wander in the hotel gardens on winter evenings for fear that wild animals may be prowling about! A few minutes' walk above the hotel there is a small zoo containing takins, curious animals that look like a cross between a goat and a moose.

The **Motithang Hotel** itself is a splendid building reserved for tourists and certain distinguished guests, others of whom may be housed at Kungachoeling, the State Guest House, which is nearby. The ethnic shop inside the hotel is open in the evening and has an exceptionally fine selection of handicrafts, especially textiles.

A good way to return to the city is by following Thori Lam, Thongsel Lam, then Thori Lam once again, coming out at the top of the main street, at the level of the third roundabout.

Changangkha Area

This district gets its name from **Changangkha Lhakhang,** which lies on top of the knoll that stands out above Thimphu and from where the view of the valley is superb. This place has a special magical atmosphere with its prayer flags floating in the wind and its feeling of riding above the hurly-burly of the city.

Changangkha Lhakhang is one of the oldest temples in the Thimphu valley, having been built in the 15th century by a descendant of Phajo Drugom Shigpo, the founder of the Drukpa school in Bhutan. The main statue here is an image of Avalokiteshvara. One of the most remarkable paintings on the wall opposite the entrance is of Tsangpa Gyare Yeshe Dorje (1161–1211), the founder of the Drukpa school in Tibet.

Around the knoll of Changangkha, the many Bhutanese houses with their little gardens give the neighbourhood a rural charm. A very good walk with a magnificent view runs along the foot of the knoll and avoids the main thoroughfares. It goes from Changangkha to Memorial Chorten along Rabten Lam.

Simtokha Dzong

Simtokha Dzong (Sinmo Dokha) lies six kilometres (nearly four miles) south of Thimphu where the roads from Thimphu, Paro/Phuntsholing and Punakha/Wangdi cross. Its strategic position is evident since it controls all the approaches from and to Thimphu. This dzong, whose complete name is San Ngag Sabdon Phodrang, 'the palace of profound Tantric teachings', was the first dzong to be built by Shabdrung Ngawang Namgyel. Its construction started in 1629 and it was consecrated in 1631. The dzong was attacked by the army of the Five Groups of Lamas in 1634, but the Shabdrung's army was victorious. In 1671, the dzong was restored by the Third Desi, Minjur Tenpa. In 1961, the Third King, Jigme Dorji Wangchuck, decided to turn the dzong into a centre for traditional studies for lay students who would be trained as teachers of Dzongkha. Today the school has 200 students, and it became *(following pages) The 'Judge of the Dead' with his mirror in which he sees all actions—in front, one of his helpers weighs good and bad deeds on a scale*

163

co-educational in 1989.

The main temple is in the **central tower**. The Guardians of the Four Directions are represented under the porch of the entranceway, along with a magnificent Wheel of Life. A widely seen design is painted on the right-hand wall: a flaming sword placed over a book and a lotus. A bird with two heads stands on each side of the sword. The lotus represents Guru Rinpoche in his form as Padmasambhava; the book, which represents knowledge, and the flaming sword, which cuts through ignorance, are the attributes of the great Tibetan king, Trisong Detsen. The two-headed yellow waterfowl symbolizes the Indian masters, Santarakshita and Kamalasila, and the two-headed green parrot represents two great translators of religious texts from Sanskrit into Tibetan. These paintings were partially restored in 1983 in memory of a Japanese woman, Mrs Sugiura, who died in Bhutan. This is explained in a Japanese and Dzongkha inscription on the left side of the wall.

The **statues in the sanctuary** inside are certainly among the most impressive and beautiful in Bhutan. They are very large and they show the extraordinary degree of skill that has been achieved in metalworking. They represent the historical Buddha and his two main disciples, Maudgalayayana and Sariputra. Along the walls stand statues of the eight principal bodhisattvas: Maitreya, Manjushri, Vajrapani, Avalokiteshvara, Samantabhadra, Kshitigarbha, Akashagarbha and Sarvanivarana Vishkambhini.

The **paintings in the sanctuary** represent the Sixteen Arhats (actually 18, as two were added to the original list, but the identifying name remains unchanged). They are of the highest quality due as much to their composition as to the rich colours and the fine lines of the drawings. Equal in excellence are the paintings in the chapel of Avalokiteshvara on the left side of the big hall. There, too, the paintings are among the finest to be seen anywhere in Bhutan. They show the Drukpa Kagyupa lamas and the first three Buddhist Kings of Tibet surrounded by the first translators of holy texts. In this chapel the statues of Avalokiteshvara and Tara, his female counterpart, are also of exceptional quality.

On the right side of the big hall, a door flanked by two figures in armour signals the entrance to the *Gonkhang*, the temple of fearsome deities.

forest takes about five hours and passes through several different levels of vegetation. It has no view, and since the route is not frequently used nowadays, it may be necessary to beat a path through the tunnels of greenery. The first village is **Tonshinkha** where the Indian saint, Ngagi Rinchen, is said to have drawn a thousand pictures of Buddha on a rock with one magic gesture. From there the path goes down by much gentler slopes and crosses rice fields for a couple of hours to the village of **Sirigang**, situated on the motor road north of Punakha Dzong at an altitude of 1,350 metres (4,430 feet).

The South: Chhuzom to Phuntsholing

The trip of 141 kilometres (87 miles) from Chhuzom to Phuntsholing takes four and a half hours by car. The road from Thimphu to Phuntsholing via Chhuzom was only finished in 1962. Before that it took at least five days to reach the plain and to struggle across a region of leech-infested jungle.

After leaving the Paro road at Chhuzom, the Phuntsholing road enters a gorge and, a true miracle, it remains straight and flat for four kilometres (two and a half miles)! The road follows Thimphu's river, the Wang Chhu, which takes its name from Wang, the region of Thimphu, and makes its way southward through the mountains. You need a sharp eye in order to spot **Dobji Dzong** perched upon its rock; it used to guard the narrow gorge but today it serves as a prison.

After the defile comes the assault of the **Chapcha Pass**, situated at 2,900 metres (9,500 feet). From here, the entire Wang Chhu gorge can be seen with the naked eye, all the way to the last range before the Plain of Bengal, a mere 50 kilometres (just over 30 miles) away as the crow flies.

Chapcha, situated on the southern face of the mountains, is made up of numerous houses scattered over the slope, and a little dzong in the process of restoration, which can be reached by a 15-minute walk from the road. The people of Chapcha are considered well-off by other Bhutanese because their soil is suitable for growing potatoes and, above all, they own trucks for transporting merchandise between India and Bhutan.

After descending from the Chapcha Pass, the road runs along the side of the mountain and arrives at **Bunakha**, lying at 2,200 metres (7,220 feet) where a little restaurant is kept going by the BTC. The village of Bunakha, with its shingle roofs, lies below the level of the restaurant.

Some 15 minutes later, the road passes through **Chimakhoti**, a straggling new village that only came into existence with the building of the road and t' ɔ construction of the Chhukha hydroelectric plant. The latter is at the bottom of the gorge at the outlet of a natural lock through which the Wang Chhu passes. Built with Indian aid, this plant is one of the most important in the Himalayas (336 megawatts) and a large part of the electricity is exported to India. A bridge crosses the river at the outlet of the lock and this unofficially marks the half-way point between Thimphu and Phuntsholing. A small restaurant next to the bridge does good business. **Chhukha Dzong**, which formerly stood on the valley floor and constituted a stopping place on the trail from the south, no longer exists, but Chhukha is now the name of a newly created district which extends as far as Phuntsholing.

The road now runs along the mountainside which forms the right bank of the Wang Chhu and enters a zone of subtropical forest. There is no sign of habitation on this portion of the route until it reaches Gedu, 30 kilometres (18.6 miles) further on. There is, however, a small canteen at a spot named **Taktichu** which serves a few south Indian specialities. A few kilometres beyond Taktichu on the other side of the valley, a splendid waterfall plunges 200 metres (650 feet) into the the river below. The area beyond Taktichu is often foggy, which makes it look like a landscape in a Chinese painting, with great banks of mist floating in the valley. From here on it is also the domain of leeches and in the rainy season the paths alongside the road abound with them.

The way through **Gedu** settlement is strewn with pot-holes, tree trunks, and trucks. Houses made of boards line both sides of the road. Gedu is a recent creation which owes its existence to the installation of a big plywood factory. A small café will give you a chance to recover from Gedu's humidity and get something to eat.

Half an hour after leaving Gedu, you arrive at what I call the 'balcony of the Himalayas', the last mountain chain before the Plain of Bengal. A pass, at an altitude of 2,200 metres (7,220 feet), is marked by many prayer flags. From here you will have a magnificent view in fine weather. The wooded spurs of the Himalayas seem to mount an onslaught as they rise towards the pass and beyond, the vast plain spreading out endlessly towards the horizon. On the right, the valley of the Torsa River bores through the mountains. It takes roughly an hour to cover the 30 kilometres (18.5 miles) of vertiginous descent through tropical jungle and the 'Sorchen Bends'. At the bottom, Phuntsholing is located on the left bank of the Torsa River at the exact point where the plain meets the mountains. At Phuntsholing, as at Samdrup Jongkhar in Bhutan's far southeast, it is strikingly obvious how the Himalayas form a mighty barrier rising like a wall from the plain.

In former times, the trail did not pass through Phuntsholing but through Pasamkha, also called Buxa Duar, which is slightly to the east of Phuntsholing.

Five kilometres (three miles) before reaching Phuntsholing, a police checkpoint is set up at a spot called **Kharbandi**. Here the Bhutanese police check over travellers' papers and permits for visiting the interior of Bhutan. Not far from the police checkpoint there is the big Kharbandi Technical School and, just beyond that, Kharbandi Monastery comes into sight on the left.

On the last hillock, at an altitude of 400 metres (1,300 feet), **Kharbandi Monastery** stands above the Plain of Bengal like a sentinel. The monastery was founded in 1967 by the Royal Grandmother, Ashi Phuntsho Choegron. From the monastery garden there is a beautiful view over the plain and the town of Phuntsholing. The Eight Kinds of Chortens encircle the main temple which contains paintings of the life of Buddha and statues of Shabdrung Ngawang Namgyel, Guru Rinpoche and the historical Buddha. After a rapid descent through jungle where teak trees are easily recognizable by their huge flat leaves, the road enters Phuntsholing.

Phuntsholing

Phuntsholing is a true example of a frontier town where different ethnic groups mingle: Bhutanese in national costume, suffering from the hot climate; Bengalis in light dhotis; Nepalese wearing their characteristic hats; and Indian businessmen carrying their briefcases. Despite an effort to give the town a Bhutanese appearance, the various buildings are more or less devoid of charm. The centre of the city is made up of wholesale and retail shops selling groceries, paper products, tyres, construction materials and plumbing fixtures.

A small public park allows the inhabitants to stroll in the fresh air at day's end, and a temple was built in the middle of it in 1982. Named the **Zangdopelri**, it represents the heaven of Guru Rinpoche. On the ground level there are statues of the Eight Manifestations of Guru Rinpoche arranged as a tree of life, and paintings of the life of Buddha. On the next floor are the Eight Bodhisattvas and statues of Avalokiteshvara with a thousand eyes and a thousand hands, and of Shabdrung Ngawang

Namgyel. On the top floor, the main statue is of Amitabha.

The frontier post stands beside a wonderfully decorated gate which marks the entry into Bhutan. On the far side of it is the little Indian town of Jaigaon, all noisy hustle and bustle.

Hotels and Restaurants

Phuntsholing has one hotel of international standards, the Druk Hotel, which also boasts a good restaurant. A new hotel, the Namgel, slightly cheaper but of a good standard, has just opened on the main square. For visitors on a tight budget, there are a number of local hotels which are more or less clean. The Kunga, situated just opposite the Druk, is a good, simple hotel and its restaurant, which serves Indian food, is very good.

The Road to Punakha and Wangdi Phodrang

The road to Punakha and Wangdi Phodrang, and beyond to Central and Eastern Bhutan, branches off a short distance before Simtokha Dzong. One or two kilometres (about a mile) after the crossroads, there is a very fine view back to the dzong.

The road climbs rapidly after that and the sharp bends may seem even more numerous than usual! The first hamlet is Oesepang, famous for its experimental potato farm. Five kilometres (three miles) further on, the road passes through the village of **Hongtso,** where there is a checkpoint for inspecting the travel permits of foreigners. Hongtso is 19 kilometres (nearly 12 miles) from Thimphu. The ancient village of Hongtso is set back from the road, and not far from it rises the large Hongtso Lhakhang which was founded in 1525 by the 14th Drukpa hierarch of Tibet, Ngawang Choegyel. The houses lining the road belong to Tibetans who have become Bhutanese citizens.

Four kilometres (two and a half miles) beyond Hongtso, and three quarters of an hour after leaving Thimphu, the traveller arrives at the **Dochu La Pass,**[7] which lies at an altitude of 3,050 metres (10,000 feet). The pass is marked by a large Bhutanese chorten and prayer flags. There is a log cabin where you can spend the night if you want to see the sunrise over the Himalayas in the right season. Indeed, Dochu La, or rather the lookout point 500 metres (1,640 feet) lower, offers the most spectacular view over the high peaks of the eastern Himalayas. However, the peaks can be seen only in the clear weather during mid-October to mid-February, and it is extremely unusual to see them at any other season unless, by chance, torrential rain has cleared the atmosphere. If that should happen, get to Dochu La as early as possible, since the mist rises again very quickly.

The pointed peak standing opposite Dochu La is Masangang, at 7,158 metres (23,484 feet), which dominates the region of Laya. Next are Tsendagang, at 6,960 metres (22,835 feet), Terigang, at 7,060 metres (23,163 feet), then Jejegangphugang, at 7,158 metres (23,484 feet), Kangphugang, at 7,170 metres (23,524 feet), Zongaphugang, at 7,060 metres (23,163 feet)—a table-mountain that dominates the isolated region of Lunana, and finally Gangkar Punsum, the highest peak in Bhutan, at 7,497 metres (24,596 feet).

The descent from Dochu La into the Punakha valley and Wangdi Phodrang is long, as the altitude difference between the pass and the valley is 1,700 metres (5,580 feet), the valley lying at an altitude of 1,300 metres (4,265 feet). The road passes first through a temperate type of leafy forest where rhododendron and magnolia bloom in March and April, then a semi-tropical zone where orange trees, banana trees and cactuses are found in abundance.

It takes about two hours to cover the 65 kilometres (40 miles) between Thimphu and Lobeysa, where the road to Punakha and the road to Wangdi Phodrang separate. A few kilometres before Lobeysa, the road leads into a reforested area where the Chir pine grows, a species of pine unique to the semi-tropical regions of the Himalayas.

Near Lobeysa, the temple standing on a round hillock is called **Chime Lhakhang**. It was built in 1499 by the 14th Drukpa hierarch, Ngawang Choegyel, the site having formerly been blessed by the famous 'divine madman', Drukpa Kunley, who built a chorten there. The temple is a pilgrim site for women who are unable to bear children. From Lobeysa the road turns northward and runs along a dry valley for 12 kilometres (seven and a half miles) to Punakha.

Punakha

Punakha, at 1,350 metres (4,430 feet), was nothing more than a dzong as recently as 15 years ago. Then a central school was constructed and the village expanded in the mid-1980s. The small size of the place is surprising considering the primordial role that Punakha has played in the history of Bhutan and the fact that it was the country's winter capital for 300 years.

Punakha Dzong, or Punthang Dechen Phodrang, was built in 1637 by Shabdrung Ngawang Namgyel. However, the site had already been occupied as far back as 1328 by a saint, Ngagi Rinchen, who built a temple there which can still be seen today opposite the great dzong and which is called the **Dzongchung**, meaning 'the little dzong'. In addition, Guru Rinpoche blessed the site in the eighth century and issued a prophecy which said that 'on the front edge of the hill that looks like an elephant's trunk, a man named Namgyel will come and build a fortress.'

When the Shabdrung arrived at the confluence of the Pho and Mo rivers, he set up a camp there and that very night had a dream in which he heard the prophecy of Guru Rinpoche. He decided then and there to build a dzong on that spot and place there the Ranjung Karsapani, the exceedingly sacred relic that he had brought with him from his monastery at Ralung in Tibet. This was a statue of Avalokiteshvara which had appeared miraculously from a vertebra of Tsangpa Gyare, the founder of the Drukpa school in Tibet, at the time of his cremation. This relic was so sacred that the Tibetans attacked Punakha Dzong in order to take it back but were repulsed by the Bhutanese. This episode gave rise to the festival of Punakha, the Punakha *Serda*, which takes place every year at the end of the winter (see page 103).

Exactly covering a spit of land at the confluence of the two rivers, the dzong resembles a gigantic ship. The Shabdrung made Punakha his winter capital since it was situated at a fairly low altitude, and the government moved every year from Thimphu to Punakha until the early 1950s, when Thimphu was established as the permanent capital. The Shabdrung died in 1651 while he was in meditation at Punakha and his body is preserved in one of the dzong's temples, the **Machen Lhakhang**. The monks of the central clergy, true to ancient custom, still migrate from Thimphu and come back to spend the six coldest months in Punakha.

The monks' **great assembly hall** was constructed at the time of Tenzing Drugda, the Second Desi (1656–67), and the central tower was rebuilt at the time of Minjur Tenpa, the Third Desi (1667–80). The dzong was damaged six times by fire, once by floods and once by an earthquake. The coronation of Ugyen Wangchuck, the First King of Bhutan, took place at Punakha Dzong on 17 December 1907.

In the first courtyard, which is the area of administration, there stands a large chorten which was finished in 1981. The dzong is the administrative headquarters for Punakha district, which is the largest in Bhutan. The second courtyard is now practically non-existent since a

temple to the Tantric deity Cakrasamvara was built there in 1983. The dzong includes 21 temples, the biggest being the monks' assembly hall which is in the 'prow' of the dzong in the third courtyard. The main statue is a magnificent Vajrasattva. The porch of the assembly hall is decorated with the same cosmic mandalas that are found at Paro (see page 140), and with a Wheel of Life.

The motor road continues for 30 kilometres (18.5 miles) north of the dzong, starting at the point where there is a small restaurant serving basic food. The countryside in this part of the valley is much more beautiful than the part leading up to the dzong: rice fields, little hamlets, rivers and sand banks are followed by a semi-tropical forest which stretches on to Tashinthang at the end of the road. From here it is a 12-hour walk through more forest to reach Gasa Dzong which controls the route to the regions of Laya and Lunana.

Wangdi Phodrang

Wangdi Phodrang, or simply 'Wangdi', is at an elevation of 1,350 metres (4,430 feet). It is 71 kilometres (44 miles) from Thimphu, a trip that takes about two and a half hours by car. Nine kilometres (six miles) straight south from Lobeysa, the road arrives at the base of **Wangdi Phodrang Dzong**, which is perched on a spur at the confluence of two rivers. The position of the dzong is remarkable as it completely covers the spur and commands an impressive view over both the north–south and east–west roads.

At the bridge, a new motor road leads in a four-hour drive through a gorge to the southern region of **Chirang**, a realm of orange and cardamom groves. The original bridge of Wangdi Phodrang was washed away by floods in 1968. It had been built in 1685 on orders from the Fourth Desi, Tenzing Rabgye, and the massive towers which served as its piers can still be seen.

The main road now climbs the length of the spur and on the left, across the river, comes the first glimpse of the picturesque village of **Rinchengang** whose inhabitants were, and still are, celebrated stonemasons. The form of the village with its houses all attached to one another is extremely unusual in Bhutan. The road passes the entrance to a military training centre and finally comes to the central square of Wangdi Phodrang, which is marked by an antique petrol pump. All around the square, small shops, hardly more than stalls, are lodged in temporary huts while Wangdi's urbanization plan is being put into

effect. One characteristic of Wangdi is its gusty wind which blows from
the south at all seasons, raising whirling clouds of dust.

You reach the tourist inn shortly before the dzong; it contains six
rooms with rudimentary facilities and is a place to quench your thirst.
On the right-hand side of the dzong is the charming house of the District
Administrator, the Dzongdag; from the parapet there is a fine view over
the valley and the village of Rinchengang.

There are two stories which explain the origin of the dzong, one
religious and the other popular. The first one tells us that the protective
deity Mahakala appeared to the Shabdrung and made a prediction to
him, saying: 'At the top of a rocky spur where two rivers meet, at the
place where a flock of ravens (the bird associated with Mahakala) will
fly off in the four directions, there you will build a dzong.' In 1638 the
Shabdrung came to the place that the prophecy described and built a
fortress which he named Wangdi Phodrang, meaning 'the palace where
the four directions are gathered under the power (of the Shabdrung)'.

However, the popular story has it that the Shabdrung arrived at the
river and happened to see a little boy building a sandcastle. He asked for
the boy's name, which was Wangdi, and thereupon decided to name the
dzong Wangdi Phodrang, or 'Wangdi's palace'.

The dzong is roofed with shingles and has an oddly rustic, yet
disquieting, charm about it. The first courtyard, surrounded by
administrative buildings, is not a true square as its side walls make it
slightly oblong. This part was built in 1683 on orders from the Fourth
Desi, Tenzing Rabgye. The second part of the dzong is separated from
the first by a small ravine which is spanned by a bridge. This part dates
from 1638 and contains a narrow interior courtyard that ends in a flight
of steps leading to the central tower. On the far side there is another
courtyard, at the southern end of which is the monks' assembly hall,
graced by statues of the Past, Present and Future Buddhas.

The Central Road

The tarring of the central road was completed in 1985 and it brought
great changes for the residents of Central Bhutan. The two-day trip of
the 1970s from Tongsa to the capital Thimphu now takes only six hours.
However, the road is not well stabilized and heavy rains or earthquakes
frequently cause collapses between May and the end of September. If
this happens, the road may remain closed for several days or even
weeks.

Over the Black Mountains: Wangdi to Tongsa

The distance from Wangdi to Tongsa is 129 kilometres (80 miles) and the trip by car takes about four hours. The road to Central and Eastern Bhutan starts from the east side of the dzong and is flat for the first ten kilometres (six miles) or so, as far as a hamlet called Chuzomsa, or 'confluence'. There is a slate mine not far from here. Just beyond Chuzomsa, a cable lift transports goods and raw materials between the valley and Tashi La, a pass at an altitude of 2,800 metres (9,185 feet) at the top of the ridge, which gives access to the isolated valleys of Kothoka and Gogona.

The road begins its climb over the Black Mountains immediately after the bridge at Tikke. The valley is very narrow, with houses and fields perched on steep slopes. Little by little, habitations become sparser and the road starts to snake through the middle of a dense forest. At a point 40 kilometres (25 miles) from Wangdi, the featureless village of Nobding stands on a plateau surrounded by forest.

Seven kilometres (four miles) beyond Nobding, a road branches off on the right and goes for 13 kilometres (eight miles) through a forest of oak and rhododendron into the broad **Phobjika valley** at 3,000 metres (9,840 feet) where Gantey Monastery is located. Phobjika is one of the few glacial valleys in Bhutan and the valley floor is quite marshy in places. For several years, the cultivation of potatoes has brought a certain degree of prosperity to the peasants. Phobjika is also the chosen home of the rare black-necked crane which migrates from the Central Asiatic Plateau to escape its harsh winters. The other side of the pass that overlooks the valley is a realm of high-altitude dwarf bamboo, the favourite food of yaks.

Gantey Monastery

Gantey Gompa, the Gantey Monastery, is perched atop a small hill that rises from the valley floor. The monastery is surrounded by a large village inhabited mainly by the families of the 140 *gomchens* who take care of the monastery. In winter these families, together with the monastery's ten monks, move away to another monastery, a day's walk to the south. Gantey, which is now controlled by the government, is the only Nyingmapa monastery on the western side of the Black Mountains and is also the biggest Nyingmapa monastery in Bhutan. It is directed by Gantey Tulku, the ninth reincarnation (*tulku*) to bear that name.

Gantey was founded by Pema Trinley, the grandson of Pema Lingpa, the famous Nyingmapa saint of Bhutan. Pema Lingpa visited this area and predicted that a monastery would be established by one of his descendants near the summit (*tey*) of a mountain (*gang*). Thus, in 1613, Pema Trinley established the monastery and became the first Gantey Tulku. The religious tradition of Pema Lingpa is still taught there. The second tulku, Tenzing Legpe Dondrub (1645–1726), enhanced the size of Gantey while keeping up good relations with the Drukpas, and rebuilt the monastery in the form of a dzong.

The entrance to the monastery displays a large painting of Hayagriva. The monks' dwellings are all around the courtyard, while the central tower houses five temples. The porch of the central tower contains paintings of cosmic mandalas, a Wheel of Life, Zangdopelri — the heaven of Guru Rinpoche, as well as a rare (in Bhutan) picture of the mythical land of Shambala shown inside its circle of snow-capped mountains.

The road continues for a few more kilometres beyond the monastery to the village of Phobjika. The valley of Gantey is one of the most beautiful spots in Bhutan. The surprise of finding such a wide, flat valley without any trees after the hard climb through dense forest is augmented by an impression of vast space, an extremely rare experience in Bhutan where most of the valleys are tightly enclosed. The round trip to Gantey Gompa takes about three hours from the junction with the main road.

The Pele La Pass

After the junction, the main road twists up the steep mountainside for 14 kilometres (nine miles) to the Pele La Pass. The forest is made up almost entirely of rhododendron and magnolia, which can be seen in April and May. If the winter has been cold, there is also a good chance you will see herds of yaks that have not yet been taken up to the high pastures — the vision of yaks browsing under rhododendron in full bloom is certainly a sight never to be forgotten. However, it is advisable to be cautious and not get too close to yaks as they are nervous animals and may attack you without provocation.

Just before the pass, if the weather is clear, the high range of the Himalayas can be seen, particularly the peak of Jhomolhari, at 7,219 metres (23,685 feet), to the west.

The Pele La, at 3,300 metres (10,825 feet), is marked by a large prayer flag, and the ground is covered with high-altitude dwarf [8] bamboo. The Pele La is traditionally considered the boundary between Western and Central Bhutan and in former times the jurisdiction of the Tongsa Penlop extended just to the pass. The landscape which spreads out on the far side of the pass is completely different from that on the western side. Herds of animals graze on gentle slopes covered with dwarf bamboo and there is practically no forest.

On the far side, 11 kilometres (seven miles) beyond the pass, a plateau divided into large fields appears on the right at the head of which is the large village of Rukubji. The road continues downwards and comes to the bottom of a valley at the bridge of Nikkarchu, near to which a few houses have recently been built. This is the starting point of a path that goes to the isolated northern region of Lunana; the walk requires four or five days and the path crosses several very high passes, among which is the fearsome Rinchenzoe at 5,400 metres (17,715 feet). The whole region, including the areas between Gantey Gompa and the Pele La, the part between Rukubji and Nikkarchu and other areas to the north, is the domain of yak- and sheep-herders and is called in Bhutan the 'Black Mountain Bjop'.

Chendebji Chorten

After Nikkarchu, the road enters Tongsa district where it follows the river along a narrow, enclosed valley for about ten kilometres (six miles). On the right-hand side it passes the picturesque village of Chendebji which is reached by an ancient bridge roofed with bamboo matting. The great, whitewashed stone chorten then appears at a bend in the road. Chendebji Chorten is Nepalese in style, with eyes painted at the four cardinal points. It was built during the first half of the 18th century by a lama named Shida, in order to nail into the ground a demon who had been terrorizing the inhabitants of this valley and the Ada valley just over the ridge. A long stone *mani* wall stands in front of the chorten bearing an inscription that tells the story of its founding. On the left side, a chorten was constructed in Bhutanese style by H M the Queen Mother in 1982.

There are 42 kilometres (26 miles) between Chendebji and Tongsa. The road emerges from the gorge and follows the Mangde River valley, then it turns and heads straight north to Tongsa. The landscape is dramatic and the road is hewn into the side of the rock with a sheer drop on the right. The route runs parallel to a road that is visible on the other side of the valley leading south to Shemgang Dzong then to Geylegphug on the Indian border.

You will see Tongsa Dzong at the bottom of the valley 20 kilometres (12 miles) before reaching it. There is a splendid lookout point with a view over Tongsa at the place where the old track branches off. This old footpath leads down to the bottom of the gorge, crosses the stream, then climbs very steeply up to the gate of the fortress. The paved road was not able to follow this ancient route so it makes a detour of 14 kilometres (nine miles) into a side valley before arriving at Tongsa from the west. It is worth noting that this region grows a species of cherry that flowers in the autumn, at which time the whole gorge is dotted with pink trees.

The Important Stages of Life

Birth The birth of a child, whether boy or girl, is always welcome. The mother receives no visitors except for family during the first three days after the birth. A *lhasang*, or purification ceremony, is then performed in the house, after which visitors may present themselves. The customary gifts in a village are eggs, rice or maize in diverse forms, while in a town they are children's clothes and nappies (diapers). A little money is always given to the newborn to bring good luck. The mother is given a rich diet and encouraged particularly to drink a hot alcoholic beverage made with *ara*, butter and eggs that is supposed to increase her milk supply. This beverage is also served to visitors and the atmosphere is very jolly.

Naming the Child The child is not named immediately; if possible, it is named by an eminent religious personage or the lama-astrologer whom the parents visit. The child's horoscope, *kyetsi*, is then established. It gives the date of birth by the Bhutanese lunar calendar and the list of rituals to be performed each year, or in the event of problems. The birth also has to be registered with the state.

Marriage No special ceremony takes place at puberty and the next important stage is marriage. The marriage can be a completely informal affair or it can be a complicated ceremony, depending on the status of the families and the way the young people came to know one another. It can be a marriage of love or an arranged marriage; in the latter case, both the young people are consulted by their families about the choice of a partner, who usually belongs to the family of friends so they are already acquainted with each other. This kind of arranged marriage is unlike those in other parts of Asia where the future spouses are total strangers. Moreover, there is always the possibility of refusing. Even in a love marriage, the partners want their parents to approve of their choice. If the families disapprove, the young people either comply with their parents' wishes or they run away together, presenting their parents with a *fait accompli*.

A marriage between two people of affluent families is a social occasion. At an auspicious hour prescribed by the astrologer, the bridegroom and his friends go to fetch the bride at her home and bring her and her friends back to his house. Two members of the family stand in front of the door holding a bowl of milk and a bowl of water, symbolizing prosperity for the new couple's life.

The *marchang* ceremony is performed next and then the couple sits down near the monks who intone the marriage ritual. The religious ceremony does not carry the same weight as the sacrament in some Christian weddings. The couple then exchange cups of alcohol and are declared man and wife. The families, followed by friends, cover them with white scarves and the gifts pile up, especially fabrics that are always presented in quantities of three, five or seven. A copious meal (with plenty to drink) and dancing end the day.

Among members of the population who are less well-off, young people simply start living together, thus declaring themselves married in the eyes of society. Very often the marriage is not even announced verbally; it is just a fact. Nowadays, the legal registration of a marriage is encouraged by the government but it is hardly ever done outside the towns.

Divorce is frequent and if it is the woman who seeks the divorce, her new companion has to pay a fine to the former husband.

Promotions A promotion up the social ladder is blessed in much the same way as a marriage by monks who perform a ritual in the home of the person being promoted. He sits on a raised seat and receives the traditional gifts of cloth or money accompanied by a white scarf from visitors.

Funerals A funeral is by far the most important and costly ceremony because of all the expenses it entails. Death does not mean the end but simply the passing into another life, so everything must be done to make it happen in the most favourable way. As rapidly as possible after death has occurred, monks, lamas or *gomchens* must be called to perform the ritual to help the conscious principle to exit from its carnal envelope and read the *Book of the Dead*. This reading guides the dead person through all the stages that his conscious principle must pass through, and it explains the visions that he will see. This intermediate state between death and the conscious principle's reincarnation in another body is called the *bardo*.

The rituals are complex and can last for 49 days without interruption if a family is very well off. Most often the rituals last for seven days with more on the 14th, 21st and 49th days. Those that take place between the 21st and the 49th days have to be performed in a temple and not in the house. After the 49th day, a ceremony intended to purify the atmosphere and bring prosperity to the living takes place in the house of the deceased.

From the moment of death, the deceased is placed in a curled-up position on a catafalque covered with a multicoloured cloth, which, for most of the time, is placed outside the house. Visitors who come to offer condolences to the family place a gift of money and a white scarf on the catafalque. Meals are served to the deceased throughout the period following death and until all rituals are finished.

The cremation of the body takes place on a day decided by the astrologer but at least three days after the death. If the deceased comes from an affluent background or is a monk or lama, the body is placed in a special clay construction which acts as a funeral pyre. Otherwise it is wrapped in a white shroud and simply placed on the funeral pyre. When the fire is lit, relatives and friends throw white scarves and money into the blaze while praying for a good reincarnation for the deceased. During the next three years, an important ritual should take place on the anniversary of the death, the most extensive being the one performed after the third year, marking the true end of funeral observances.

After the cremation, the ashes are usually scattered in the river or mixed with clay to become votive tablets. Then, depending on the piety and affluence of the family, prayer flags and chortens are raised to bring merit to the deceased. Small children are not cremated but are exposed to vultures or thrown into the river.

Central Bhutan

Tongsa Dzong

The landscape around Tongsa is spectacular, and for miles on end the dzong seems to tease you so that you wonder if you will ever reach it. Backing on to the mountain and built on several levels, the dzong fits narrowly on a spur that sticks out into the gorge of the Mangde River and overlooks the routes south and west. The view from the dzong extends for many kilometres and in former times nothing could escape the vigilance of its watchmen. Furthermore, the dzong is built in such a way that in the old days, no matter what direction a traveller came from, he was obliged to pass by the dzong. This helped to augment its importance as it thus had complete control over all east–west traffic. Above the dzong a watchtower, the Ta Dzong, strengthened its defence.

Tongsa means 'the new village' and the founding of Tongsa first dates from the 16th century, which is indeed relatively recent for Bhutan. It was the Drukpa lama, Ngagi Wangchuck (1517–54), the great-grandfather of Shabdrung Ngawang Namgyel, who founded the first temple at Tongsa in 1543. He was meditating nearby when he saw a light at the furthest point of the spur. He took this to be a sign and decided to build a temple. The original site is situated today at the end of the dzong, at the 'temple of chortens'.

In 1647, the Shabdrung had begun his great work of expansion and unification and, realizing all the advantages that could be gained from Tongsa's position, he constructed the first dzong at the place where his ancestor had erected the temple. The dzong was called Choekhor Rabtentse Dzong. In 1652, Minjur Tenpa, the future Third Desi of Bhutan who at that time was Penlop of Tongsa, had the dzong enlarged. It was changed still further in 1771 when a temple of Maitreya was added. Since the earthquake of 1897 the dzong has been repaired several times, in particular by the First King, Ugyen Wangchuck.

Inside the Dzong

At an altitude of 2,200 metres (7,220 feet) the dzong is a masterpiece of architecture, a maze of courtyards, passageways and corridors containing, in addition, 23 temples. The most important ones are those dedicated to the great Tantric deities Yamantaka, Hevajra and Kalacakra. They include the **Maitreya temple**, constructed in 1771, which contains a big statue of the Buddha of the Future erected by Sir Ugyen Wangchuck at the beginning of this century; and the **temple of Chortens**, built on the place where the original temple stood. This temple contains the funerary chorten of Ngagi Wangchuck and some superb paintings of the Sixteen Arhats and Akshobya.

In the **entrance to the central tower** there is a painting of Zangdopelri, the paradise of Guru Rinpoche. You can also see paintings of Punakha Dzong and of the chorten of Swayambunath in Nepal, which was formerly a Bhutanese possession, and finally a painting of the cosmic mandala according to the *Abidharmakosha*.

The dzong also has a **printing house** where the printing of religious texts is still done by the traditional xylographic method (see page 113). The Drukpa monastic community is about 200 members strong. Most of them move in summer to Kurjey Monastery in the Jakar valley of Bumthang where there is no state monastic community.

If you can visit the dzong, you should go through the door on the right, on the level below that of the small police post. In the old days, this door marked the end of the hard climb up from the river to the entrance of the dzong. To experience what it must have been like, go down the slippery steps along the precipice and then look up at the dzong. Its size and power are completely overwhelming and it is easy to understand the psychological effect it had upon travellers arriving at Tongsa.

Today the dzong is the administrative seat for Tongsa district, but in the 19th century it could have been considered the capital of Bhutan due to the importance and power of its governors, the Tongsa Penlops. They controlled all of Eastern and Central Bhutan, including the fertile strip in the south. In the middle of the 19th century, one governor became more powerful than any of the others. This was Jigme Namgyel, the father of Ugyen Wangchuck who was to be the First King of Bhutan. Jigme Namgyel came from the region of Kurtoe (now Lhuntshi district) but he made his whole career at Tongsa Dzong and played a dominant national role as well. His son, Ugyen Wangchuck, became Penlop of Tongsa in his turn and from that time on, the Crown Princes of Bhutan have received the title of Tongsa Penlop. Jigme Dorji Wangchuck, the Third King of Bhutan, was born in Tongsa in 1928 and the house of his birth can be seen on the left of the road, in the U-turn which leads to the main street.

The watchtower, the Ta Dzong, stands on the side of the mountain east of the dzong. Unlike that of Paro, which is round, the Tongsa watchtower has a fairly narrow tower section and two wings which extend in front of the main part of the building. Its most important temple, established in 1977, is dedicated to King Gesar, the hero of a great epic.

Tongsa Village

Up until 1982, the three or four old houses that made up the village of Tongsa lay in the shadow of the dzong on a narrow piece of land near the stream, to the left of the entrance to the dzong. Then, in that year, the old village was razed to the ground and a new village started to develop along the road above the dzong. The impressive size of the houses, built in Bhutanese style, makes them appear like a rampart overlooking the dzong. Due to the configuration of the landscape, the village of Tongsa is hardly more than one street lined by well-stocked little shops and small friendly restaurants.

Most of Tongsa's shopkeepers are Bhutanese of Tibetan origin, and the restaurants are likely to serve Tibetan specialities such as fried dumplings stuffed with ground meat (*shabale*) and steamed bread with a soup (*trimomo*). One place that can be heartily recommended is Yangkhyil, on the right at the end of the street. The owner is a fine cook and her rooms are clean and cheap. In winter, a wood stove is lit in the common room, which is much needed as Tongsa is always somewhat damp, hemmed in as it is by the mountains.

There is another little tourist hotel above the dzong, near the high school and the hospital. The rooms there are more comfortable but much more expensive and the food, also very expensive, is not as good as the food at Yangkhyil.

Shemgang Region (Khyeng)

Tongsa lies at the junction of the east–west road with the southern road. The road to the south runs for 237 tortuous kilometres (147 miles) to the southern agricultural zone and the commercial border town of Geylegphug. This road crosses part of a large region formerly known as Khyeng, which nowadays is divided into the districts of Shemgang to the west and Mongar to the east.

For the first 15 kilometres (nine miles) or so, the southern route runs parallel to the Thimphu road, then it turns towards the southeast. It follows the side of the mountain and offers some fine, clear views over the Mangde River valley.

Some 20 kilometres (12 miles) south of Tongsa, **Kunga Rabten**, the winter palace of the Second King, Jigme Wangchuck, can be seen below the level of the road. It is a splendid building which belongs today to the National Library. It is worth stopping and going into the inner courtyard to look at the woodwork and decorations.

The road goes through several small villages. The mountain slope on this side is fairly gentle which allows for some farming. Then the valley grows narrower and the road goes down to 1,400 metres (4,560 feet) in the river gorge. This area is wild and almost uninhabited.

Shemgang Dzong finally comes into view at the top of a ridge. It is only 107 kilometres (66 miles) from Tongsa but the poor condition of the road means that four hours of driving are required to reach it. Shemgang is built on an open ridge, which gives it the advantage of an unbroken view over the whole area. The disadvantage is that it gets battered by the wind and in spite of its relatively low altitude of 1,900 metres (6,235 feet) it can be cold there.

A Tibetan Drukpa lama, Drogon Shangkyeme, built the first temple on the site of Shemgang as early as 1163. The temple took his name as Shang Gang, 'Shang's mountain', which local pronunciation turned into Shemgang. His youngest brother was the chaplain of the king of Khaling in Eastern Bhutan. This king behaved very badly towards his subjects, so the lama wrote to his brother advising him to leave the king's service and come to join him at Shemgang. He also wrote to the king saying that he was unwell and wanted his brother to come and visit him. Unfortunately the two letters got mixed up as they were being delivered. The king was furious to read what the lama of Shemgang had written to one of the lama's subjects and sent assassins to kill him. But even after his death, Drogon Shangkyeme's temple continued to prosper. In 1963, when Shemgang district was created, the Third King, Jigme Dorji Wangchuck, ordered that Shemgang Dzong be restored.

The Ancient Region of Khyeng

The village of **Nabji** lies across difficult terrain, two days' walk from Shemgang. Here stands a stone pillar which commemorates a peace treaty between King Sendhaka (Sindhu Raja) and King Na'oche in the eighth century. This makes it one of the most ancient historical monuments of Bhutan.

The ancient region of Khyeng, which stretched east to Mongar and

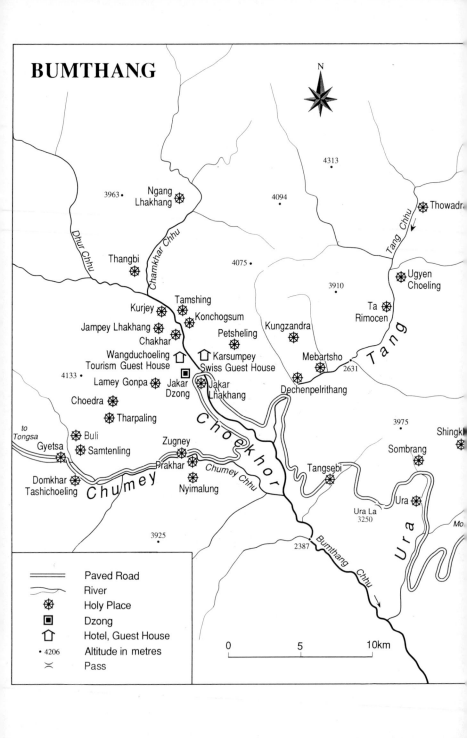

south practically to Geylegphug, was divided into a multitude of little kingdoms until the 17th century. The most important of these were Buli and Nyakhar. Buli, in particular, was visited in 1478 and 1497 by the Nyingmapa saint, Pema Lingpa, who founded a temple there. After the Drukpa conquest in the middle of the 17th century, the kings lost whatever importance they may have had but their descendants still call themselves 'king', as a purely honorific title.

In 1963, the region of Khyeng was divided into the districts of Mongar and Shemgang. There also exist ties with the Bumthang valleys which go beyond simple language affiliation. The old nobility of Bumthang owns land in the Khyeng region and their herds of animals are moved there from Bumthang for the winter. And it is from Khyeng that Bumthang's weavers get their supplies of raw material for making vegetable dyes.

Shemgang is a land of steep, forest-covered mountains except for pockets such as Buli where rice is cultivated. The rivers cut deep gorges and valleys are rare. The people speak Khyengkha, a language which is really a dialect of Bumthangkha, and they are highly esteemed for their knowledge of forest plants.

Descending in steps from 1,900 metres (6,235 feet) to 200 metres (655 feet), most of the district is covered by a tropical forest that conceals rare orchids and carnivorous plants. This is where most of Bhutan's production of bamboo- and rattan-ware takes place. Many plants which still grow wild form an important part of the people's diet: bananas, mangoes, yams, bamboo shoots, young ferns, certain orchids and a very rare plant which tastes like potatoes when it is boiled; and even, in hard times, certain poisonous roots of fern or poisonous beans which, once they have been boiled or left to soak, become edible. Nettles are used to make a very strong type of cloth.[9] Though Shemyang may be lacking in spectacular historical sites, it makes up for that by being a paradise for botanists and ethnobotanists.

The Road from Tongsa to Bumthang

It takes less than two hours to cover the 42 kilometres (26 miles) from Tongsa to the village of Gyetsa in the upper Chumey valley. The road passes through Tongsa village just beneath the Ta Dzong and then rises rapidly through a series of hairpin bends. The view over Tongsa and the dzong is marvellous on this side of the valley as well. After running across cultivated slopes for a few kilometres, the road enters a very ancient forest where the large trees are often bare but where magnificent rhododendron grow.

At a distance of 29 kilometres (18 miles) from Tongsa, the road reaches the Yutong La Pass, at 3,400 metres (11,155 feet), and once again the landscape that spreads out ahead looks very different. The rhododendron is still there, but there is now a dense forest of conifers which stretches as far as the eye can see. After 13 kilometres (eight miles), the road comes out into a wide, open, cultivated valley. This is the Chumey Valley, the first of Bumthang's four valleys.

The Bumthang Valleys

A *bumpa* is an oblong-shaped lustral water vase and Bumthang means 'the plain shaped like a *bumpa*'. The religious connotation of the name aptly applies to the sacred character of the region. It would be difficult to find so many important temples and monasteries in such a small area anywhere else in Bhutan.

Bumthang is the general name given to a complex of four valleys — Chumey, Choekhor, Tang and Ura — with altitudes varying from 2,600 metres (8,530 feet) to 4,000 metres (13,125 feet). Today it is a district with its administrative headquarters at Jakar (also spelled Byakar but always pronounced Jakar). Choekhor and Chumey are agricultural valleys; Tang and Ura are given over more to yak- and sheep-breeding.

Because the valleys are wide and open, and the mountains have relatively gentle slopes, there is a feeling of spaciousness that is unequalled in any other part of Bhutan except the Phobjika valley in the Black Mountains. Bumthang is a joy for hikers as the valleys are fairly flat, the slopes are usually gentle, and there are many little hamlets where you can get some idea of what life in a rural area is like.

Bumthang was converted to Buddhism by Guru Rinpoche in the eighth century and was the home of famous saints of the Nyingmapa school such as Longchen Rabjampa (1308–63), Dorje Lingpa (1346–1405) and above all Pema Lingpa (1450–1521), who was born in Bumthang. His descendants scattered through Central and Eastern Bhutan and contributed to the spread of the Nyingmapa school. Dorje Lingpa and Pema Lingpa were also *tertons*, or 'discoverers of religious treasures' (see page 56).

After remaining more or less independent for centuries, Bumthang was conquered by the Drukpas in the middle of the 17th century.

In former times the Bumthang valleys were fairly poor and isolated, but since the construction of the east–west road the area has undergone significant economic development. In addition, projects financed by Switzerland and an Indian hydroelectric project have helped to bring a certain degree of prosperity. This can be seen in the number of new houses built in the past five years.

The Chumey Valley

The Chumey valley begins at Gyetsa and has an average altitude of 2,700 metres (8,860 feet). It is a wide valley dotted with villages and temples. People here grow wheat, barley, potatoes and above all buckwheat, which used to provide the staple diet of Bumthang in the form of pancakes and noodles.

Just after the village of Gyetsa on a small knoll to the right of the road, there is the ancient little **Buli Lhakhang** founded at the beginning of the 14th century by a descendant of Dorje Lingpa. Much higher up the mountain, the buildings of Tharpaling Monastery can be seen and, higher still, those of Choedrak Monastery.

Tharpaling Monastery

The site of Tharpaling, at 3,600 metres (11,810 feet), was established by Longchen Rabjampa, the great philosopher of the Dzogchen, a sect within the Nyingmapa school. Longchen Rabjampa (1308–63) was obliged to flee from Tibet and lived in exile in Bumthang for ten years. He built several temples there, among them Tharpaling, which was constructed in 1352. The monastery prospered and was always an active centre of Nyingmapa teachings, especially in the 18th century while Jigme Lingpa (1730–98), another great Dzogchen philosopher, was staying at Tharpaling.

The temple on the ground floor, the **Tsongkhang**, is adorned with statues of Longchen Rabjampa, Guru Rinpoche, Trisong Detsen, the eighth century Tibetan king, and Jigme Lingpa. The small temple on the upper floor was restored in the time of the First King, Ugyen Wangchuck. It contains very beautiful paintings of the heaven of Amitabha; also of Longchen Rabjampa, Shabdrung Ngawang Namgyel, and a rarely seen form of Guru Rinpoche as Guru Dewa. The principal statues are those of Samantabhadra, Guru Rinpoche and Longchen Rabjampa.

In 1985, a **monastic school** was founded above the main complex. There are about 15 cells for monks and a central room with paintings of the lineage of Longchen Rabjampa which are well worth seeing.

Above Tharpaling Monastery is **Choedrak**. Guru Rinpoche had meditated at this spot and that is the reason why Lorepa (1187–1250), a Drukpa Kagyupa lama from Tibet, decided to live and build a temple there in 1234. Unfortunately, it is said that after his departure for Tibet, the place was besieged by a demon and nobody dared to go to Choedrak. It was not until the 18th century that Ngawang Trinley, the great monk from Si'ula Monastery in the Punakha region, succeeded in vanquishing the demon and repairing the monastery which had fallen into ruins.

On the way down from Tharpaling and Choedrak, **Samtenling Monastery** is on a forested knoll not far from the path. It, too, was founded by Longchen Rabjampa in the 14th century but it was severely damaged by a fire in the mid-1980s.

The tarmac road follows the middle of the valley and a few kilometres after Gyetsa it comes to the village of Domkhar where, on the right side of the road, slightly above the village, there stands the old palace of **Domkhar Tashichoeling**. Like Kunga Rabten in the Tongsa region, this was a royal palace built in 1937 as the summer residence of the Second

King. Nowadays, Domkhar Tashichoeling belongs to the government, which has plans to turn it into a centre for Buddhist studies.

Four kilometres (two and a half miles) beyond Domkhar, the road comes to the **Chorten Nyingpo Lhakhang**. Here a small hydroelectric power-station which provides for Bumthang's needs was finished in 1989 with aid from India. The temple perched on a hillock overlooking the river was founded in 1587 by Tenpe Nyima, Shabdrung Ngawang Namgyel's father.

Zugney Village

Just after the bridge comes the village of Zugney. This village is worth a stop for there are many weavers here. With scarves tied on their heads in the Bumthang style, they weave woollen *yatras* on pedal looms as well as belts on backstrap looms. *Yatras* are rolls of patterned twill-weave woollen cloth which are Bumthang's speciality and which can be used as bed covers, cushions or even garments. The Chumey valley is famous for the quality of its *yatras*, and especially the house of Gyamtshola in Zugney.

But Zugney has an even more important claim to glory than its *yatras*. The tiny temple on the right side of the road is said to have been founded by the Tibetan king, Songtsen Gampo, in the seventh century! The principal statue in the sanctuary is that of Buddha Vairocana, which is generally a sign of antiquity for a temple. Vairocana can be recognized by the wheel which he holds in his hands. The splendid new paintings were created in 1978 by Lopen Pemala, the Director of the National Library, who is a native of Zugney.

Pra (Prakhar)

Two kilometres (just over one mile) beyond Zugney, the road skirts **Pra,** or **Prakhar**, a picturesque village perched on a small plateau in a bend of the river. Pra was built at the end of the 16th century by a certain Tenpe Nyima who happens this time not to be father of the Shabdrung but the grandson of Pema Lingpa, the Nyingmapa saint. Tenpe Nyima had a vision and knew that he must construct a temple on this spot. As he built it, the temple seemed somehow to be growing in size at night as well, and the villagers observed that white monkeys were working on the temple after dark. The place takes its name from this event: Prakhar means 'white monkey'. Tenpe Nyima's father, Lama Dawa Gyeltsen, is embalmed in a chorten that stands in the main temple. The descendants

of this lineage have given Bhutan many great reincarnations and eminent personages on both regional and national levels.

Hidden in the woods half an hour's walk from Pra is the Nyingmapa monastery of **Nyimalung**. Created in 1900 by Dori Tulku, a Tibetan monk sponsored by the Lord of Pra, this monastery has acquired a high reputation for the quality of its teachings, for the virtuosity of its musicians and for the discipline which prevails there. It has about a hundred monks.

The last village in the Chumey valley is Nangar. From there the road starts to climb towards the **Kiki La Pass** at 2,900 metres (9,515 feet), which separates the Chumey valley from the Choekhor valley where Jakar Dzong serves as the district seat. In the Chumey valley, the road covers 18 kilometres (11 miles) from Gyetsa to Kiki La. In clear weather the view from Kiki La is magnificent. The vast sweep of Choekhor extends from the foot of the pass: Jakar Dzong rises on the left, the great Kurjey Lhakhang bars the bottom of the valley, and in the distance snowy peaks stand out against the sky.

The Choekhor Valley

There are barely nine kilometres (five and a half miles) from Kiki La to Jakar Dzong, or rather the village of Jakar which has grown up on the flat ground at the base of its hill. A roundabout situated on the east–west road in the centre of the village is the meeting point where people can wait for a vehicle or bus going in any direction. The village is named Chamkhar but is more normally referred to as Jakar.

Jakar is in the process of urbanization and on the right, towards the river, a broad, somewhat boggy area regards itself as the new commercial section. A number of wooden shacks already contain little shops and bars. Most of the shopkeepers are Bhutanese of Tibetan origin. Beyond a wind-battered bridge, the road on the right leads to the Tang and Ura valleys and onwards to Eastern Bhutan. Just above the bridge, a new temple with lovely architecture is almost finished and is worth a visit. This temple belongs to Namkhe Nyingpo, the reincarnation of one of Guru Rinpoche's disciples.

The road on the left of the bridge follows the left bank of the river towards the north. It runs through the farm of a Swiss project and a mechanical workshop which is the only place for 400 kilometres (250 miles) where you can get a punctured tyre mended! A small shop sells delicious cheese made by the Swiss method, apple or peach brandy, cider and apple juice and honey.

From the mechanical workshop, a narrow rough road climbs up for a good kilometre (nearly a mile) above the farm to the Karsumpey plateau, where the **Swiss Guest House** is located. Primarily reserved for Swiss people working in Bhutan, it is open to others if there is room, at a moderate price. With its good country cooking, common room, communicating bedrooms, and toilets under the apple trees at the bottom of the garden, the place seems like an Alpine mountaineering hut with the added attractions of good company and a warm atmosphere.

A Walk in the Valley

The road which continues beyond the farm offers the chance of a fine walk in the valley. Five kilometres (three miles) to the north it comes back to the river where there is a bridge over to the right bank. In this way you can make a loop on foot of about ten kilometres (six miles) over flat terrain. This walk should preferably be taken in the morning because it often rains in the afternoon and the wind may blow in gusts. (It is possible, however, to go as far as Tamshing Monastery by car.) Just after the farm there is a good view of the buildings on the other side of the river: Wangduchoeling Palace and the small houses containing prayer wheels, and after the palace, an enormous building with remarkable architecture which is a brand new hospital.

The road goes through fields, and about three kilometres (two miles) further, at a place where the opposite bank of the river forms a cliff, you will see the 'iron castle' **Chakhar**. According to Bhutanese tradition, this was the residence in the eighth century of King Sendhaka, the king who invited Guru Rinpoche to Bhutan.

One kilometre (just over half a mile) further, the road skirts a tiny temple surrounded by a wall, on the right. This is **Konchogsum Lhakhang** (also called Tsilung) which was founded, according to the saint Pema Lingpa, as far back as the eighth century. The temple is famous for its bell, which bears an inscription from the eighth century inside and which must have been cast for the Tibetan royal family so that they could hear 'the sound of Buddhism'. The bell was stolen and transported to Bhutan where its chimes could be heard all the way to Tibet. A Tibetan army was sent to fetch it back but its bell was so heavy that the soldiers could not lift it and, whether accidentally or not, they let it fall, which explains why it is broken. In any case it remained in Bhutan.[10]

In 1039 Bonpo Dragtshel, the first active *terton* ('discoverer of religious treasures') in Bhutan, discovered texts which had been hidden by Guru Rinpoche at this spot. It is said that the king of the water deities rose out of the lake beneath the temple and offered Bonpo Dragtshel a stone pillar and a stone scroll.

Another story in the oral tradition claims that the saint Pema Lingpa in the 15th century also discovered religious treasures here, which he found in the subterranean lake. He then sealed up the entrance with a block of stone and set his lotus seal on it. The stone can be seen in the middle of the courtyard. As for the pillar which stands in front of the surrounding wall, it is perhaps an ancient megalith reconverted, such as one often finds in Bhutan.

The main statue in the sanctuary is Buddha Vairocana, which seems to indicate the antiquity of the temple. The other statues are of Guru Rinpoche, Avalokiteshvara, and the great Nyingmapa masters who have already been mentioned: Pema Lingpa and Longchen Rabjampa. On the walls there are paintings of Guru Rinpoche as well as Pema Lingpa, Longchen Rabjampa and Jigme Lingpa.

Tamshing Lhakhang [11]

Tamshing Lhakhang, founded in 1501 (completed in 1505) by Pema Lingpa, is important on more than one count. It contains paintings of fundamental interest for the history of painting in this region and it is also, along with Gantey Gompa in the Black Mountains, one of the only places where Pema Lingpa's tradition of religious teachings still continues today. A small monastic community which came from the mother-monastery of Lhalung in Tibet in 1959 has settled at Tamshing, and young monks are being educated in the tradition of Pema Lingpa.

The temple was restored at the end of the 19th century, probably at the time of the eighth reincarnation of Pema Lingpa, Kunzang Tenpe Nyima (1843–91), since he is the last historical personage to figure in the paintings. The temple itself is made up of a vestibule and two sanctuaries, one above the other, with a path for circumambulation running around it.

The **36 paintings in the vestibule** on the ground floor date from the same period as the construction of the temple and are still in good condition. Since they are probably the oldest extant paintings in Bhutan, they are of enormous interest for the history of both art and religion, and by some miracle they have escaped the repaintings which are so frequently sponsored by the faithful as acts of piety. Each painting consists of a central figure surrounded by smaller personages who form his entourage and are placed on either side in small horizontal compartments. The colours are evenly applied and the lines are drawn firmly and clearly. All the figures conform to the iconographic canons laid down by Pema Lingpa.

On the left of the vestibule, starting from the door, there are: the Wheel of Life; the goddess Mahakala; the indigenous deity Shanpa Marnak; Sogdu, a divinity from Lhamo's entourage; the indigenous deity Shanpa Ngamo; Pema Lingpa, always recognizable by his hat, which is like Guru Rinpoche's, and the Vase of Long Life which he holds in his hands; the seventh Karmapa Choedra Gyamtsho (1454–1506); Guru Rinpoche's consort Yeshe Tsogyel; Guru Rinpoche; Jampel Shenyen, the direct disciple of Garab Dorje and holder of the Dzogchen teachings; Garab Dorje, the first to receive the Dzogchen teachings directly from Buddha Vajrasattva; the blue Buddha Vajradhara; the white Buddha Vajrasattva; the green Buddha Amogasiddhi; the red Buddha Amitabha; the yellow Buddha Ratnasambhava; the blue Buddha Akshobya; the white Buddha Vairocana holding a wheel; and a painting which is nowadays effaced.

At the exit of the circumambulation path, the series resumes with Amitayus, in sexual embrace, Guru Dragpo, a terrifying form of Guru Rinpoche in red, holding a scorpion in his left hand; a form of Avalokiteshvara in sexual embrace, Hayagriva in sexual embrace; Samantabhadra in sexual embrace; followed by his terrifying form, also in sexual embrace; Manjushri; the deity Yama in sexual embrace; Avalokiteshvara; Vajrapani; Prajnaparamita; Vajrakila (Phurpa) the dagger-deity in sexual embrace; Vaisravana; Mahakala; Ekajati, the god with one eye and one tooth; and Rahu (Za), the elipse-deity whose body is covered with eyes; the two latter deities are both protective gods of the Nyingmapa school.

In the **circumambulation path**, the paintings cannot be dated. On the interior wall they represent Pema Lingpa's lineage and on the exterior wall the Sixteen Arhats separated by the Buddha of Medicine.

The **sanctuary on the lower floor** is dedicated to Guru Rinpoche and his Eight Manifestations. The right-hand wall displays paintings of the Norbu Gyamtsho, a lineage of Guru Rinpoche particular to Pema Lingpa. The left-hand wall has the lineage of Pema Lingpa himself, ending with his eighth incarnation, Kunzang Tenpe Nyima. These

paintings were restored on the initiative of the Royal Grandmother, Ashi Choegron.

In the **vestibule in front of the sanctuary** there is a coat of mail attributed to Pema Lingpa, who had knowledge of metallurgy. Tradition says that if a person walks three times around the sanctuary wearing this coat of mail, a part of his sins will be wiped away.

The ceiling of the upper floor is extremely low. It is said that Pema Lingpa was a short man and that his measurements were used as the gauge for the temple. The upper floor would thus have been scaled to his size.

The first paintings in the **left-hand gallery** are of the Thousand Buddhas (1,004) followed by the Twenty-One Taras, feminine emanations of Avalokiteshvara. The outside wall of the circumambulation path is covered with pictures of the Three Bodies of Buddha (Amitabha, Avalokiteshvara and Padmasambhava). They are simple figures elegantly drawn in yellow on a red background. On the inner wall are paintings of the religious cycle called *Sampa Lhundrup*, very popular with the Nyingmapas, in which 13 forms of Guru Rinpoche are represented. Next, the Eighty-Four Mahasiddhas are painted in a landscape of green hills. The right side of the gallery is taken up by a continuation of the Thousand Buddha images. The west part of the gallery over the entrance is occupied by the *Gonkhang*, the temple of fearsome deities.

The upper temple is dedicated to Buddha Amitayus whose statue graces the holy of holies. The wall on the right is decorated with a painting of Samantabhadra, coloured dark blue. He is surrounded by the Four Bodhisattvas and several eminent Nyingmapa lamas, among them Jamyang Khyentse Wangpo (1820–92) and Kongtrul Lodroe Thaye (1813–99). The left-hand wall has a painting of Buddha Vajrasattva coloured white, holding a diamond-thunderbolt and a bell; he is surrounded by the other Four Bodhisattvas. Like the paintings in the sanctuary below, these in the upper sanctuary date from the end of the 19th century.

From Tamshing Monastery there is an excellent view of the Kurjey complex on the other side of the river. A little bit north of Tamshing, a footbridge crosses the river and from there it is only a ten-minute walk to Kurjey Lhakhang.

Shortly after leaving Tamshing on the way to the footbridge, you will notice, about 100 metres (328 feet) above the road, the small

Padmasambhava Lhakhang which was erected on one of Guru Rinpoche's meditation sites. It was first founded by Pema Lingpa in 1490 and its name at that time was Dekyiling. It was restored by the Royal Grandmother, Ashi Pemadechen.

The Kurjey Lhakhang Complex

In addition to the walking route, a tarmac road gives access to the Kurjey Lhakhang, leaving from the village of Jakar and following the right bank of the river.

Kurjey's site is one of the most sacred in Bhutan as Guru Rinpoche meditated here and left the imprint of his body on a rock (*kur* means 'body', *jey* means 'imprint').

In the eighth century, Bumthang was under the rule of a king named Sendhaka (Sintu Raja) whose home was the 'iron castle', Jakar. This king was at war with his southern neighbour, King Na'oche. The latter killed the son of King Sendhaka, who became so distraught that he forgot to worship his personal deity, Shelging Karpo. The angry god withdrew the king's vital principle and as a result he fell gravely ill. As nothing seemed able to save him, his ministers decided to call Guru Rinpoche whose supernatural powers were well known throughout the Himalayas.

When Guru Rinpoche arrived in Bumthang, he went to a place a short distance north of Chakhar where there was a large rock resembling a diamond-thunderbolt on the summit. Here lived the deity Shelging Karpo. Guru Rinpoche meditated there for a while, leaving the imprint of his body on the rock. Then he asked the king's daughter, whom he had taken to be his wife, to go and fetch some water in a golden ewer. While she was doing so, he changed into his Eight Manifestations and began to dance in the meadow. So amazing was this spectacle that all the local divinities, except Shelging Karpo, came to watch.

When the king's daughter came back, Guru Rinpoche transformed her into five princesses, each holding a golden ewer in her hand. The ewers reflected the sun's rays directly at Shelging Karpo's rock. Curious about this unusual flashing, Shelging Karpo decided to take the form of a white lion and come out to see what was going on. This was the moment Guru Rinpoche had been waiting for.

Turning himself into the holy griffon, *garuda* (*jachung*), he swooped down, seized Shelging Karpo and forced him to give back the king's vital principle. At the same time he made him promise not to cause any trouble for Buddhism and to become a protective deity. Guru Rinpoche planted his pilgrim staff in the ground where it grew into a cypress tree which has a descendant said to stand to this day in front of Kurjey Lhakhang.

As for Shelging Karpo, he is still the deity of Kurjey. King Sendhaka recovered his health and converted to Buddhism. Guru Rinpoche compelled the two kings to meet each other and make peace at a place in the Black Mountains called Nabji, where a stone pillar commemorates this meeting (see page 193). This episode constitutes the first conversion to Buddhism in Bumthang.

The actual Kurjey complex is made up of three temples facing south. The **first temple** on the right is the oldest and was built on the rock where Guru Rinpoche meditated by Minjur Tenpa in 1652 while he was Tongsa Penlop and before he became the Third Desi of Bhutan. Below the roof there is a carving of Guru Rinpoche as Garuda subduing the white lion (see above). The temple has two sanctuaries. The upper one is dedicated to the Past, Present and Future Buddhas, whose images stand in the sanctuary. On the wall to the right are painted the Twenty-One Taras and on the left are various gods associated with riches.

The **second temple** is the holiest because this is the site of a cave containing a rock with the imprint of Guru Rinpoche's body. The cave cannot be seen as it is concealed by a large statue of Guru Rinpoche. His Eight Manifestations are displayed on the altar.

Just to the left of the entrance is the figure of Shelging Karpo and an altar dedicated to him. On the right of the door, a thousand statues of Guru Rinpoche are lined up against the wall accompanied by three large statues: of the white Tara, the Goddess of Compassion; Guru Rinpoche; and either Pema Lingpa or Dorje Lingpa — the identity of this image is uncertain.

The wall opposite the door, on the right of the altar, is covered with high reliefs commissioned by the Royal Grandmother, Ashi Phuntsho Choegron, some 30 years ago. They represent Guru Rinpoche and his Twenty-Five Disciples, his Eight Manifestations and various other forms accounted for in the tradition of Pema Lingpa. The ceiling is decorated with a magnificent mandala dedicated to the teaching of the Gondu.

Leaving the sanctuary, you will notice two holes in the rock to the left of the entrance. They offer a way to purify sins. The sinner is supposed to enter on one side, worm his way as best he can through the rock and come out the other side. If he gets stuck it is because he has committed too many sins and will only be able to free himself by saying prayers. (Just in front of the steps leading to the temples there is a fairly small rock with a hole which you could also try to go through!)

The second temple was built in 1900 by Ugyen Wangchuck, the First King of Bhutan, while he was still the Penlop of Tongsa. The temple was built to house a monumental statue of Guru Rinpoche. It was modelled under the advice of the great Nyingmapa lama, Rigzin Khamsum Yondrol. He said that the blessings brought about by the presence of this image would contribute to the prosperity and stability of the whole country. The image of Guru Rinpoche is about ten metres (over 32 feet) high and is surrounded by the Eight Manifestations. An image of the historical Buddha sits on the left side of the altar and Zangdopelri, the paradise of Guru Rinpoche, is on the right. Facing the entrance, a second, smaller statue of Guru Rinpoche was commissioned by the Minister of Home Affairs in the early 1960s.

To the left of the window there is a large painting of the fourth reincarnation of Pema Lingpa, Ngawang Kunzang Dorje (1680–1723), and on the right is a painting of Shabdrung Ngawang Namgyel bracketed on his right by Umze Tenzing Drugye (First Desi of Bhutan from 1651 to 1656), and on his left by Pekar Juney (First Je Khenpo).

The porch at the entrance to the temple contains particularly fine paintings of the Guardians of the Four Directions and various indigenous deities who were vanquished by Guru Rinpoche and transformed into protectors of Buddhism. Here we find Dorje Legpa coloured red, holding a diamond-thunderbolt and riding on a goat; Ekajati, dark red, with one tooth and one eye; Yak Du Nagpo, the guardian deity of the Ura valley, coloured black and mounted on a black yak; Kyebu Lungten, the guardian deity of the Four Valleys of Bumthang, red, wearing armour and mounted on a red horse; and of course Shelging Karpo, Kurjey's god, coloured white and riding a white horse.

A **third temple** is under construction. It is sponsored by H M the Queen Mother of Bhutan, Ashi Kesang, who also commissioned 108 small stone chortens to be erected. These will enclose the whole Kurjey complex, transforming it into a three-dimensional mandala along a pattern set by the Samye Monastery in Tibet.

In front of the temples there are three chortens, one of them made up of a heap of stones which are dedicated to the Three Kings of Bhutan. As there are no representatives of the state clergy permanently established in Bumthang, the monks from Tongsa spend the summer at

Kurjey and perform numerous rituals here including a *Tshechu* festival (see page 102).

Thangbi Lhakhang

A walk of one and a half hours north from Kurjey leads to Thangbi Lhakhang. The fourth Shamar Rinpoche of the Karmapa religious school came to Bumthang from Tibet in the 15th century in order to establish a monastery. In 1470 he founded Thangbi, located in the middle of a wide, fertile plateau overlooking the river. Following a quarrel with Pema Lingpa, Shamar Rinpoche had to leave Thangbi. The iron chain curtain hanging in the entrance is said to have been forged by Pema Lingpa who took over the monastery.

The temple has two sanctuaries and a rather large temple of terrifying deities, the *Gonkhang*. The sanctuary on the ground floor contains recent statues of the Past, Present and Future Buddhas and three clay statues which probably date from the end of the 15th century. Of exceptional craftsmanship, these are portraits of lamas, one of whom is the fourth Shamar Rinpoche (1453–1524).

On the upper floor, the vestibule of the sanctuary contains two remarkable paintings of Guru Rinpoche's heaven, Zangdopelri, and the heaven of Amitabha. The main statue is an image of Jowo, Buddha as a young prince.

Jampa Lhakhang

From the Kurjey complex, a tarmac road heads south along the right bank of the river to the temple of Jampa (Maitreya) and beyond that to the village of Jakar. It is equally possible to return to the village on foot, five kilometres (three miles) away.

Like Kyichu Lhakhang in the Paro valley (see page 122), this temple is said to be the first that King Songtsen Gampo of Tibet constructed in Bhutan in the seventh century. It is one of the 108 temples built by him throughout Tibet and the Himalayas to overcome a demon giantess. While Kyichu Lhakhang was erected on the demon's left foot, and was one of the temples built 'to subjugate regions beyond the frontiers', Jampa Lhakhang was placed on the demon's left knee and was one of the temples built 'to subjugate the frontiers'.

When Guru Rinpoche came to Bhutan, it is said that he preached the teachings of the Kagye cycle to King Sendhaka and his court from the roof the temple.

In addition to the main sanctuary containing the statue of Jampa, four more sanctuaries were added at some date after the middle of the 19th century, creating a closed courtyard in front of the main sanctuary. A caretaker from the monastic community of Tongsa looks after the temple.

It is interesting to note that the exact dates of the founding and restoration of the different sanctuaries are not known, except that the temple was partially restored by Ugyen Wangchuck's brother-in-law, the Jakar Dzongpon, Chime [12] Dorje, in 1905.

Inside the Lhakhang It is not known exactly when the **main sanctuary** was restored, but it was probably at the beginning of the 20th century judging by the style of the paintings. Like all very ancient temples, the sanctuary consists of a central shrine with a circumambulation path. The central shrine contains a large statue of Maitreya, framed on either side by Four Bodhisattvas. On one side of the doorway leading into the main shrine there is a painting of the historical Buddha and, on the other, a painting of the Eight Manifestations of Guru Rinpoche. The circumambulation path is covered with paintings of the Thousand Buddhas, 1,004 to be exact.

The **sanctuary of Dukikhorlo**, or Dukhor (Kalacakra), is on the right of the main sanctuary, forming the right side of the courtyard. It was built by Jigme Namgyel or Ugyen Wangchuck — it is not clear which — at the end of the 19th century.

Kalacakra, the Wheel of Time, is considered to be the most complex of the cycles of Tantric teachings, and is the one most recently divulged. According to Himalayan tradition, it was preached by Buddha and then kept secret for several centuries in the kingdom of Shambala. After reappearing in India around AD 966, it was introduced into Tibet in 1026.

The deity who symbolizes Kalacakra is coloured dark blue, with 32 arms, one yellow leg and one red leg. He is in sexual embrace with his consort, who is orange. The temple's main image represents this deity and the smaller statues represent his entourage. The splendid paintings devoted to the Karling Shitro cycle are of 'the peaceful and terrifying Deities according to Karma Lingpa' who appear in the intermediary state between death and rebirth.

The *Gonkhang* is situated near the Dukhor sanctuary.

The **Chorten Lhakhang** is in the extension of the Dukikhorlo Lhakhang. It was built by Ashi Wangmo, the present King's great-aunt, who was a Karmapa nun. This temple is dedicated to the first Benchey Desi, a reincarnation of the Karmapa school who died around 1940 and was one of the Wangchuck family's chaplains. His chorten is in the middle of the temple. On the right-hand wall there is a painting of the lineage of the Karmapas, and the left wall shows the Thirty-Five Buddhas of Confession.

The **Guru Lhakhang** forms the left side of the courtyard. It was founded by the Jakar Dzongpon, Tsondru Gyeltsen, in the middle of the 19th century. The main statue is of Guru Rinpoche flanked by images of Avalokiteshvara and Amitayus. On the wall to the right are the Twenty-One Taras. On the left-hand wall are Avalokiteshvara with a thousand eyes and a thousand hands, and Sukhavati — the Western Heaven of Amitabha. On the right of the window there is a painting of Pema Linga and, on the left, the protective deity Gompo Maning (one aspect of Mahakala).

The Sangye Lhakhang is above the entrance. This 'temple of Buddhas' was founded by the Second King, Jigme Wangchuck. The main statues represent the Buddhas of the Seven Ages. The wall on the right shows the cycle of Gondu. On the left are Guru Rinpoche and his Eight Manifestations, Avalokiteshvara and the Medicine Buddhas whose principal figure is dark blue, holding a myrobalan fruit in his hand.

Chakhar

Not far from Jampa Lhakhang, set back on the edge of the plateau overlooking the river, is the residence of Chakhar, where King Sendhaka's 'iron palace' stood in the eighth century. A temple seems also to have been founded on this spot by the saint Dorje Lingpa in the 14th century. The head of the family who lives at Chakhar is said to be descended from Dorje Lingpa and he bears the name of Chakhar Lama. He takes care of the annual festival of Jampa Lhakhang, with which bonds continue to survive after many centuries. The present house dates from the beginning of this century.

Wangduchoeling Palace

As the road approaches the village of Jakar, the building with interesting architecture on the left is the regional hospital, built with Swiss aid in 1988–9. This hospital has an allopathic unit as well as a traditional

medicine unit. Just after the hospital, beyond the archery range, the tall structure that comes into view is the Wangduchoeling Palace. The palace, which is private property, was built on a site called Shamkhar, already inhabited in the eighth century. This palace was constructed in 1856 by the Tongsa Penlop, Jigme Namgyel, whose son, Ugyen Wangchuck, the future First King, was born here.

A tourist guesthouse has been built in traditional style in the palace gardens. The rooms are clustered in small buildings opening on to the garden and are nice and comfortable. Each room has a wood stove and the bathrooms have hot water. The lavishly painted dining room is located in a separate building. Although it is simple, the guesthouse is well maintained and offers what one hopes is the best of Bumthang. The cook makes laudable efforts and the food is good but the prices are unbelievably high.

Jakar Dzong

The road to Jakar Dzong branches off the main road on the right just after the archery field. Jakar Dzong (sometimes written Byakar) sits on a little spur overlooking the valley. The 'dzong of the white bird' is very elegant and more modest in size than the dzongs mentioned so far. It is the administrative seat of the district but it has the odd distinction of being the only dzong in Bhutan that does not contain a Drukpa monastic community.

The dzong was founded as far back as the Shabdrung's great-grandfather, the Drukpa lama, Ngagi Wangchuck. After he had founded Tongsa, Ngagi Wangchuck came to Bumthang where, with the help of donors, he started to build a monastery. One day he saw a white bird flying over the construction site towards the ridge where the dzong now stands, and there the bird stayed. Ngagi Wangchuck took this to be an omen and he decided to change the location of the monastery. In 1549 the monastery was finished and he named it 'the monastery of the white bird'.

After Shabdrung Ngawang Namgyel had firmly established his power, he ordered the Tongsa Penlop, Minjur Tenpa, to repair the monastery and build it into a dzong, which he did in 1646. During the struggle for effective control of Central Bhutan which took place in the 1650s after the Shabdrung's death, the dzong was damaged. It was repaired much later in 1683 by the Fourth Desi of Bhutan, Tenzing Rabgye, who added a tower as a water reservoir. The dzong was badly damaged again in the earthquake of 1897 and was rebuilt on a smaller scale by the future First King, Ugyen Wangchuck, in 1905.[13]

Coming into the dzong through the courtyard for administration, you will then pass below the central tower which contains a temple to Maitreya. A second temple, dedicated to the lineage of the Drukpa lamas, has as its principal statue a representation of Tenpe Nyima, Shabdrung Ngawang Namgyel's father. A small passage then leads to the courtyard formerly reserved for monks. The part on the right was the Kunre, the monks' assembly hall, which contains a statue of the deity Phurpa.

Four kilometres (two and a half miles) above the dzong is the superb palace-monastery of Lamey Gompa, 'the unsurpassed monastery', which is home to a Forest Institute today. It is one of the finest examples of palatial architecture in Bhutan. Lamey Gompa was built at the beginning of the 19th century by the Tongsa Penlop, Sonam Drugyel, who was King Ugyen Wangchuck's maternal great-grandfather. The King restored Lamey Gompa just the way it looks today, and the place became the residence of his two daughters, both very pious.

Jakar Lhakhang

Many houses have recently been built along the road that runs from the base of the hill where the dzong stands to the roundabout in the village. However, on the left side of the road, only minimally distinguished by the gold ornament on its roof, is Jakar Lhakhang, one of the oldest temples in Bhutan.

It was founded in 1445 by a descendant of Dorje Lingpa and it contains some very fine paintings, in particular a superb image of Ushnishavijaya (Tsugtor Namgyelma) represented in a chorten. The temple appears to have been restored at the end of the 19th century since there is a picture of Shabdrung Jigme Choegyel (1862–1904). The principal statue is of Guru Rinpoche.

The Tang Valley

From Jakar, the road crosses the bridge and branches to the right, following the left bank of the river southwards. Five kilometres (three miles) further, the road turns to the east and enters the southern end of the Tang valley, whose average altitude is 2,800 metres (9,185 feet). The road passes Dechenpelrithang, an experimental sheep-breeding farm, and after crossing a bridge it ascends in a series of sharp bends and goes

on towards the Ura valley.

The unpaved road into the Tang valley branches off to the left, one kilometre (half a mile) beyond the sheep farm, and climbs steeply to cross over the first line of hills. From here the valley stretches out northwards.

It is also possible to reach Tang on foot from the Choekhor valley. The shortest route is the one which starts above the Swiss farm and climbs up to Petsheling Monastery then follows the ridge to a small pass after which it comes down not far from Kungzandra Monastery. This hike takes about four hours.

The Tang valley is still relatively poor compared to the other Bumthang valleys. Its agricultural yields are meagre and people there mostly raise sheep. The unpaved road now reaches part of it, but since the north of this valley is a dead end, it lies some distance off the east–west axis of road connections.

Mebartsho

The Tang River cuts through the first line of hills, forming a narrow gorge which contains one of the great pilgrimage sites of Bhutan — Mebartsho, 'the flaming lake'.

This is where Pema Lingpa found the treasures hidden by Guru Rinpoche and thus became a *terton*, a 'discoverer of religious treasures'. The story is well known in Bhutan, and goes as follows. One day, in the year 1475, when Pema Lingpa had gone to look for mushrooms in the forest, he met a stranger who said he had come to see him, gave him a scroll and disappeared. The scroll declared that Pema Lingpa should go and fetch the religious treasures hidden in a rock called Naring on the opposite side of the river. So Pema Lingpa headed for the gorge, accompanied by five friends. Just before arriving there, Pema Linga began to behave strangely, as though he were in a trance. He plunged into the river, went over to the rock, fetched the books and came back to the other side again. His friends were absolutely astonished.

In the autumn of that same year, Pema Lingpa returned to the gorge and, in the presence of a large number of people, stood at the edge of the river with a lighted lamp in his hand, saying: 'If I be a demon, let me die! If I be the spiritual son of Guru Rinpoche, let this lamp not go out and let me find the religious treasures!' With that he plunged into the river and came out with a statue of Buddha and a skull sealed full of miraculous substances. And the lamp was still burning. So that seems to be how the place got the name of Mebartsho, 'the flaming lake'. This name also refers to a prophecy contained in the *Pema Thangyig*, a text discovered a century earlier by Ugyen Lingpa (1329– 67).

Mebartsho, in fact, is not a lake but a gorge through which the river rushes. It is a great pilgrimage site; visitors launch small lighted lamps on the water. Images of Pema Lingpa and his two sons have been carved on the rock. There is no sanctuary.

Kungzandra Monastery

This monastery, at 3,350 metres (10,990 feet), is located in the hollow of a cliff which rises above the valley. You need about one and a half hours to reach it on foot. It is one of the places where Guru Rinpoche meditated, as did his disciple Namkhe Nyingpo, and a little temple is said to have been established there at the end of the eighth century. However, the present site was founded in 1488 by the saint Pema Lingpa who was born close by at Chel, and he made it one of his residences. Apart from Pema Lingpa's living quarters, the monastery consists of three temples: the Wangkhang, in which the principal statue is Avalokiteshvara with a thousand eyes and a thousand hands; Oezerphug, the meditation cave of Pema Lingpa's son, Dawa Gyeltsen; and the Khandroma Lhakhang, which contains a gilded copper statue of Pema Lingpa.

Four kilometres (two and a half miles) from the foot of the Kungzandra cliff, after passing a school, the road arrives at **Rimocen Temple**. The temple is dominated by an enormous rock which was one of Guru Rinpoche's meditation places. He left numerous marks on it, and the name of the temple means 'the one with drawings (or marks)'. The religious master Longchen Rabjampa predicted in the middle of the 14th century that a temple would be built on this spot. At the end of the 14th century, the saint Dorje Lingpa erected a little temple which was restored at the end of the 19th century by one of his distant descendants, the Tongsa Penlop, Tshokye Dorje.

Ugyenchoeling Palace

The road ends three kilometres (two miles) beyond Rimocen, almost opposite the lordly residence of Ugyenchoeling, which is still private property. A half-hour's walk leads to the hilltop from which Ugyenchoeling overlooks the surrounding countryside.

The site was occupied in the middle of the 14th century by the Nyingmapa master, Longchen Rabjampa, who built a little retreat there. At the end of the 14th century, the saint Dorje Lingpa decided to settle at the place where the great master had meditated and there he discovered numerous religious treasures. Of all the places in Bhutan where Dorje Lingpa lived, Ugyenchoeling seems to have been his favourite. His direct descendants took over his possessions and contributed to the spreading of his teachings.

The original monastery seems to have been preserved up until the middle of the 19th century when Tshokye Dorje, Tongsa Penlop and the 15th blood-descendant of Dorje Lingpa to be born at Ugyenchoeling, built the palace which is seen today. The structure was very badly damaged in the earthquake of 1897 and Tshokye Dorje's grandson, the Jakar Dzongpon, Ugyen Wangdi, had to rebuild a large part of it at the beginning of this century.

Thowadra Monastery

Beyond Ugyenchoeling, four hours' walk to the north, another monastery nestles into a cliff that appears to block the Tang valley. Thowadra, meaning 'the highest rock', is at an altitude of 3,400 metres (11,155 feet). It was blessed by the presence of Guru Rinpoche who came there to meditate and left many marks on the rock. This is where Guru Rinpoche is said to have left behind a wooden bird which was used to expel a wicked king from the Khenpalung valley north of Bumthang. Thowadra is also one of the 'gates' leading into this secret valley, which was sealed up by Guru Rinpoche after he drove out the king.

Thowadra was founded in 1238 by Lorepa (1187–1250), the Drukpa Kagyupa lama who had established Choedrak Monastery at another of Guru Rinpoche's meditation places. A Nyingmapa monastic community was brought here at the end of the 18th century by Changchub Gyeltsen (also called Jigme Kundrel), a disciple of the great Dzogchen master, Jigme Lingpa (1730–98).

The Ura Valley

From Tang it is 50 kilometres (32 miles) across a pass to the Ura valley, the last and highest of the Bumthang valleys. To get there the road climbs through amazingly open countryside, only occasionally running into a forest.

Large sheep pastures line the road 20 kilometres (12 miles) beyond

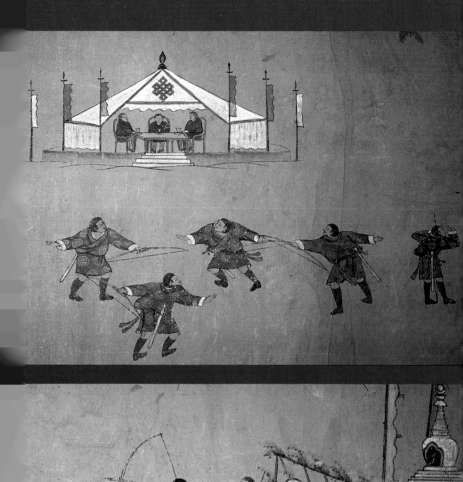
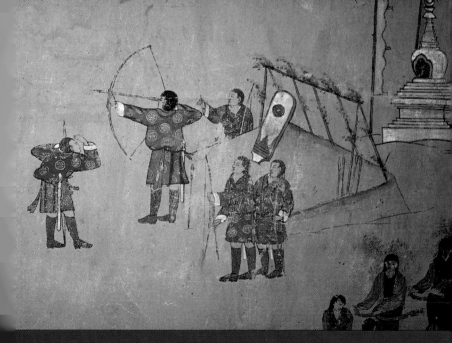

Archery and Other Sports

Archery Archery is Bhutan's national sport and is played practically all year. Spectators marvel at the dexterity of the Bhutanese and gasp at other members of a team who stand close to the target and sidestep the flying arrows with amazing speed. Archery is an integral part of all festivities and is usually accompanied by a banquet.

Bows and arrows are made of a special kind of bamboo and the tension can be as high as 60 pounds. Two painted wooden targets 30 by 120 centimetres (12 by 47 inches) are placed at each end of the range which measures 120 metres (394 feet) in length! The two targets are used alternately. Two teams of eleven archers compete, each man shooting two arrows, and the first team to get 33 points wins the match. There are three sets and the method of scoring is complicated because arrows that land within an arrow's length of the target also count.

Each team is encouraged by its supporters and 'cheer leaders'. These are women who dance and sing, extolling their team while teasing and mocking the adversaries with bawdy comments to make them lose their concentration.

Women are not allowed to touch a bow. The day before an important match, the archers will not only make offerings to local deities but will refrain from sleeping at home. The best archers wear multicoloured scarves tied to the back of their belts, and each time an arrow hits the bull's-eye a short victory dance is performed by the team.

Dego *Dego* is a traditional sport played by monks, since archery is forbidden to them. It is a game something like bowls or the French game of pétanque, which involves throwing a stone of a certain weight underhand to get it as close as possible to a small stick driven into the ground. A competitor can also dislodge his opponent's stone.

Pundo *Pundo* is a game played by laymen which consists of throwing a stone weighing about one kilo (over two pounds) as far as possible. This time the throwing movement is from the shoulder, with the stone held flat in the hand.

Kuru *Kuru* is a game like darts played out of doors, with the target some 20 metres (65 feet) away.

Soksom *Soksom* consists of throwing a javelin a distance of 20 metres (65 feet).

Games of Strength *Keyshey* and *Sherey parey* are games of strength that pit two men against each other. The first one resembles wrestling, while the second is more like 'iron hand'; one fighter's fist is clasped in the two hands of his opponent and if he can get it free he is declared the winner.

Others Nowadays, two Western sports have found favour with the public: football and basketball. And one Korean sport, Taekwondo, has also made a remarkable breakthrough.

the southern tip of the Tang valley, and the big village of Tangsibi can be seen below the road level. Five kilometres (three miles) further is the Ura La Pass at 3,600 metres (11,810 feet), marked by a chorten. About one kilometre (half a mile) before reaching the top of the pass there is a magnificent view in clear weather of Bhutan's highest peak, Gankar Punsum, at 7,239 metres (23,750 feet), its massive white summit etched against the sky.

The road descends into Ura by long loops across fields and pastures. Villages in the region of Ura characteristically have very closely clustered houses, which is unusual in Bhutan. Ura's main occupation is raising sheep and yaks, but the introduction of potato farming ten years ago has brought a certain degree of prosperity to people living in the harsh climate of this valley. Women can still be seen wearing black sheepskins on their backs, the sheepskin serving as both a waterproof coat and a cushion for sitting on the ground.

Sombrang and Shingkhar

Just before the road reaches the floor of the valley, above the road on the right can be seen the village and monastery of Sombrang, where Pema Lingpa's ancestors settled in 1228. A good hour's walk from the road across the small pass that overlooks Sombrang brings you to the village and monastery of Shingkhar at 3,400 metres (11,155 feet). The monastery was founded by the Nyingmapa master, Longchen Rabjampa, in around 1350.

Ura Village

Most of Ura village lies on the right side of the road. Perched at an altitude of 3,100 metres (10,170 feet), the village is composed of big houses crowded close together and roofed with shingles. Above the village, a new temple dedicated to Guru Rinpoche was inaugurated in 1986. The old families of Ura have provided numerous high officials to Bhutan since the inception of the monarchy.

Eastern Bhutan

The Road from Ura to Mongar

The distance from Ura to Mongar is 141 kilometres (88 miles). At the far end of the Ura valley, the road starts to climb towards the highest pass in Bhutan, the Thumsing La, at 3,800 metres (12,465 feet), and passes through a forest of conifers with an underbrush of rhododendron. The pass, which lies about 30 kilometres (19 miles) further, is often hidden in mist, or covered with snow in winter. A sign put up by a road construction crew invites all comers simply to 'BASH ON REGARDLESS!'. This kind of sign, and others warning about unexpected curves — even though the road is nothing but curves — are a delight to newcomers.

The mountains of Eastern Bhutan can be seen in clear weather. From the pass, the road plunges down in a long series of bends through a dark coniferous forest. The whole descent is dizzying and lasts for a good three hours, and at the bottom the lowest point has an altitude of only 650 metres (2,130 feet)! From the pass, the forest lasts for about 20 kilometres (12 miles), then the road comes out at 3,000 metres (nearly 10,000 feet) on to the plateau where Sengor is situated. This is the last village where Bumthangkha is spoken.

After this brief opening out of the landscape, the road plunges once more into forest, this time composed of both deciduous trees and conifers, the latter disappearing progressively before the road comes into the semi-tropical zone at about 1,800 metres (5,900 feet). Bamboo and liana then take over the scene. The 20 kilometres (12.5 miles) between Sengor and Namning is perhaps, for the uninitiated, the most hair-raising stretch of road in Bhutan. The route is literally dug out of the rock and bordered by a vertiginous drop. The heavy atmosphere is made worse by the constant humidity, the frequent fog and the absence of any human activity. A small memorial has been put up for the 247 Indian and Nepalese workers who lost their lives while constructing this road.

Namning is scarcely more than a name but this is where the road enters the semi-tropical zone. More houses are to be seen from here on, some of them roofed with bamboo matting, the typical roofing material of Eastern Bhutan. Numerous cows graze at the edge of the road. The first fields of corn, Eastern Bhutan's staple food, now appear surrounded by clumps of bamboo and banana trees. The temperature rises noticeably and it is really warm by the time you reach the road maintenance camp at Lingmithang, 37 kilometres (23 miles) beyond Namning.

Shortly before Lingmithang, near an area called Saling, the **ruins of Shongar dzong** can just be seen peeping through the thick jungle on the right. This fortress, built in 1100 by a lord from Ura, was abandoned around 1800 when Mongar Dzong was established. Up until that time it had been one of the most important dzongs of Eastern Bhutan, as it controlled the route between the centre and the east of the country.

Four kilometres (two and a half miles) further, the road reaches its lowest point of 650 metres (2,130 feet) at the bridge over the Kuru River. The big chorten here, built in Nepalese style, was founded about 1800 by the last Shongar Dzongpon, Kunzang Wangdu, who enshrined the precious religious objects of Shongar Dzong inside it when the dzong was abandoned in favour of Mongar.

After crossing the river, the road starts climbing again and zigzags up the side of the mountains where Mongar is located. The road branches 13 kilometres (eight miles) from the bridge. One road goes to Lhuntshi Dzong, 65 kilometres (40 miles) to the north; the other continues to climb through a light forest of leafy trees and Chir pine for 12 kilometres (seven and a half miles), to arrive at last at Mongar, at 1,700 metres (5,575 feet).

Mongar

Mongar is the district headquarters and hardly more than a stopping place surrounded by fields of corn. It is also the first town which is built on a mountainside instead of in a valley. This is characteristic of Eastern Bhutan where the valleys are usually little more than riverbeds and the mountain slopes which rise abruptly from the rivers flatten out as they appproach their summits. Looking up at those steep slopes from a river, one would never imagine that the upper parts of the mountain were so densely populated.

The western and southwestern parts of Mongar district used to belong to the ancient district of Khyeng (see page 193). The true land of the 'Eastern People', the Sharchopas, begins beyond Mongar. The language of these people is very different from Khyengkha and, although it is commonly called Sharchopkha, its correct name is Tsangla.

Mongar Dzong was established at the beginning of the 19th century when the site of Shongar was abandoned. The present dzong dates from 1953, when it was founded on orders from the Third King, Jigme Dorji

Wangchuck. Besides its function as an administrative centre, it houses the region's Drukpa monastic community. The dzong's central tower contains two temples.

Near the dzong there is a large tourist guesthouse with rudimentary facilities but a very pleasant garden and it enjoys a lovely view over a wide area. On the main street which runs below the dzong, some small shops sell packets of tea and the usual biscuits, and there is a small daily vegetable market very early in the morning. Mongar is lucky enough to have a good hospital.

The Road from Mongar to Lhuntshi

Mongar is only 77 kilometres (48 miles) from Lhuntshi but the road is so bad that it often takes more than four hours to cover this distance. Even worse, the Mongar road is sometimes cut off for weeks on end and then Lhuntshi becomes one of the most isolated districts in Bhutan. The road to Lhuntshi branches off from the Bumthang–Lingmithing road 12 kilometres (seven and a half miles) below Mongar. After running for a few kilometres through open countryside on the side of the mountain, the road turns north and goes down into the gorge of the Kuru River, following its left bank at an altitude of 1,100 metres (3,610 feet). The landscape is spectacular, with cliffs and a coniferous forest from which turpentine is extracted. Lemon grass also grows in abundance.

The first hamlet is Aotsho, followed by Gurgaon, both of them new settlements which came into being after the road was built. The old villages are higher up on the mountainside, invisible from the road. Lhuntshi, like Mongar and Tashigang, is a densely populated district but you would have to climb for hours in the mountains to realize this.

After about 30 kilometres (19 miles), the road reaches Thangmachu. Here a bridge crosses over the river to the right bank, thus giving access to Lhuntshi Dzong which lies 13 kilometres (eight miles) beyond it. The dzong perches on a spur and appears to block the end of the narrow valley completely. The road which leads to it is very steep, climbing from 1,350 to 1,700 metres (from 4,430 to 5,570 feet) in only four kilometres (two and a half miles).

Lhuntshi scarcely deserves to be called a village. It is basically just a dzong and a school. It is the headquarters of Lhuntshi district which, from Thangmachu, was formerly called Kurtoe. The language spoken in the Kurtoe region is closely related to Bumthangkha and Khyengkha, as numerous families from Bumthang emigrated to Kurtoe in the 16th and

17th centuries. In particular, Kurtoe is the cradle of the Royal Family, the Wangchucks. Their exact point of origin is the village of Dungkhar, two days' walk north of the dzong, where one of Pema Lingpa's sons emigrated in the 16th century.

The region is famous for its weavers who, in the dim light of their homes, make superb dresses called *kushutara*, woven with a brocading technique (see page 89). The village of **Gompa Karpo**, a four-hour walk east of the dzong, and **Dungkhar** village are especially renowned for the fine quality of the fabrics they produce.

Lhuntshi Dzong

The original foundation of Lhuntshi Dzong seems to go back to Pema Lingpa's son, Kunga Wangpo, in 1543. Then in 1552, the Drukpa lama, Ngagi Wangchuck, who had already established temples at Tongsa and Jakar, arrived in Kurtoe and set up a little dzong at a place called Linglingthang. After a successful military campaign against the lords of Kurtoe in 1654, the Tongsa Penlop, Minjur Tenpa, had a dzong constructed at Lhuntshi (Lhundrup Rinchentse) in 1654. The dzong was restored in 1962 and again between 1972 and 1974. It is the administrative centre of the district and it houses a monastic community of about a hundred monks.

The dzong contains five temples and a *Gonkhang*. The three temples in the central tower are a temple dedicated to Guru Rinpoche, while the *Gonkhang* is dedicated to Mahakala and the temple is dedicated to Amitayus. The assembly hall of the monks, the Kunre, is on the upper floor in the wing on the right. Its principal statues represent the Past, Present and Future Buddhas. On the ground floor of this wing there is a temple dedicated to Avalokiteshvara. The upper floor of the left-hand wing contains a temple of Akshobya. The woodwork on the railings of the galleries is extremely fine.

To see and appreciate Lhuntshi district properly, with its many small villages and ancient temples, you should really explore on foot.

The Road from Mongar to Tashigang

This trip of 96 kilometres (60 miles) takes three hours and generally presents no serious difficulties since the Kori La Pass is only 2,450 metres (8,000 feet) high. The first part of the journey is through a leafy forest filled with ferns. The Kori La lies 18 kilometres (11 miles) beyond Mongar; it is marked by a pretty chorten and a stone wall. Seven kilometres (four miles) after the pass comes the village of **Nagtshang** where one of the small kingdoms of Eastern Bhutan was located before the Drukpa conquest in the 17th century.

The road descends rapidly through corn fields and banana groves and arrives, about ten kilometres (six miles) below, at the famous zigzags of Yadi. **Yadi** is a recent settlement which has grown up beside the road at 1,500 metres (4,920 feet) and is composed of a few small shops and a school. After 20 kilometres (12 miles) of interminable bends through a rather sparse forest of conifers, the road reaches its lowest point on this section of the journey, at 700 metres (2,300 feet). This is at a bridge over the Sheri River, a small tributary of the Gamri River, which flows below Tashigang. Halfway up the mountain facing the bridge, the outline of a large chorten in Nepalese style can just be seen.

The road now follows the Gamri River (the Manas River) northwards. An unsurfaced road branches off 13 kilometres (eight miles) beyond the bridge over the Sheri River to the big monastery of Dametsi. This road climbs for 20 kilometres (12.5 miles) before reaching Dametsi, at an altitude of 2,400 metres (7,875 feet). From here, Sherubtse College, the University of Bhutan situated at Kanglung, can be seen on a plateau directly opposite. Once more it becomes evident that in most cases in Eastern Bhutan, due to its peculiar geography without open valleys, the distance in kilometres or miles on the motor road has very little to do with the actual topography. It is a 50-kilometre (30-mile) drive, passing by way of Tashigang, to get from Dametsi to Kanglung.

Dametsi Monastery

Dametsi, situated on the flat top of a hill, is the biggest and most important monastery of Eastern Bhutan, where Pema Lingpa's teachings were faithfully transmitted. Dametsi Ugyenchoeling, to use its full name, is a Nyingmapa monastery which became state property in 1982.

The history of the founding of Dametsi is very complicated and there are several versions. It was founded at an unknown date towards the end of the 16th century by Choeden Zangmo[14] (born about 1535), who was a great-granddaughter of Pema Lingpa. It is here that Choeden Zangmo's brother, Kunga Nyingpo (born 1557), had his vision of the famous dance, the 'Drummers of Dametsi'. The family line started by Choeden Zangpo was called the 'Dametsi Choeje' and many eminent Bhutanese lamas, including two Shabdrungs, were born into this family.

The monastery was probably restored at the end of the 17th century because it has the architecture of a dzong, and again at the beginning of the 20th century because there are pictures of Shabdrung Jigme Choegyel (1862–1904) and the First King, Ugyen Wangchuck.

Some of the paintings were completely redone in the 1950s and again in 1985.

The temples are located in the central tower. On the top floor is the *Gonkhang* and below it a temple dedicated to the 'Five Sisters of Long Life', indigenous goddesses who became protectors of Buddhism. The ground floor is occupied by the big Guru Lhakhang that contains the funerary chorten of the temple's foundress, Choeden Zangmo.

Apart from a few ordained monks, the main religious community consists of 78 *gomchens* who live around the monastery with their families, as is the case at Bhutan's other great Nyingmapa monastery, Gantey Gompa in the Black Mountains.

Tashigang

The town of Tashigang lies 20 kilometres (12.5 miles) beyond the point where the Dametsi road branches off. The main road continues to follow high above the right bank of the Gamri River and then enters Tashigang district, the most densely populated district in Bhutan with 150,000 inhabitants.

As soon as the road crosses the old Chagzam 'iron bridge', Tashigang Dzong comes into view at the top of a spur overlooking the river. The upper slopes of the mountains throughout Tashigang district are covered with little villages, and the deforestation there has been extreme. After a steep eight-kilometre (five-mile) climb, the road reaches Tashigang where the altitude is 1,150 metres (3,775 feet).

The road from Thimphu to Tashigang, known in Bhutan as the 'Lateral Road', covers a distance of 580 kilometres (360 miles). It was begun in 1965 but the difficulties encountered during its construction were so great that it was not finished until 1975. The paving of the surface took another ten years.

After Thimphu, Tashigang is the biggest urban centre in mountainous Bhutan. It has a true atmosphere of its own which helps to make it one of the most pleasant towns in Bhutan. The mild climate and flowering bougainvillea contribute to this atmosphere: people chat on their doorsteps or in front of their stalls, women stop to gossip in the middle of the road, bistros are full until quite late at night, people from the Merak and Sakteng valleys stroll about with their little yak-hair hats

pulled down on their heads; everybody comes to watch the arrival of a car or the evening bus in the small square in the middle of town. It is reminiscent of an unspoiled village in the south of France, except for the costumes!

The topography of Tashigang town, built on a spur and backing on to the side of a mountain, defies any precise description. The commercial district is immediately at the back of the spur where the dzong stands, while the school, the hospital and the tourist guesthouse have been built somewhat higher and more to the north, in a kind of small cirque.

There are three social gathering places in Tashigang that you should know about: the Ugyen Newly, a small, typically Bhutanese, hotel-restaurant; the Punsum, a small restaurant-bar run by the enterprising Karma who always knows how many 'mud puppies' (sweet tea and rum) you have drunk and how much fried rice you have gobbled up (this is the unofficial headquarters for the volunteer teachers, mostly Canadians, who have taken up their abode in Eastern Bhutan); and finally the Norkhyil Bar which is on the road leading to the dzong. Since Tashigang is the centre of a region where several international development projects are under way, including a big irrigation project, do not be too surprised to encounter quite a lot of Western faces.

Tashigang Dzong

The dzong stands at the extreme end of the spur, overhanging the Gamri River by more than 400 metres (1,300 feet). Unlike most other dzongs, it has only one courtyard. It serves as the administrative seat for the district. A Drukpa monastic community also occupies part of the dzong.

The dzong was built in 1659 by Pekar Choepel on orders from the Tongsa Penlop, Minjur Tenpa, after Eastern Bhutan had finally been conquered by the Drukpas. The dzong was named Tashigang, the 'fortress of the auspicious mountain'. The site had probably been occupied since the 12th century when Serdung, one of the kings of Eastern Bhutan, settled there and built a fort which he named Bengkhar.

The dzong commands a remarkable view over the surrounding countryside. Furthermore, it is practically impregnable, being protected on three sides by the river and ravines, and from behind by the mountain. The dzong was enlarged by the Fourth Desi of Bhutan, Tenzing Rabgye (r. 1680–94), and restored in around 1950 by Dasho Dopola.

The dzong includes a *Gonkhang* and several temples: the Lam

Lhakhang dedicated to the Eight Great Indian Masters of Buddhism; the Guru Lhakhang; the Tshogshing Lhakhang where the lineages of the Drukpa, Karmapa, Nyingmapa, and Dzogchen Nyingmapa lamas are represented; and the working hall of the monks—the Kunre. In the central tower are the *Gonkhang* dedicated to Mahakala; the Tshechu Lhakhang, where images of Guru Rinpoche and his Eight Manifestations are displayed for worship; and a meditation room.

If you have a car and a whole day at your disposal, it is worth making a trip to Chorten Kora by way of Gom Kora and Tashi Yangtse. The distance is 50 kilometres (31 miles), which takes about two hours by road.

Gom Kora

From Tashigang, you must go back down to Chagzam, the 'iron bridge' which was initially constructed by the Tibetan lama Thangton Gyelpo in the 15th century (see page 144). Here you take the road on the right which continues to follow the right bank of the Gamri River. The bottom of the gorge, formed by the denuded mountains, has an altitude of only 750 metres (2,460 feet) and it can get very hot.

At a point 24 kilometres (15 miles) from Tashigang, you can see the temple of Gom Kora on the right, set on a small alluvial plateau overlooking the river. Behind the little temple is an enormous black rock surrounded by rice fields and clumps of banana trees. It is like an oasis in an arid landscape.

Gom Kora is one of the famous places where Guru Rinpoche meditated in order to subdue a demon who dwelt in the big rock. It was vanquished after Guru Rinpoche turned himself into Garuda, the mythical griffin. The big rock contains the special feature of a 'sinner's path' through which a person must wriggle in order to expiate his or her sins. The little temple, which was established in the second half of the 17th century on orders from Minjur Tenpa, contains statues of Guru Rinpoche and Avalokiteshvara.

Two kilometres (just over one mile) after Gom Kora, the road arrives at Doksum, a village halting-place at a spot where two valleys come together. In certain seasons many of the women sit weaving outside their houses.

The left-hand road rises rapidly into the Tashi Yangtse valley which is full of rice fields. Six kilometres (four miles) from Doksum, a road branches off to the right and leads after eight kilometres to the ridge of

Ranthong Woom, at 2,100 metres (6,890 feet), where **Tsenkharla,** a ruined castle, stands. It is possible that this site was the one occupied in the ninth century by Prince Tsangma when he fled from Tibet to take refuge in Eastern Bhutan.

Tashi Yangtse Dzong

The road now enters a gorge filled with lush vegetation where you can sometimes see monkeys playing. Some 20 kilometres (12.5 miles) further, little Tashi Yangtse Dzong comes into view on the left, on the far side of the river. Tashi Yangtse Dzong, at an altitude of 1,850 metres (6,000 feet), was established just after the Drukpa conquest in around 1656 but was completely renovated in 1976. It looks more like a large house than a dzong.

In former times Tashi Yangtse was important because it lay on one of the caravan routes leading from Western and Central Bhutan. Instead of going from the Ura valley (Bumthang) to Tashigang by way of Mongar, muleteers would go from the Tang valley to Lhuntshi via the Rodong La Pass and from there to Tashi Yangtse before coming down to Tashigang. Today, Tashi Yangtse is an administrative subdivision of Tashigang.

Chorten Kora

Still heading northwards in the gorge, the road passes near a pretty little chorten, and four kilometres (two and a half miles) further it opens out into a cirque with terraced rice fields all along the gentle slopes. Near the river, the gigantic Chorten Kora finally appears.

Constructed in Nepalese style, this chorten is entirely whitewashed. It is said that after Guru Rinpoche had overcome the demons in the Bumdeling valley, where Chorten Kora forms the southern tip, he predicted that a great chorten and a temple would be built at this spot. Local tradition has it that a Bhutanese brought a model of this chorten from Nepal carved in a radish. The chorten is believed to have been founded by the 13th Je Khenpo, Yonten Thaye, in 1782. The chorten was restored at the time of the Second King, Jigme Wangchuck.

Under the porch leading to the little temple near the chorten, there is a very unusual rendering of the Wheel of Life. The main statue in the temple is of Guru Rinpoche.

A great religious festival takes place annually at Chorten Kora some time around and is followed by another one at Gom Kora. Masses of people from all parts of Eastern Bhutan come for these celebrations.

The South: Tashigang to Samdrup Jongkhar

The building of the 180 kilometres (119 miles) of road from Tashigang to Samdrup Jongkhar was begun in 1963 and finished (unpaved) in 1965. Today it is paved, and the trip south takes six hours.

The university town of **Kanglung** is located on a dry ridge 25 kilometres (16 miles) south of Tashigang. This is the only University of Bhutan, Sherubtse College, founded in 1978. The vast campus takes up most of the ridge and it houses more than 300 students in Arts, Sciences, and Commerce. The new Zangdopelri Temple was built in 1978 by the late Minister of Home Affairs, Tamshing Jagar. The students gather at a little restaurant called 'Phala', named after its owner. Close to Kanglung, the new zonal headquarters have been established at Yongphula.

For most of the trip the road goes from ridge to ridge, giving lovely glimpses of the surrounding countryside. Some 32 kilometres (20 miles) from Kanglung, the little village of **Khaling** nestles in a mountain hollow at 2,100 metres (6,890 feet) and here it is possible to see Bhutanese paper being made (see page 113). About ten kilometres (six miles) further, the road reaches its highest point, hardly 2,450 metres (about 8,000 feet), which is very low for Bhutan.

Some 20 kilometres (12.5 miles) from this high point, the road goes through the village of **Wamrong**, at 2,000 metres (6,560 feet), then passes the large Riserboo Hospital. Another 20 kilometres (12.5 miles) brings it to the place where a road branches off to Pemagatsel, a new district created a dozen years ago which covers part of an ancient region called Dungsam. Unlike Western Bhutan where the route goes over passes between one valley and another, the road here follows ridges almost the whole way and is marked throughout with stone chortens. Most of the dwellings are raised on stilts and roofed with bamboo matting.

The last ridge before the plain is reached 80 kilometres (50 miles) south of Wamrong. The town of **Deothang**, at 870 metres (2,850 feet), holds little of interest today except for a Technical Training College and the road maintenance headquarters for the east. However, up until 1865 there was an important fort standing on the ridge overlooking the road. This fort, known at the time as Dewangiri, was dismantled by the British during the Anglo-Bhutanese War of 1865. The British suffered a crushing defeat here and when they recaptured Dewangiri they hurried to destroy all trace of their earlier humiliation.

From here the road descends fairly rapidly to the plain through a dense tropical forest with an abundance of teak, bamboo and ferns.

Samdrup Jongkhar

This small frontier town is situated 18 kilometres (11 miles) from Deothang at the precise point where the mountains meet the plain. It is the headquarters of a district boasting a brand new dzong, although it is basically a town of small shopkeepers who serve all of Eastern Bhutan as far as Mongar and Lhuntshi. The tropical heat gives it a languid air which is accentuated by a lack of busy traffic. Apart from a tourist guesthouse standing in a garden, there are two hotels that are simple but adequate: the Shambala and the Mountain, which stand side by side. The rooms are more comfortable at the Mountain but the food is better at the Shambala.

Terms of Address

The male members of the royal family are called *Dasho* and the female members are called *Ashi*.

A Minister is called *Lyonpo* (pronounced 'Lonpo'); a vice-minister and all high ranking oficials including judges are called *Dasho*.

A common man with a certain amount of education and all teachers are called *Lopen*, but current convention styles the director of a department as *Dasho* out of respect, even if he has not received the red scarf; however, it would be incorrect to address him as *Dasho* in any official correspondence.

A monk is called either *Gelong* or *Lopen* according to his rank.

The wives of officials are called *Aum* (pronounced 'Am').

In Western Bhutan, villagers are called *Lopen* to be polite or if a person is educated; otherwise simply *Apa* or *Ap* followed by his first name.

To call a child you do not know, use *Alou* for a boy and *Bum* or *Bumo* for a girl. A married woman is addressed as *Am* or *Ama*. If people are old enough to be grandparents, they may be respectfully called *Agye* (for male) and *Angye* (for female).

In all cases these terms of address may be followed by the first name or the entire name of the person, but never directly by the last name.

Trekking and Mountaineering

General Advice

Trekking in Bhutan is very different from the kind of trekking you may be familiar with in other parts of the Himalayas. Here there is no easy-going trekking. There is an enormous gulf between accepting the idea of difficulties and actually being confronted with those difficulties on the ground.

Trekking in Bhutan is for true trekking adventurers.

The climate is much windier, damper and colder than Nepal. The changes in weather are spectacular, and when bad weather moves in it may last for several days. The valleys are narrow and once the clouds have swallowed them up, they seem unable to be dislodged. The monsoon arrives around the middle of June and does not really finish until the end of September, leaving only a short time for high-altitude treks above 4,000 metres (13,000 feet) before snow starts falling.

The starting points of treks in Bhutan are generally higher by about 1,000 metres (more than 3,000 feet) than in Nepal, a factor which should not be taken lightly.

Furthermore, it is unthinkable to go trekking alone or without the help of somebody who knows the way. Bhutan is sparsely inhabited, there are no detailed trekking maps and none of the routes are marked. It is easy to get lost by taking paths that peter out in pastures or forests, and there is no one to ask for directions.

The scarcity of houses means also that there is nowhere to spend a night and you must carry food for several days, as well as utensils. Even if you should happen upon a village, it is most unlikely that the inhabitants would agree to give up their own provisions, even for money. In some places rice is an excellent medium of exchange, but rice is unbelievably heavy to carry! Of course, there is always the option of using extreme restraint like the famous Robert Rieffel who went off on a seven-day trek with three kilos (six pounds) of raisins as his only source of food!

So, you do need to go with a guide, have a tent, and take provisions.

The Bhutanese who go along on the trek also need their rations of rice and hot peppers or else they won't walk or, at the very least, will be bad tempered. They loathe having to eat a snack lunch of sandwiches in the middle of the day; they settle down, light a fire and prepare a hot meal and cuss these crazy Westerners who are always hurrying to get on to some destination which they are going to reach sooner or later anyway.

The last point of difference with Nepal is the question of carrying the gear. In Bhutan there are no porters. Peasants have enough to do at home and do not need to hire themselves out as porters in order to live. They don't want to leave their fields during spring and autumn, their busiest seasons, which happen to coincide neatly with the trekking seasons.

Some people rent their horses or yaks as beasts of burden. However, they may be late, very late indeed, or have forgotten where they were supposed to meet the trekkers, or have any number of good excuses for not showing up. It all becomes more complicated when you realize that it is obligatory to change animals whenever you enter a new district, and the boundary lines may be in the middle of nowhere. A certain degree of patience and a philosophical outlook are necessary, especially if you are above 4,500 metres (14,500 feet) in some desolate area, far from any village or means of communication, and the yaks which should have been waiting for you are not.

Finally, the possibilities for evacuation are very limited and can take a lot of time because the Bhutan Tourism Corporation has to ask permission from the Indian army to use one of their helicopters and the latter, naturally, only fly in calm weather. Besides, the helicopter will not usually take more than two people at a time. The price is around US$600 an hour and you have to count on at least four or five hours for an evacuation.

Logistics and organization in Bhutan, in contrast to Nepal, are fairly complicated and should not be underestimated. However, if you want to walk through wild, unspoiled country, on routes where you will not meet a white face at every turn, Bhutan is the place to come.

What to Bring

The Bhutan Tourism Corporation takes charge of the material organization of all the treks. It also supplies tents and small mattresses, but you need to bring the following:

Plan to bring your own sleeping bag and personal equipment. Also bring several pairs of socks because paths often turn into rivers. Some people prefer to walk in rubber boots which keep their feet dry, but this is a personal matter and you should make sure you have boots which do not rub. Garments and shoes made of Goretex are ideal for Bhutan, while canvas desert boots (Pataugas) are totally useless because of the permanently wet paths. An umbrella is more useful than a raincoat, which makes you sweat, but this again is a matter of choice. In Thimphu you can buy excellent umbrellas which triple as sunshades and walking sticks, and also plastic sheets to cover your backpack. Wrap everything you own in plastic rubbish bags inside your backpack, and bring extras with you as this kind of bag is not available in Thimphu. Also bring toilet paper, a torch (flashlight)—the head-lamp type with a halogen bulb is the most practical for trekking—with extra batteries, all your own photographic equipment, a water flask, a multi-purpose pocket knife, a hat, glasses, sunscreen lotion, antibiotic ointment and an antihistamine cream for insect bites. A small plastic water-jug (available in Thimphu) is useful for washing in the stream.

As in Nepal, leeches can be a nuisance at certain seasons. You make them drop off by dabbing them with salt, and then disinfect the wound thoroughly. The bites are not painful but they bleed for a long time and can easily become infected.

Treks

The cost of a trek is around US$90 per day per person, which includes guide, horses, cook, food and tents.

It is not possible here to describe in detail every trek offered by the Bhutan Tourism Corporation but a little information about each one follows:

Druk Path This is a short, four-day trek which leads from Thimphu to Paro or vice versa, crossing the chain of mountains that separates the two valleys. Although there are very few houses to see, there are wonderful lakes teeming with fish at 4,000 metres (13,000 feet) and spectacular rhododendron that bloom in May. In winter and in clear weather, there is a magnificent view over the high Himalayas. This trek can be done in all seasons, but the best time is from October to the end of May.

Bumthang Trek This four-day trek is ideal for average walkers as the altitude does not go over 3,400 metres (11,155 feet). There are no views over the high peaks, but the trek crosses several villages and wends through the Bumthang countryside, giving an exceptional opportunity to be in contact with rural life. This trek can be done in October and November or from February to May.

Gantey Gompa Trek This is another good trek for average walkers. It takes three days and gives you a chance to visit the isolated valleys of

Gantey Gompa/Phobjika, Gogona and Kothoka. Although this trek can be done any time from October to May, it is best done in April when the rhododendron is flowering.

Punakha Trek and Samtengang Trek These two treks are perfect for beginners. They take only three or four days, altitudes are low, at 1,500–2,000 metres (5,000–6,500 feet), and they go through several villages.

Merak Sakteng Trek This five-day trek goes from Tashigang in Eastern Bhutan into the isolated Merak and Sakteng valleys at 3,000 metres (9,850 feet). The trek, meant only for good walkers, is especially beautiful in May when the rhododendron is out. These valleys are famous for their population of semi-nomadic yak-herders, who differ completely from other Bhutanese both in language and costume. This trek is not recommended in winter partly because of the cold but partly because so many of the inhabitants migrate southwards at that time of year. The best months are May, September and October.

Jhomolhari Trek This is a superb seven-day trek for strong walkers It goes into Northern Bhutan to the land of yak-herders, to the base of Mount Jhomolhari, at 7,316 metres (24,000 feet) and on to remote Lingshi Dzong. There are fabulous views of the mountains and exceptional flora. You will encounter many yak-herders but few villages. The maximum altitude is 4,900 metres (16,000 feet). This trek can be done from the end of April to November, with the possibility of snow during these two months.

Rather than proceeding straight to Thimphu via the Yele La Pass, at 4,900 metres (16,000 feet), to Shodu and Barotag, I would strongly recommend that you take the same route back, coming and going by way of Paro; the path from Shodu to Thimphu is awful and can really spoil the trek. The best time to go is October, but August and September are the best months for seeing the flora.

Laya Trek This trek takes about ten days and goes from the sub-tropical Punakha valley, at 1,300 metres (4,265 feet), up to the high Laya region, at 4,000 metres (over 13,000 feet), where yak-herders live at the foot of Mount Masang Gang, at 7,200 metres (23,620 feet). The route passes by hot springs and Gasa Dzong, and through different levels of vegetation before reaching the village of Laya, where the women wear black yak-hair costumes and strange, conical bamboo hats. This trek combines a variety of landscapes, villages, and beautiful views of the peaks. It can be done in May, June, September, October and November.

It is not advisable to go during the monsoon because leeches swarm in the jungles between Punakha and Gasa.

Lunana Trek This is the most difficult and the longest trek (18 days) and it requires not only excellent health but also a high spirit of adventure. It starts off taking the same route as the Laya Trek. After reaching Laya, it turns eastwards and crosses the Ganglakarchung Pass, at 5,100 metres (16,730 feet), into the Lunana region where habitation is concentrated in the villages of Thega and Chezo. It is the most difficult region of Bhutan to reach, lying at 4,000 metres (13,000 feet) at the foot of peaks that soar up to 7,000 metres (23,000 feet). The inhabitants are farmer-herders who are famous for their difficult character. The trek then heads south, and after crossing the Rinchenzoe Pass, at 5,220 metres (17,125 feet), it hits the tarmac road at the Nikkarchu bridge. The trek can be done from mid-June to mid-October, but there is always the possibility of snow.

Snowman Trek The Lunana Trek can be combined with the Jhomolhari Trek to become the Snowman Trek, a long trek taking more than three weeks which is considered to be one of the most difficult in the world. It covers a distance of 356 kilometres (221 miles), crosses eight passes, three of which are over 5,000 metres (16,400 feet), and stays at an average altitude of 4,000 metres (over 13,000 feet).

For more information about treks, write in English to the Trekking Manager, Bhutan Tourist Corporation, PO Box 15, Thimphu, Bhutan (Asia); Telex (0890) 217 BTC TPU.

Mountaineering

Bhutan has only been open for mountaineering since 1983. All mountain climbing is tightly controlled by the government, which only gives permission to two or three teams a year. There are 21 peaks over 7,000 metres (23,000 feet) but only certain ones are open. The cost per day is the same as for trekking but you also have to pay climbing fees. Bhutanese personnel will not go beyond the base camp, and climbers are totally responsible for organizing the climb.

A booklet entitled *Bhutan Mountaineering Regulations* is available from the Bhutan Tourist Corporation. It is best to write giving the exact date of the proposed climb and ask which mountains are open for that year.

Peaks below 6,000 metres (19,700 feet) can be climbed without prior permission in the course of treks.

Bhutan's mountains are not as high as those in Nepal but they are reputed to be difficult, due undoubtedly to the harsher climatic conditions and to the fact that serious reconnaissance still remains to be done.

National Parks

Bhutan is very conscious of the need to protect its environment. Starting its development later than most countries means that Bhutan has been able to learn from the mistakes of others. Its emphasis is on the conservation of forests and rare flora and fauna. Many animals are protected: musk deer, takin, red panda, black-necked crane, blue sheep, snow leopard, golden langur, etc. A Royal Society for the Protection of Nature has been established which works with the Forest Department and the World Wide Fund for Nature (WWF). The latter gives funds and technical assistance for developing parks and nature reserves, and helps to promote an awareness of ecology among children.

Parks and Nature Reserves

Jigme Dorji Wangchuck Sanctuary, 7,813 sq km (over 3,000 sq miles), created in 1974. It occupies the whole northern strip of Bhutan. All the other reserves are in the southern strip of Bhutan, near the Indian border.

Manas Wildlife Sanctuary, 463 sq km (179 sq miles), created in 1966. This park is the pilot project for the Royal Society for the Protection of Nature and the WWF.

Mochu Wildlife Reserve, 175 sq km (68 sq miles), created in 1974.

Pochu Wildlife Reserve, 140 sq km (54 sq miles), created in 1974.

Sinchula Reserved Forest, 80 sq km (31 sq miles), created in 1984.

Pochu Wildlife Reserve, 140 sq km (54 sq miles), created in 1984.

Sinchula Reserved Forest, 80 sq km (31 sq miles), created in 1974.

Sumar Wildlife Reserve, 160 sq km (62 sq miles), created in 1984.

Dungsam Wildlife Reserve, 180 sq km (70 sq miles), created in 1984.

Neoli Wildlife Sanctuary, 40 sq km (15 sq miles), created in 1984.

Khaling Wildlife Reserve, 233 sq km (90 sq miles), created in 1974.

Namgyel Wangchuck Reserve, 195 sq km (75 sq miles), created in 1974.

Zhoshing Reserved Forest, 5 sq km (2 sq miles), created in 1984 to protect the species of bamboo that is used for making traditional bows fo archery.

Two more reserves in the centre of the country have been proposed: the Black Mountain Reserve, southeast of Wangdi and southwest of Tongsa, and the Thumsing La Reserve, which would stretch from Namning in Eastern Ura to the Ura valley in Bumthang.

Some Bhutanese Customs

A whole book could be written about Bhutanese customs, but here there is only room to pick out those that may be problematic to you.

Showing Respect

As in most other Asian countries, a sense of hierarchy and respect for superiors or older people plays an important part and conditions people's attitudes. This respect is mixed with awe when it comes to religious personages. It shows itself in various ways in daily life: the body inclined slightly forward if one is standing up; legs held straight against the chair, knees covered with the ceremonial scarf when sitting down; right hand placed in front of the mouth to avoid defiling the air with one's breath when speaking; no smoking. Using the word 'la' at the end of a sentence (even in English!) is another sign of respect.

Important religious figures are greeted in the same way as gods, with three prostrations. It is good to leave small offerings of money in temples and monasteries, just as it is advisable not to speak too loudly and to take off one's shoes as a sign of respect for the holiness of these places. Umbrellas and hats are not allowed in monasteries or dzongs.

The head is considered the most sacred part of the body and the feet are the most impure, which means in practice that you must never touch another person's head, nor extend your feet out in front of you. Thus, when sitting on the ground, you should sit cross-legged, or with legs folded to one side if the first position is too uncomfortable, and avoid crossing your legs when sitting on a chair.

Face

The rules of politeness and honour are complex and some of their manifestations may cause you bewilderment. For instance, it is impolite to say 'no', so a Bhutanese will answer any question in the affirmative, or he may evade it altogether if he sees that he is going to have to say 'no' and thus lose face in front of his questioner, or make the questioner lose face.

It is also bad manners to appear too sure of oneself or too firm in one's opinions since that leaves no honourable way out in case of disagreement or failure. The word 'perhaps' and conditional clauses are therefore widely used. A suggestion is more congenial to the Bhutanese way of thinking than a statement.

Exchanging Presents

Exchanging presents is much more important here than in the West. There are three ways of designating a gift according to social status: from an inferior to a superior, from a superior to an inferior, or between people of the same rank. A present should always be reciprocated after a certain length of time unless it came from a superior. When food is given in a receptacle, the latter must be returned with some sweets (candy) in it because an empty container infers an absence of prosperity. Gifts should never be opened in front of the donors, so do not expect your gift to be opened and appreciated in your presence. It is not the custom to send a thank-you note.

When the great events of life take place (marriage, promotion, death) it is the traditional custom to present three—or five, seven or nine depending on the status of the donor—pieces of cloth called *zon* accompanied by a white scarf, a *kata*. Today, the white scarf is still obligatory but some people prefer to give money in an envelope instead of the pieces of fabric, which entail a very good knowledge of the proper ceremonial practices.

It is also the custom to give presents when somebody is leaving on a trip. This can be anything from a bottle of local alcohol to a fine piece of cloth or a little pocket money for the children.

Host and Guest

To receive a guest without offering a cup of tea or a glass of alcoholic drink is the height of rudeness. In a private home, a guest should take at least two cups or glasses (sips can suffice) of whatever beverage is offered. You should not accept what is offered too quickly. If you are playing host, don't take a guest's initial refusal at face value, but go on insisting.

When you are invited to a meal with a family at home, different drinks with appetizers will be served before the meal (see Food and Drink, page 30) and this 'cocktail hour' may last for more than an hour. Very often, if you are visiting a humble family that you do not know very well, the hosts will not stay with their guests but will disappear until it is time to serve the meal. Much to their surprise, guests are left alone in the 'parlour', which is most likely to be the private chapel. The master of the house may then be present at the meal but not eat with the guests and there is no necessity to make conversation during the meal as there is in the West. Eating is a serious business which does not allow for distractions, so conversation is supposed to take place before it starts.

When the meal is over, guests do not sit around and chat as they do in the West, but get up and go almost as soon as they have swallowed their last mouthful. This rule holds for official banquets as well, and the guest of honour should always be the one to give a signal when it is time to leave or nobody else will dare to move. Since many foreigners do not know about this custom of leaving as soon as the meal is finished, the situation can become a little awkward as an air of impatience subtly overtakes the Bhutanese guests.

Attending a Ceremony

One of the most important official customs, obligatory for both Bhutanese men and women, is the wearing of ceremonial scarves to visit dzongs or monasteries or to attend official ceremonies.

The most common official ceremonies are of two kinds. The first is a ceremony of blessing and prosperity, called *Shugdrel*, performed by monks. The second, conducted by a layman or a monk, is a ceremony of propitiation to the local protective deities, the *Marchang*. A vessel filled with local beer (*chang*), with four horns made of butter on its rim, is placed on a tripod. A local official or monk then takes a little of the alcoholic liquid in a ladle and after raising it towards the sky and saying a prayer he pours a small amount of it on the ground. Then a prayer flag is blessed.

Practical Information

Useful Addresses

Bhutan Tourist Corporation PO Box 159, Thimphu, Bhutan.
Tel. 2647, 2854, 2479. Telex: (0890) 217 BTC TPU BT.
The Royal Bhutanese Embassy Chandragupta Marg, Chanakyapuri,
New Delhi 10021, India. Tel. 699 227/8. Telex: 31-2220 Druk In.
The Royal Bhutanese Embassy House No. 58, Road No. 3A,
Dhanmondi R.A. Dhaka, Bangladesh. Tel. 505 418.

Druk Air

Bhutan: Chorten Lam, Thimphu. Tel. 2215. Telex: (0890) 219
Drukair.

India: Malbros Travels, 403 Nirmal Towers, Barakhamba Road,
New Delhi 10001. Tel. 332 2859. Telex: 31-61773.
Druk Air Corporation Calcutta, 48 Tivoli Court, 1A
Ballygunj Circular Road, Calcutta 700019, India.
Tel. 441 301/2.

Nepal: Shambala Travels, Durbar Marg, Kathmandu.
Tel. 225 166. Telex: 2627.

Thailand: Thai International, 485 Silom Road, Bangkok.
Tel. (02) 233 3810.

US: Bhutan Travel Service, 120 East 56th Street, Suite
1430, New York, NY 10022, USA. Tel. (212) 838 6382.
Telex: 220 896 BTS UR.

Glossaries

Historical Figures, Saints and Others

Acaryas Religious masters of India

Arhats The first persons to attain the state of Buddhahood; called 16 Arhats but usually 18

Ashi Kesang Queen Mother of Bhutan

Ashi Pemadechen One of the Royal Grandmothers

Ashi Phuntsho Choegron One of the Royal Grandmothers

Barawa (1320–91) Founder of the Barawas

Bonpo Dragtshel First active Terton

Chagzampa Builder of bridges; also see Thangton Gyelpo

Changchub Gyeltsen (Jigme Kundrel) Disciple of great Dzogchen master, Jigme Lingpa

Choeden Zangmo Great grandfather of Pema Lingpa; founded Dametsi monastery

Dawa Penjor One of the Penlops of Paro

Dorje Droloe Terrifying manifestation of Guru Rinpoche

Dorje Lingpa (1356–1405) Nyingmapa saint and philosopher of Dzogchen sect

Drubthob The 'realized one'; also see Thangton Gyelpo

Drukpa Kunley (1455–1529) The 'divine madman'

Gampopa Obtained teachings on Buddhahood from the Mahasiddhas

Garab Dorje The first to receive the Dzogchen teachings directly from Buddha Vajrasattva

Gongzim Sonam Tobgye Son of Kazi Ugyen Dorje

Guru Dragpo Terrifying form of Guru Rinpoche in red

Guru Rinpoche Principal aspect of Padmasambhava, converted Bhutan to Buddhism in the eighth century.

Gyelchok Brother of Gyelzom; founded Paro Dzong

Gyelwa Lhanangpa (1164–1224) Founder of the Lhapa school

Gyelzom Brother of Gyelchok

Jampel Zhenyen Direct disciple of Garab Dorje and holder of the Dzogchen teachings

Jamyang Khyentse Wangpo (1820–92) Eminent Nyingmapa lama

Jigme Dorje Wangchuck Third King of Bhutan (r. 1952–72)

Jigme Lingpa (1730–98) Great Dzogchen philosopher

Jigme Namgyel Father of Ugyen Wangchuck

Jigme Singye Wangchuck Present King, Fourth King of Bhutan, ascended in 1972

Jigme Wangchuck Second King of Bhutan

Karmapa Choedra Gyamtsho (1454–1506)
Kazi Ugyen Dorje Adviser to Ugyen Wangchuck
Kongtrul Lodroe Thaye (1813–99) Eminent Nyingmapa lama
Kunga Gyatso 12th Desi
Kunga Nyingpo (b. 1557) Brother of Choeden Zangmo
Kunga Wangpo Son of Pema Lingpa
Kunzang Tenpe Nyima (1843–99) Eighth reincarnation of Pema Lingpa
Kunzang Wangdu Last Shongar Dzongpon
Langchen Pelkyi Singye Pupil of Guru Rinpoche; meditated near Takstang
Langdarma Tibetan king, assassinated in AD 842
Lhapa Branch of the Drigung Kagyupa school; established pre-Drukpa
Loden Chogse One of the eight manifestations of Guru Rinpoche
Longchen Rabjampa (1308–63) A Nyingmapa saint and philosopher of the
Dzogchen sect
Lorepa (1187–1250) Drukpa Kagyupa lama
Machig Labdoenma (1055–1145 or 53) Famous Tibetan yogin
Mahasiddhas 84 Indian saints; first to receive Tantric teachings
Marpa Obtained teachings on Buddhahood from the Mahasiddhas
Maudgalayayana Disciple of Buddha
Milarepa (1040–1123) 12th-century poet-saint; obtained teachings from the
Mahasiddhas
Minjur Tenpa Third Desi of Bhutan; previously Tongsa Penlop
Namkhe Nyingpo Disciple of Guru Rinpoche
Ngagi Wangchuck (1517–54) Great-great-grandfather of Shabdrung
Ngawang Namgyel
Ngawang Choegyel 14th Drukpa hierarch; great-grandfather of
Shabdrung Ngawang Namgyel
Ngawang Kunzang Dorje (1680–1723) Fourth reincarnation of Pema Lingpa
Ngawang Trinley Great monk from Si'ula Monastery in Punakha region
Nyangrel Nyima Oezer Discovered the Kagye texts at Memorial Chorten
Nyima Oezer One of the eight manifestations of Guru Rinpoche
Old Man of Long Life Chinese Taoist god of longevity; adopted into
Bhutanese popular iconography
Padmasambhava One of the eight manifestations of Guru Rinpoche
Pekar Juney First Je Khenpo
Pelkyi Dorje A monk who assassinated anti-Buddhist Tibetan king,
Langdarma in AD 842
Pema Gyelpo One of the eight manifestations of Guru Rinpoche
Pema Karpo (1527–92) Famous Drukpa scholar
Pema Lingpa (1450–1521) Reincarnation of Guru Rinpoche and Longchen
Rabjampa
Pema Trinley Founder of Gantey Gompa; grandson of Pema Lingpa
Phadampa Sangye (d. 1117) Tibetan saint

Phajo Drugom Shigpo (1208–76)   Founder of Drugpa Kagyupa school in Bhutan

Rakshas   Aids to the God of the Dead

Relpachen   King of Tibet

Rigzin Khamsum Yondrol   Great Nyingmapa lama

Rinzing Nyingpo   Nyingmapa master

Sariputra   Other main disciple of Buddha; also see Maudgalayayana

Sendhaka, King   Invited Guru Rinpoche to Bhutan; first to convert to Buddhism in Bumthang

Sengye Drathok   One of the eight manifestations of Guru Rinpoche

Serdung   Twelfth King of Eastern Bhutan

Shabdrung Jigme Choegy (1862–1904)

Shabdrung Ngawang Namgyel (1594–1651)   Unified Bhutan under Drukpa authority

Shakya Rinchen   Ninth Je Khenpo

Shakya Sengye   One of the eight manifestations of Guru Rinpoche

Sheldrup Oezer   34th Je Khenpo

Sherab Gyeltshen   25th Je Khenpo (r. 1836–39)

Shinje Choekyi Gyelpo   God of the Dead

Sonam Drugyel   A Tongsa Penlop

Sonam Gyeltshen   Nyingmapa lama of Kathogpa branch

Songtsen Gampo   King of Tibet

Tenpe Nyima   Grandson of Pema Lingpa (not same as below)

Tenpe Nyima   Shabdrung Ngawang Namgyel's father

Tenzing Drugda   Second Desi; half brother of Shabdrung Ngawang Namgyel

Tenzing Legpe Dondrub   Second Tulku of Gantey

Tenzing Rabgye (1638–96)   Fourth Desi (r. 1680–94)

Thangton Gyelpo (1385–1464)   Tibetan lama; also see Chagzampa and Drubthob

Trakthung Dujom Lingpa   Previous incarnation of Dujom Rinpoche

Trisong Detsen   King of Tibet

Tsangpa Gyare Yeshe Dorje (1161–1211)   Founded the Drukpa Kagyupa school in Tibet; prophesied the conversion to Buddhism of the southern valleys

Tshering Penjor   Paro Penlop

Tshokye Dorje   One of the eight manifestations of Guru Rinpoche

Tshokye Dorje   Tongsa Penlop

Tsondru Gyeltsen   Jakar Dzongpon

Ugyen Lingpa (1329–67)

Ugyen Wangchuck   Last Tongsa Penlop; became First King of Bhutan in 1907

Ugyen Wangdi   Tsokye Dorje's grandson, and a Jakar Dzongpon

Umze Tenzing Drugye   First Desi

Yeshe Tsogyel   One of Guru Rinpoche's consorts

Yonten Thaye   13th Je Khenpo

Deities in the Buddhist Pantheon of Bhutan

Akshobya (Mitrugpa)
Amitabha (Oepame) Buddha of Infinite Light
Amitayus (Tshempume) Buddha of Infinite Life
Amogasiddhi (Donyondrub)
Avalokiteshvara (Chenrezig) Bodhisattva of Compassion
Avalokiteshvara Mahakarunika (Thuje Chenpo)
Avalokiteshvara with 1,000 eyes and 1,000 hands (Chagton Chenton)
Avalokiteshvara with 11 heads (Chuchije)
Buddha (Sangye)
Cakrasamvara (Demcho Khorlo Dompa)
Dorje Legpa Protector of Buddhism
Ekajati Protector of Buddhism
Genyen Dorje Dradul Protector of Buddhism
Ging Part of Guru Rinpoche's retinue
Gompo Maning One aspect of Mahakala
Gonpo Jarodonchen Mahakala with a raven's head
Guyasamaja (Sangdu)
Hayagriva (Tamdrin) Drukpa tutelary deity
Hevajra (Kyedorje)
Humrel Gompo Guardian deity of Paro
Jhomo Goddess
Jowo Buddha as a prince aged eight
Kubera/Vaisravana (Namthoese/Namse) God of Wealth
Kyebu Lungten Protector of Buddhism; guardian deity of the Four Valleys of
    Bumthang
Maha... (Palden Lhamo)
Mahakala (Yeshe Gompo) Protective deity of Bhutan
Maitreya (Jampa)
Manjushri (Jampelyang) Bodhisattva
Menlha The Medicine Buddha
Pehar Guardian deity
Prajna Paramita
Rahu (Za) The elipse deity
Ratnasambhava (Rinchenjune)
Samanysbhadra (Kuntu Zangpo) The supreme Buddha of the Nyingmapa
Shanpa Marnak
Shanpa Ngamo
Shelging Karpo Deity of Kurjey
Shinje Choekyi Gyelpo God of the Dead
Sogdu Divinity from Lhamo's entourage

Tara (Drolma) Feminine emanation of Avalokiteshvara
Tsheringma Goddess of Long Life
Tsholing Terrifying deities who are seen as protectors of the religion
Ushnishavijaya (Tsugtor Namgyelma)
Vairocana (Namparnanze)
Vajrabhairava, Yamantaka (Dorje Jigje)
Vajradhara (Dorjechang)
Vajrakila (Phurpa/Phurbu) The dagger deity
Vajrapani (Chana Dorje)
Vajrapani Bodhisattva
Vajrasattva (Dorje Sempa)
Vajravarahi (Dorje Phagmo)
Yak Du Nagpo Protector of Buddhism; guardian deity of the Ura Valley
Yama
Yamantaka

Dzongkha Words

Abhidharmakosha Fifth-century text by Indian scholar Vasubandhu
Agye Term of address for a male grandparent
Alou Term of address for a boy
Am, Ama Term of address for a married woman
Angye Term of address for a female grandparent
Anim Nun
Apa, Ap Term of address in Western Bhutan
Ara Common alcoholic drink
Ashi Title given to women of the Royal Family; comparable to princess
Atsara Clown
Aum Term of address in Western Bhutan
Banchung Small double basket made of bamboo
Bardo Intermediary state between death and rebirth
Bla Life energy
Bodhisattva (Changchub Sempa) Enlightened Being; a person who has the spiritual possibility of obtaining Buddhahood but who chooses to reincarnate in order to help release others from the Cycle of Reincarnation.
Brgyad Eight, pronounced 'gye'
Brogpa Yak-breeder and -herder
Bum, Bumo Term of address for a girl
Bumpa Water vase
Bundi Bags
Bura Bhutanese raw silk
Buta Noodles

Cham Religious dances

Chang Alcoholic drink made from grain

Changkhang Bar; wine shop

Chasipangkhep Ceremonial cloths

Chetrum There are 100 *chetrums* in one *ngultrum*

Chhu Water, river

Choesham Private chapel in the interior of a house

Choeshe Religious song, dance

Chogu Ritual or religious ceremony

Chorten Buddhist funerary monument (*Stupa* in Sanskrit)

Chos skad The religious language, Classical Tibetan

Churpi Yak cheese

Dametsi Ngacham Well-known dance

Damulu Small drum

Dasho A non-transferable title given by the King to certain officials; carries a red scarf and a sword

Datsi Soft fresh cheese, small and round

Dego Traditional sport played by monks

Desi (formerly called *Deb Raja* by the British) Temporal Ruler of Bhutan at the time of the Shabdrungs (1651–1905)

Doe Construction of coloured thread

Doma A chew composed of areca nut, lime and betel leaf

Dorje (*Vajra* in Sanskrit) Diamond-thunderbolt

Dorje Lopen Principal assistant to the Je Khenpo, in charge of religious teachings. One of four high Lopens masters

Dranyen Cham Dance celebrating the founding and spreading of the Drukpa school

Dranyen Seven-stringed lute

Drape Lopen Master of grammar

Dratshang Lhentshog Independent organ of the state clergy, headed by the Je Khenpo

Drilbu Bell

Dromchoe Festival dedicated to Yeshe Gompo (Mahakala) or Palden Lhamo

Druk Dragon

Druk Yul The Dzongkha name for Bhutan

Drukpa Name given to the mountain Bhutanese from the Central Himalayas who practise Tantric Buddhism

Drukpa The official religious school of Bhutan

Duar An Indian word meaning 'gate', which refers to the traditional 18 entrances to Bhutan from the plains of India

Dungchen Musical instrument. A long trump

Dungkhag Sub-district

Dungpa Assistant administrator of a district

Durdag A dance
Dzong Fortress, seat of civil and religious power
Dzongdag Literally 'dzong master'. District Administrator
Dzongde *Chichab* Zonal Administrator
Dzongde Zone, made up of four districts
Dzongkha Bhutan's national language, also called Zhungkha
Dzongkhag District
Dzongpon The old term for Dzongdag, head of a dzong, now no longer used
Eze Spicy Bhutanese salad
Gang Mountain
Garuda (*Jachung*) Griffin
Gelong Ordained celibate monk; wears monk's robes
Gesasip Flattened maize
Getre Retired monk
Ging A dance
Ging dang Tsholing The Dance of the Ging and the Tsholing
Go Men's costume
Gomchen A half-religious, half-lay person
Gompa Monastery
Gonda Secret teachings of the deity Gondu
Gondomaru Dish with scrambled eggs cooked in butter
Gondu One of the three principal cycles of the teachings of the Nyingmapa
    school. The other two are the *Phurpa* and the *Kagye*.
Gonkhang Temple of terrifying and protective deities
Gup Village headman
Guru Tschen The Dance of the Eight Manifestations of Guru Rinpoche
Gyaling Oboe
Gyelpo Losar Official lunar New Year
Hema Chillies
Hemadatsi Hot peppers with cheese; Bhutan's national dish
Je Khenpo Head Abbot of Bhutan; head of the religious Drukpa Kagyupa
    school of Bhutan
Kabne Ceremonial scarf for men
Kabze A dessert
Kada/Kata White scarf presented at official occasions and ceremonies
Kadrinche Thank you. (There is no word for 'please'. In Dzongkha, a
    different form of the verb denotes politeness.)
Kagye Secret teachings of Guru Rinpoche
Kalacakra (*Dukikhorlo/Dukhor*) Wheel of Time
Kangling Trumpet made from a femur
Karma Consequences of actions in previous lives
Kata Ceremonial white scarves
Kera Belt

Keyshey Game of strength between men

Kha Language

Khamar White scarf worn by *Gups*

Khilkhor Master of arts

Khyil Khor (Mandala) Mystic cosmic diagram

Kira Woman's dress

Koenyer Caretaker, sacristan of a temple

Koma Clasps attaching a woman's dress at the shoulders

Kousouzangpo Hello; literally, 'You are well'

Kudun Master of discipline

Kule Buckwheat pancakes

Kunre Monks' assembly hall

Kuru A game like darts

Kushutara Fancy woman's dress

Kyetsi Horoscope

La Kind of soul

La Mountain pass

La, lasso la Polite term for finishing a sentence

Lags Yes, pronounced 'la'

Lam Neten Abbot of a regional Drukpa monk-body

Lama 'Religious master'. May be celibate or married, may wear monk's robes or not

Lha Divinity or deity

Lhakhang Temple, sanctuary

Lhasang Purification ceremony at birth of child

Lim Flute

Lomba Holiday in Paro and Ha: last day of tenth lunar month and first two days of 11th lunar month

Lopen (pronounced *Lopoen*) Literally 'master'; title given to anybody who has received a traditional education, but most particularly certain learned monks

Lung Collective initiation by a great master into one special text or cycle of texts

Lyonpo (pronounced *Lonpo*) Minister; wears an orange scarf and a sword

Makara Giant fish

Mandala (*khyil khor* in Dzongkha) Mystic cosmic diagram

Mantra Inscription, verbal formulae with precise objectives

Marchang Ceremony of propitiation to the local protective deity

Masheer A river fish, sometimes compared to tropical salmon

Mathra Check woollen material

Mensimathra Kind of material

Mewang Blessing by fire

Mithun Native bull with spectacular horns

Momos Tibetan 'ravioli'

Nadja Indian-style tea

Naga Dragon-snake

Namshe Conscious principle, which transmigrates when the human body dies

Nga Double-sided drum

Ngalongs A name given to Western Bhutanese

Ngultrum (Nu.) Unit of currency, contains 100 *chetrum*

Nirvana State where all suffering has been annihilated

Nyingmapa Important religious school in Central and Eastern Bhutan; founded by Guru Rinpoche in the eighth century.

Nyinlo New Year in the Eastern regions

Onju A woman's blouse

Onsham Fancy woman's dress

Pa School, sect

Pan Chew like *doma* used in the south of Bhutan

Patang Straight sword worn by Dashos and other dignitaries

Pchie Roasted flour

Pechung Bags

Penlop Title given to the governors of the three big provinces of Paro, Tongsa and Daga from 1651 to 1905. No longer used except for the title of Tongsa Penlop which is usually conferred on the Crown Prince.

Phagshapa Strips of pork-fat

Pholey Moley Dance of the Princes and Princesses

Phurpa (Kila) Ritual dagger

Phurpa Secret teachings of the deity Phurpa

Piwang Two-stringed viol

Pooche Printed flannelette

Pundo Game played by laymen

Rabde Regional Drukpa monastic community

Rachung Ceremonial scarf for women

Raksha Marcham Dance of the Judgement of the Dead

Resho Cotton paper

Rimro Ritual or religious ceremony

Rolmo Cymbals; also see *silnyen*

Serda Procession at the end of the Punakha Dromchoe

Serthra Check woollen material

Seudeu Kind of cheese

Seudja Tea churned with salt and butter

Shabale Fried dumplings

Shabdrung Title given to the reincarnations of Shabdrung Ngawang Namgyel

Shacham Dance of the Four Stags

Shanag A dance that purifies and protects

Sharchopkha Name incorrectly given to the language of Eastern Bhutan. Its real name is Tsangla.

Shawa Shachhi Dance of the Stags and the Hunting Dogs
Shedra Monastic school
Sherey parey Game of strength between two men
Shugdrel Ceremony of blessing and prosperity
Silnyen Cymbals
Sip Flattened rice
Sog Life principle
Sogshing 'Tree of Life' of an image which is inscribed with prayers
Soksom Javelin game
Sonam Losar Old agricultural New Year
Supari A chew like *doma* used in the south of Bhutan
Sutras Scriptures
Tahr A mountain goat
Takin A high valley animal
Taktsang A tiger's lair
Tantras Body of esoteric texts
Terma Religious treasure
Terton 'Discoverer of religious treasures', *termas*, which were hidden by
  Guru Rinpoche to be discovered by a predestined person for the benefit of all
  beings
Tey Summit
Thangka Religious banner; may be painted, embroidered or appliquéd
The Tanjur The Commentaries of Buddha
Thondrol (Thangdroel) Huge religious banner that brings 'liberation by sight'
Thukpa Noodle soup
Toego Woman's jacket or man's shirt
Torma Sacrificial cake offered to gods during ceremonies
Trimomo Steamed bread
Tsampa Roasted flour; also see *pchie*
Tsangthra Check woollen material
Tsasho Bamboo paper
Tsechu 'Tenth Day'. Religious festival honouring Guru Rinpoche
Tsenyi Lopen Master of philosophy
Tsho Lake
Tshongkhang Shop, store
Tsipe Lopen Master of astrology
Tulku Reincarnation
Tungam A dance
Umdze Choirmaster
Utse Central tower of a dzong
Vinaya Texts laying down the rules of monastic discipline
Wang Collective blessing
Yangpe Lopen Master of songs and liturgy

Yatra Rolls of patterned woollen cloth
Zangdopelri The heaven of Guru Rinpoche
Zao Toasted rice
Zem Rectangular basket with lid to be slung over flanks of animals
Zi White-lined, etched agate
Zon Piece of cloth presented as traditional custom

Common Trees and Plants

Botanical Name	Local Name	English Name
Abies densa	Dunashing	Fir
Acer	Chalam	Maple
Aconitum	Tsenduk	Aconite
Albezzia	Kabasisis	Silk Tree (in tea plantations)
Alnus	Gamashing	Alder
Areca	Domashing	Areca nut
Artemisia	Khempa	Wormwood
Cannabis satatavia	Keha	Hashish
Castanopsis	Sokey	Chestnut
Cinnamomum	Patashing	Camphor
Citrus	Humpa	Lemon
Cornus capitata	Phatsishing	Dogwood
Cosmos	Jaga Meto	Cosmos
Cupressus	Tsende	Cypress
Daphne	Deshing Nap	Daphne (for paper)
Datura	Dushing	Datura
Delonix regia	Gulmohan	Flame Tree
Diospyros kaki	Andey	Japanese Persimmon
Duabanga	Lampatey	—
Edgeworthia	Deshing Kap	Edgeworthia
Erythrina	Chatseshing	Coral Tree
Eucalyptus	—	Eucalyptus
Ficus elastica	—	Rubber
Ficus religiosa	Pipal	Pipal
Gerardina hitrpphylla	Zocha	Nettle
Gentiana	Pangen meto	Gentian
Hibiscus	Hibiscus	Hibiscus
Juniperus	Shup	Juniper
Larix	Booshing	Larch
Magnolia globosa	Magnolia	Magnolia
Oroxyllum indica	Tsampakha meto	—

Picea smithania	Bashing	Norway Spruce
Pinus roxburghii	Theythong	Chir Pine
Pinus wallichii	Tomphushing	Himalayan Blue Pine
Populus	Kashing	Poplar
Primula	Chukameto	Primrose
Quercus	Jeeshing/Gomshing Sishing	Oak
Rhododendron	Etometo	Rhododendron
Rhus	Chokashing	Asiatic Sumac (lacquer tree)
Salix	Changma/Lambashing	Willow
Shorea robusta	Sal	Sal
Tecoma grandis	Teak	Teak
Tsuga domosa	Sershing	Hemlock
Zanthoxyllum	Thinye	Szechuan Pepper

Bibliography and Recommended Reading

**Recommended reading

Adams, Barbara S. *Traditional Bhutanese Textiles* (Bangkok, Orchid Books, 1984).

Aris, Michael. *Bhutan: The Early History of a Himalayan Kingdom* (Warminster, Serindia, 1979).

Aris, Michael. *Views of Medieval Bhutan, The Diary and Drawings of Samuel Davis, 1783* (London/Washington, 1982).**

Asian Culture Centre for UNESCO 'Bhutan', *Asian Culture* No. 35, Summer/ Autumn 1983 (Tokyo, 1983).

Barker, David K. *Designs of Bhutan* (Bangkok, White Lotus, 1985).

Bartholomew, Mark. *Thunder Dragon Textiles from Bhutan* (Tokyo, 1985).

Berry, Steven K. *The Thunder Dragon Kingdom: A Mountaineering Expedition to Bhutan* (Marlborough/Seattle, 1988).

Blofield, John. *The Way of Power: A Practical Guide to the Tantric Mysticism of Tibet* (London, 1970).**

Bogle, George *see* Markham, Clements R.

Bonn, Gisela. *Kunst und Kultur im Reich der Drachen* (Koln, 1988).**

Bose, Kishen Kant *see* Eden, Ashley.

Coelho, V H. *Sikkim and Bhutan* (Delhi, Indian Council for Cultural Relations, 1970).

Collister, Peter. *Bhutan and the British* (London, Serindia, 1987).**

Dago Tshering (ed). *Bhutan: Himalayan Kingdom* (Royal Government of the Kingdom of Bhutan, Thimphu, 1979).**

Dalai Lama Tenzing Gyatsho. *Teachings of the Dalai Lama.*

Das, Nirmala. *The Dragon Country* (New Delhi, 1973).

Deb, Arabinda. *Bhutan and India: A Study in Frontier Political Relations (1772 – 1865)* (Calcutta, 1976).

Dowman Keith (tr.). *The Divine Madman: The Sublime Life of Drupka Kunley* (London, 1980).

DRUK LOSEL, Quarterly published by the Department of Information, Royal Government of Bhutan, Thimphu.

Eden, Ashley. *Political Missions to Bootan, comprising the reports of the Hon'ble Ashley Eden, 1864, Capt. R. B. Pemberton, 1837, 1838, with Dr. W. Griffith's Journal, and the account by Baboo Kishen Kant Bose* (Calcutta, 1865. Reprint: New Delhi, 1972, with the addition of *The Truth about Bootan by one who knows it,* originally published in Calcutta, 1865).

Edmunds, Tom Owen. *Bhutan: Land of the Thunder Dragon* (London, 1988).**

Gerner, Manfred. *Bhutan: Kultur und Religion im Land der Drachenkonige* (Stuttgart, 1981).

Griffith, William. *Journal of Travels in Assam, Burma, Bootan, Afganistan and the Neighbouring Countries* (Calcutta, 1847). Chapters XI, XII and XIII reprinted under the title: *Bhutan 1837–1838* (Kathmandu, 1975).

Haab, Armin. *Bhutan, Furstenstaat am Gotterthron* (Gutersloh, 1969).

Hasrat, Bikrama Jit. *History of Bhutan: Land of the Peaceful Dragon* (Education Department, Royal Government of Bhutan, Thimphu, 1980).

Hickman, Katie. *Dreams of the Peaceful Dragon: A Journey into Bhutan* (London, 1987).**

Imaeda, Yoshiro and Doffu Drukpa. *Tashigomang of Bhutan* (Tokyo, 1982).

Imaeda, Yoshiro *see* Van Strydonck, Guy.

Karan, Pradyumna P. *Bhutan: A Physical and Cultural Geography* (Lexington, 1967).

Kohli, Manorama. *India and Bhutan: A Study in Interrelations 1772 –1910* (New Delhi, 1982).

KUENSEL, News Bulletin (weekly), Department of Information, Royal Government of Bhutan, Thimphu.

Labh, Kapileshwar. *India and Bhutan* (New Delhi, 1974).

Markham, Clements R. *Narratives of the mission of George Bogle to Tibet and the journey of Thomas Maning to Lhasa* (London, 1879. Reprint: New Delhi, 1971).

Mehra, G N. *Bhutan: Land of the Peaceful Dragon* (Delhi, 1974).

Mele, Pietro Francesco. *Bhutan* (New Delhi, 1982).

Meyer, Fernand. *Gso ba Rigla, le système médicale tibétain* (Paris, 1988).

Montmollin, Marceline de. *Bhoutan: Pays du Dragon* (Guide Artou, Geneva, 1981).

Montmollin, Marceline de. *Collection du Bhoutan: Catalogue* (Extract from *Etudes Asiatiques,* XXXV — 2, 1981. Museum of Ethnography, Neuchatel, 1982).**

Myers, Diana K. 'Costume and Ceremonial Textiles of Bhutan', *The Textile Museum Journal 1987* (Washington, 1988).**

Nakao Sasuke. *Hikyo Butan* (Bhutan Unexplored) (Tokyo, 1959. Reprint: Tokyo, 1971).

Nishioka Keiji and Satoko. *Shinpi no okoku* (Mysterious Kingdom) (Tokyo, 1978).**

Nishioka Keiji and Nakao Sasuke. *Flowers of Bhutan* (Tokyo, 1984).

Olschak, Blanche C and Gansser, A. *Bhutan: Land of Hidden Treasures* (London/ New York/New Delhi, 1971).

Olschak, Blanche C. *Ancient Bhutan: A Study on Early Buddhism in the Himalayas* (Zurich, Swiss Foundation for Alpine Research, 1979).

Peissel, Michel. *Bhoutan, Royaume d'Asie inconnu* (Paris, 1971).**

Pemberton, R Boileau. *Report on Bootan* (Calcutta, 1839. Reprint: 7 New Delhi, 1976).

Pommaret, Françoise *see* Van Strydonck, Guy.

Rahul, Ram. *Modern Bhutan* (New Delhi, 1971).

Rahul, Ram. *Royal Bhutan* (New Delhi, 1983).

Rahul, Ram. *The Rise of Nepal and Bhutan* (New Delhi, 1984).

Ramsay, Cynthia Russ. *Bhutan: Excursion to Enchantment: A Journey through the World's Most Beautiful Places* (Washington, National Geographic Society, 1988).

Rathore, L S. *The Changing Bhutan* (New Delhi, 1971).

Rennie, David Field. *Bhutan and the Story of the Dooar War* (London, 1886. Reprint: New Delhi, 1970).

Ronalshay, Earl of. *Lands of the Thunderbolt: Sikkim, Chumbie and Bhutan* (London, 1923. Reprinted under the title *Himalayan Bhutan, Sikkim and Tibet,* Delhi, 1977).

Rose, Leo E. *The Politics of Bhutan* (New York, 1977).

Rustomji, Nari. *Enchanted Frontiers: Sikkim, Bhutan and India's North-Eastern Borderlands* (Calcutta, 1973).

Rustomji, Nari. *Bhutan: The Dragon Kingdom in Crisis* (New Delhi, 1978).

Rustomji, Nari. *Imperilled Frontiers: India's North-Eastern Borderlands* (New Delhi, 1983).

Singh, Amar Kaur Jasbir. *Himalayan Triangle: A Historical Survey of British India's Relations with Tibet, Sikkim and Bhutan 1765–1950* (London, 1988).

Singh, Mohanjeet. *Himalayan Art* (London, 1968).

Singh, Nagendra. *Bhutan, A Kingdom in the Himalayas: A Study of the Land, its People and their Government* (New Delhi, 1978).

Snelling, John. *The Buddhist Handbook* (London, 1987).**

Stein R A. (tr.). *Vie et chants de 'Brug-pa Kun-legs le Yogin* (Paris, 1972).**

Togo Fumihiko. *Himaraya no okoku Butan* (Bhutan: Himalayan Kingdom) (Tokyo, 1965).

Turner, Samuel. *An Account of Embassy to the Court of the Teshoo Lama in Tibet: Containing a Narrative of a Journey through Bootan, and Part of Tibet* (London, 1800. Reprint: New Delhi, 1971).

Van Strydonck, Guy; Imaeda, Yoshiro; Pommaret, Francoise. *Bhutan, A Kingdom of the Eastern Himalayas* (Geneva, 1984; London/New York, 1989).**

White, J Claude. *Sikkim and Bhutan: Twenty-One Years of the North-East Frontier, 1887-1908* (London, 1909. Reprint: Delhi, 1971).

Williamson and Snelling, J. *Memories of a Political Officer's Wife in Bhutten, Sikkim and Tibet* (London, Wisdom, 1989).**

Notes

1. These explanations of rituals have been given by Dagpo Rinpoche in his book *Dieux et Demons de l'Himalaya*, Paris, 1977, pp. 31–3.

2. The complete librettos of the Paro *Tshechu*, the Thimphu *Tshechu* and the Wangdi Phodrang *Tshechu* are available at the Tourist Office. I translated these programmes from Dzongkha and edited them some years ago under the name of Tashi Wangmo.

3. Cf. Yoshiro Imaeda, *Papermaking in Bhutan* (Kasama, 1988).

4. Technical information from Mireille Hellfer.

5. Cf. *280 Folk Songs of Bhutan* (in classical Tibetan) compiled by Kunzang Tobgyel and Mani Dorji, Department of Education, Thimphu, 1985.

6. No detailed explanation of the Wheel of Life will be given here. It is one of the best-known themes in Tibetan Buddhism and explanations can be found in most guidebooks and books on the subject.

7. It is technically incorrect to speak of the Dochu La Pass, the Pele La Pass, etc. because 'la' means 'pass', but it has become customary to refer to them in this way.

8. This bamboo has been identified by Chris Stapleton in 'Himalayan Bamboo Genera: Keys and Background Information', Aberdeen University Forestry Department, 1988.

9. I have made extensive use of *Flowers of Bhutan* by K. Nishioka and S. Nakao (Tokyo, 1984). K. Nishioka, who is a *Dasho* in Bhutan, has lived in Shemgang district and observed the daily customs there.

10. M Aris, *Bhutan: The Early History of a Himalayan Kingdom* (Warminster, Serindia, 1979).

11. For a detailed description of this temple see Y Imaeda and F Pommaret, 'Le monastère de Tam zhing (Tamshing) au Bhoutan central' in *Arts Asiatiques*, t.XLII (Paris, 1987), pp. 19–20; and M Aris, 'The Temple-Palace of Gtam zhing as Described by its Founder' in *Arts Asiatiques*, t.XLIII (Paris, 1988), pp. 33–9.

12. J C White, *Sikkim and Bhutan* reprint, p. 166.

13. *ibid.*

14. Cf. *Smyos rabs* by Lama Sangnag, pp. 325–45 (Thimphu, 1983).

Index